The Art
· of ·
Thinking

The Art of Thinking

· of ·

Thinking

A Guide to Critical and Creative Thought

· Fourth Edition ·

VINCENT RYAN RUGGIERO

HarperCollins*College*Publishers

Senior Editor: Jane Kinney
Project Editor: Janet Frick
Cover Designer: Kay Petronio
Text Designer: Nancy Sabato
Art Studio: Fineline, Inc.
Electronic Production Manager: Valerie A. Sawyer
Desktop Administrator: Hilda Koparanian
Manufacturing Manager: Helene G. Landers
Electronic Page Makeup: RR Donnelley Barbados
Printer and Binder: RR Donnelley & Sons Company
Cover Printer: The Lehigh Press, Inc.

The Art of Thinking: A Guide to Critical and Creative Thought, Fourth Edition

Library of Congress Cataloging-in-Publication Data

Ruggiero, Vincent Ryan.
   The art of thinking: a guide to critical and creative thought / Vincent
   Ryan Ruggiero.—4th edition
      p.   cm.
   Includes bibliographical references and index.
   ISBN 0-673-99325-6 (student edition)
   ISBN 0-673-99326-4 (instructor's edition)
   1. Thought and thinking.   2. Critical thinking.   3. Creative thinking.
   4. Thought and thinking—Problems, exercises, etc.   I. Title.
BF441.R84   1995
153.4'2—dc20   94–27207
                                                        CIP

94 95 96 97 9 8 7 6 5 4 3 2 1

To all my children, with a love that transcends time and trouble

Thinking is an art, with its own purposes, standards, principles, rules, strategies, and precautions. And it is an art well worth learning, for every important thing we do is affected by our habits of mind.

Contents

13 Refine Your Resolution of the Issue   180

PART 4   Communicate Your Ideas   187

14 Anticipate Negative Reactions   188

15 Build a Persuasive Case   198

To the Instructor

Throughout this century, many educators felt that thinking was learned automatically when certain subjects (notably science and math) were studied, and that therefore it need not be formally taught. Others believed that thinking could not be learned, at least not by the average student. As a result, schools did not generally offer formal instruction in thinking, and colleges confined their offerings to formal logic courses inaccessible to students outside the discipline of philosophy.

This situation has never gone unchallenged. There have always been dissenters, here and abroad, who urged that systematic training in thinking be offered to all students. But when they were heard at all, such people were either misunderstood, like John Dewey, or dutifully applauded and then ignored, like Alfred North Whitehead and Jean Piaget.

Now, thanks to the persistence of those prophets and that of the small but determined number of educators who continued to press for the reforms those prophets championed, a new era seems to be dawning. Many prestigious studies, beginning with the one released by the U.S. Department of Education in November 1981, call attention to the lack of critical thinking and problem-solving skills in today's students. Support for thinking instruction has been registered by numerous respected organizations, including the National Council of Teachers of English, the Presidential Commission on Excellence in Education, the College Board, the Carnegie Foundation for the Advancement of Teaching, the American Federation of Teachers, the Association of American Colleges, the National Institute of Education, the U.S. Department of Education, the Association for Supervision and Curriculum Development, and the University/Urban Schools National Task Force. Numerous colleges and universities now require students to complete one or more courses in thinking.

THIS BOOK'S PREMISES

This book has been designed both for existing courses in thinking and for those that are being instituted in various departments—philosophy, humanities, social science, and English. As the title *The Art of Thinking* suggests, this book is more comprehensive than most texts on thinking. The following four premises underlie its content and organization:

1. *The emphasis in a textbook on thinking should be more on what to* do *than on what to* avoid *doing.* Thinking is not an ivory tower enterprise. It is a practical matter. Moreover, it is active and dynamic, not reactive and static. Effective thinkers do not merely sit back and criticize others' efforts; they solve problems, make decisions, and take stands on issues. For this reason, textbooks focusing on fallacies are little more successful than music books that focus on avoiding the wrong notes or typing manuals that focus on avoiding all possible misstrokes.

2. *A textbook on thinking should introduce students to the principles and techniques of* creative *thinking.* The considerable literature that has been published on thinking in the past three decades demonstrates that the creative process and the critical process are intertwined: First we produce ideas (more or less creatively); then we judge them. It is not enough to give students *already formed* arguments for analysis; they must be taught how to generate arguments of their own.

3. *A text on thinking should teach students how to evaluate their own ideas, as well as the ideas of others.* Human beings have a great capacity for self-deception. Accordingly, it is much more difficult for students to see their own blind spots, their own prejudices, and their own errors than it is for them to see other people's. Yet it is their own weaknesses and mistakes that pose the greatest obstacle to their effective thinking.

4. *A text on thinking should teach students how to persuade others.* Many brilliant ideas have never been put into practice simply because the originator assumed that others would recognize excellence without assistance. Students need to learn how to anticipate objections to their ideas before they occur and how to overcome them.

SPECIAL FEATURES RETAINED FROM PREVIOUS EDITIONS

- Wherever possible, the chapters are presented in the sequence that occurs in actual problem solving and issue analysis. For example, expressing the problem (Chapter 7) is followed by investigating the problem (Chapter 8), producing ideas (Chapter 9), and refining the solution (Chapter 11).

- Part 2, "Be Creative," offers direct answers to the questions that most baffle students and prevent their progress in thinking. These are questions such as "How can I be more imaginative, more original in my solutions to problems?" "What should I do when I experience 'thinker's block,' when I get confused, or when I get in the rut of producing the same kinds of solution?" and "How does insight occur, and what can I do to stimulate it?"

- A separate chapter (Chapter 6) addresses the problem of motivating students to apply their thinking skills to problems and issues in every college course, as well as in everyday life. Authorities agree that to be effective, thinking instruction must focus not only on skills but also on *dispositions*.

- A separate chapter (Chapter 8) explains in detail how to investigate issues quickly, efficiently, and with ingenuity, both in the library and out.

- Chapters 14 and 15 offer specific techniques for anticipating negative reactions to ideas and a helpful approach to use in persuading others.

- Separate appendixes provide brief guides to composition; formal speaking, conversation, and group discussion; and formal logic.

- Warm-up exercises are provided at the end of each chapter, in addition to a generous supply of problems and issues. These exercises are designed to develop students' interest and build their self-confidence, thereby making the formal applications less intimidating.

- Applications are provided following the warm-up exercises in each chapter.

NEW FEATURES IN THE FOURTH EDITION

The fourth edition contains a number of significant changes, each of them a response to suggestions from instructors who have used the text in their classes. Those changes are as follows:

- Chapter 4: the addition of the distinction between language and reality.

- Chapter 12: the addition of a number of examples of arguments with hidden premises and complex arguments.

- All chapters: the group discussion and writing exercises at the end of each chapter have been revised and given greater prominence to facilitate the use of the text in composition courses and speech courses (without altering the basic format that has proven successful in creative/critical thinking courses).

- Appendix A: expansion of the writing process, with a new section on prewriting and expanded treatment of planning.

- Appendix B: the addition of a new section on formal speaking, including a sample outline and speech.

- Appendix C: expanded explanations of the errors in logic.

VARIATIONS IN TEACHING FORMAT

The Art of Thinking has been used successfully in composition courses and public speaking courses, as well as in creative/critical thinking courses; and in a number of disciplines, including business, the humanities, the social sciences, and the sciences. Instructors who find the book's table of contents not well suited to their courses or their students' needs may wish to consider one of the following alternative sequences.

For Composition Courses:

Appendix A: "A Guide to Composition"
Chapter 1: "Developing Your Thinking: An Overview"
Chapter 15: "Build a Persuasive Case"*
Chapter 2: "Establish a Foundation"
Chapters 3 through 14

For Speech Courses:

Appendix B: "A Guide to Formal Speaking, Conversation, and Group Discussion"
Chapter 1: "Developing Your Thinking: An Overview"
Chapter 15: "Build a Persuasive Case"*
Chapter 2: "Establish a Foundation"
Chapters 3 through 14

Another Alternative:

Chapters 1 through 4
Chapter 15: "Build a Persuasive Case"
Chapters 5 through 14

In this alternative, students would be directed to consult the composition, speech, and other appendixes as necessary.

ACKNOWLEDGMENTS

I wish, first, to express my appreciation to all the men and women—the prophets, the researchers, the risk takers—who labored to advance the cause of knowledge in a subject that for many decades was unfashionable. Without their contributions, this book would never have been written. I wish also to express special thanks to Jane Kinney for her editorial direction and to the following professors for their constructive criticisms and helpful suggestions:

Cynthia Doherty, Harrisburg Area Community College; Michael Berberich, Galveston College; Betty Cassidy, Adirondack Community College; Harold Hild, Northeastern Illinois University

Vincent Ryan Ruggiero

---

*Certain applications, notably 14 through 16, may not be suitable for the early weeks of a course.

Developing Your Thinking: An Overview

Claude is a high school student. His English teacher has just asked the class to identify the theme of the short story they read for homework. When no one answers, she admonishes them, "Class, you're just not thinking. Get busy and *think*."

Claude wrinkles up his nose, furrows his brow, scratches his chin, and stares up at the ceiling. "Think, think, I've got to think. What's the theme of that story? The theme, the theme, what could be the theme?" He shifts his gaze to the right and to the left, purses his lips, then reaches down purposefully, opens his book, and begins flipping pages as if looking for something. All the while his mind is repeating, "Think . . . think . . . theme. . . ."

Is Claude thinking? No. He's trying to, hoping to, but not really doing so. His mental motor is racing, but his transmission is in neutral. He's ready to go, but not going.

Let's consider another case. Agatha, a college student, is sitting in the campus cafeteria, drinking her morning coffee. To all outward appearances she is not only thinking but totally lost in thought. Here is what is taking place in her mind:

> So much work to do today . . . must remember to meet Jim at 6 P.M. . . . I'll have to begin my term paper soon . . . that Bertha is such a slob—I wish she'd clean her part of the room sometime this semester . . . my hair looks so awful—if only I could fix it like Martha's, it would look neat, yet demand little attention . . . if winter would only end, I wouldn't be so depressed—why is my mood so dominated by weather? . . . this coffee is bitter—you'd think the staff here could at least make a decent cup of coffee . . . I can't wait to get home to have a real meal again . . . wonder how much weight I've gained; perhaps jogging is the solution. . . .

Agatha's mental behavior is much closer to thinking than Claude's. Ideas, images, and notions are drifting through her mind, and she is dutifully watching them float by. But her role is passive; she is a spectator to the activity of her mind. Thinking, as we will view it in this book (and as most authorities view it), is something more than aimless daydreaming.

WHAT IS THINKING?

What, then, is thinking? To begin with, it is purposeful mental activity over which we exercise some control. *Control* is the key word. Just as sitting in the driver's seat of a car becomes driving only when we take the steering wheel in hand and control the car's movement, so our mind's movements become thinking only when we direct them.

There are, of course, as many different purposes in thinking as there are in traveling. We may be on a business trip or a pleasant drive through the countryside with no particular destination. Similarly, we may drive in varying conditions and with varying degrees of success or efficiency. We may travel in darkness or in light, proceed slowly or quickly, take the correct turn or the wrong one, arrive at our intended destination or a different one, or find that we are hopelessly lost en route. Nevertheless, as long as we are steering our mind, we are thinking.

This does not mean that thinking must always be conscious. The evidence that the unconscious mind can join in purposeful mental activity is over-whelming. The most dramatic example of this is the fact that insights often come to us when we are no longer working on a problem but have turned away from it to other activities. (We will see a number of examples of this phenomenon later, in Chapter 9.)

With these important considerations in mind, we can attempt a more formal definition of thinking. *Thinking is any mental activity that helps formulate or solve a problem, make a decision, or fulfill a desire to understand. It is a searching for answers, a reaching for meaning.* Numerous mental activities are included in the thinking process. Careful observation, remembering, wondering, imagining, inquiring, interpreting, evaluating, and judging are among the most important ones. Often several of these activities work in combination, as when we solve a problem or make a decision. We may, for example, identify an idea or dilemma, then deal with it—say, by questioning, interpreting, and analyzing—and finally reach a conclusion or decision.

There have been many attempts to explain the nature of thinking. One of the most popular notions, now largely discredited, is that thinking is entirely verbal. According to this theory, we arrange words in our minds or silently whisper to ourselves when we think. Yet if this were the case, Albert Einstein would not be considered a thinker. His thinking consisted more of images than of words.[1] Contemporary authorities agree that the form a thought takes in our minds is usually verbal, but not necessarily so. Just as we may *express* an idea in mathematical symbols or pictures, in addition to words, we may also *conceive* of it in that way.

CONTEMPORARY BRAIN RESEARCH

Throughout this century researchers have deepened our understanding of human thought. We now know that thinking is not a mystical activity, unknowable and unlearnable. Thinking occurs in patterns that can be studied and compared to determine their relative objectivity, validity, and effectiveness. This knowledge can be used to reinforce good thinking habits and to overcome bad ones. As James Mursell has observed, "Any notion that better thinking is intrinsically unlearnable and unteachable is nothing but a lazy fallacy, entertained only by those who have never taken the trouble to consider just how a practical job of thinking is really done."[2]

Brain research is an especially rich source of insights. One is that the brain is a dual organ. The breakthrough came when a neurosurgeon began treating patients with severe epilepsy in a new way. He severed the nerve fibers connecting the two hemispheres of the cerebral cortex to relieve the symptoms of the disease. The separation made it possible to study the way each hemisphere functioned. The right hemisphere, it was learned, governs nonverbal, symbolic, and intuitive responses. The left hemisphere governs the use of language, logical reasoning, analysis, and the performance of sequential tasks.[3]

Some writers used this research to bolster the notion that one hemisphere or the other usually dominates; in other words, that there are "left-brained people" and "right-brained people." Few, if any, researchers would affirm this view.

As Jerre Levy of the University of Chicago notes in reviewing studies of the brain,

> The creations of human culture derive from the fully integrated actions of the whole brain, and any further advances will require an intimate and brilliant collaborative synthesis of the special skills of both sides of the brain. All of the available data point to the validity of this conclusion; none supports the idea that normal people function like split-brain patients, using only one hemisphere at a time.

Levy argues further that the very structure of the brain implies profound integration of the two hemispheres; the *corpus callosum*, that bundle of nerves positioned between them, both connects them and facilitates their arousal.[4]

Such research has given new importance to old understanding. For decades psychologists of thinking stressed that the mind has two distinct phases—the production phase and the judgment phase—that complement each other during thinking. They stressed further that proficiency in thinking requires the mastery of all approaches appropriate to each phase and skill in moving back and forth between them.

Let's examine each phase a little more closely, noting how good thinkers use each effectively.

The Production Phase

In this phase, which is most closely associated with creative thinking, the mind produces various conceptions of the problem or issue, various ways of dealing with it, and possible solutions or responses to it. Good thinkers produce both more ideas and better ideas than poor thinkers. They become more adept in using a variety of invention techniques, enabling them to discover ideas. More specifically, good thinkers tend to see the problem from many perspectives before choosing any one, to consider many different investigative approaches, and to produce many ideas before turning to judgment. In addition, they are more willing to take intellectual risks, to be adventurous and consider outrageous or zany ideas, and to use their imaginations and aim for originality.

In contrast, poor thinkers tend to see the problem from a limited number of perspectives (often just a single narrow one), to take the first approach that occurs to them, to judge each idea immediately, and to settle for only a few ideas. Moreover, they are overly cautious in their thinking, unconsciously making their ideas conform to the common, the familiar, and the expected.

The Judgment Phase

In this phase, which is most closely associated with critical thinking, the mind examines and evaluates what it has produced, makes its judgments, and where appropriate, adds refinements. Good thinkers handle this phase with care. They test their first impressions, make important distinctions, and base their conclusions on evidence rather than their own feelings. Sensitive to their own limitations and predispositions, they double-check the logic of their thinking and the workability of their solutions, identifying imperfections and complications, anticipating negative responses, and generally refining their ideas.

In contrast, poor thinkers judge too quickly and uncritically, ignoring the need for evidence and letting their feelings shape their conclusions. Blind to their limitations and predispositions, poor thinkers trust their judgment implicitly, ignoring the possibility of imperfections, complications, or negative responses.

GOOD THINKING IS A HABIT

It is frequently said that good thinkers are born, not made. Though there is an element of truth in this, the idea is essentially false. Some people have more talent for thinking than others, and some learn more quickly. As a result, over the years one person may develop thinking ability to a greater extent than another. Nevertheless, effective thinking is mostly a matter of habit. Research proves that the qualities of mind it takes to think well, the qualities we noted in our discussion of the production and judgment phases, above, can be mastered by anyone. It even proves that originality can be learned. Most important, it proves that you don't need a high IQ to be a good thinker.[5] E. Paul Torrance has shown that fully 70 *percent* of all creative people score below 135 on IQ tests.[6]

The difficulty of improving your thinking depends on the habits and attitudes you have. Chances are you've had no direct training in the art of thinking before this, so you're bound to have acquired some bad habits and attitudes. This book will supply principles and techniques for you to master, and your instructor will supply the guidance. You must supply the most important ingredients—the desire to improve and the willingness to apply what you learn.

If at first the task of changing your habits and attitudes seems impossible, remember that a lot of other tasks seemed so, yet you mastered them: walking, for example, and eating without drooling food out of your mouth onto your high chair, swimming, hitting a baseball, and driving a car. The unfamiliar often seems daunting.

STRUCTURE OF THIS BOOK

Becoming familiar with the contents of this book will help you meet its challenge more confidently. The purpose of the book is to *teach you how to think* more creatively and critically. That may seem obvious enough, but it's easily confused with *telling you what to think.* The difference is this: Telling you what to think brainwashes you, enslaves you to others' ideas; teaching you how to think liberates you from dependency on others' ideas and helps you form sound and sensible ideas of your own. You will find this book introducing you to, or deepening your acquaintance with, a host of problems and controversial issues. It will guide the way you consider them—that is, the strategies you apply and the manner in which you apply them. But you will not find this book making up your mind for you. That task is yours alone.

The Art of Thinking is divided into four parts, each with several chapters. The first part is titled "Be Aware." Its importance is suggested by these words from philosopher Arthur Schopenhauer: "Every man takes the limits of his own field of vision for the limits of the world." One aim of this section is to broaden your outlook. Another is to clarify such important concepts as *truth, knowledge,* and *opinion,* each of them clouded today by confusion and misconceptions. Other aims are to help you arrive at a better understanding of your own strengths and weaknesses and to develop your curiosity and analytical skills. The second section of the book, "Be Creative," focuses on producing ideas and offers practice in identifying, investigating, and solving a variety of challenging problems and issues. The third section, "Be Critical," focuses on judgment. It shows you how to apply your curiosity and analytical skill in evaluating your ideas, choosing the best ones, refining them, and overcoming their flaws. Finally, Part Four, "Communicate Your Ideas," helps you prepare the ideas for presentation to other people.

The book also includes five appendixes you will undoubtedly find useful from time to time during the course:

Appendix A, "A Guide to Composition," offers suggestions that can make the process of writing easier and improve the quality of your compositions.

Appendix B, "A Guide to Formal Speaking, Conversation, and Group Discussion," explains the principles and strategies of speaking in public and exchanging ideas with others in a group. It is designed both to help you present your ideas more effectively and to make you a better listener.

Appendix C, "The Fundamentals of Logic," provides a brief overview of formal logic.

Appendix D, "Doing the Warm-up Exercises," offers tips to help you overcome "exercise block."

Appendix E, "Solutions to Sample Problems," permits you to check your answers to the sample problems that appear in the book.

Together the appendixes will help you build the kind of self-reliance and resourcefulness all good thinkers possess. Whenever you aren't sure how to begin an assignment or you encounter an obstacle as you proceed, there's no need to give up or wait for your instructor to clarify the matter in class. You can simply turn to the appropriate appendix for guidance. (Keep in mind that your instructor is likely to be more forgiving if you do an assignment incorrectly than if you don't do it at all.)

GETTING THE MOST FROM YOUR EFFORTS

There was a time when it was thought that the same occasions, places, and conditions of work are right for everyone. Today we know better. No two people are exactly alike in their needs. What works for one will not necessarily work for another. Mozart and Beethoven, for example, were both great composers. Yet they worked very differently. Mozart thought out entire symphonies and scenes from operas in his head, without benefit of notes. Later he transcribed them onto paper. Beethoven, on the other hand, wrote fragments of notes in notebooks, often reworking and polishing them for years. His first ideas were so clumsy that scholars marvel at how he could have developed such great music from them.[7]

Imagine what would have happened if Mozart had followed Beethoven's approach, and vice versa. Surely Mozart's output would have been diminished. Given the unsuitability of another approach to his temperament, it might even have been choked off altogether. And Beethoven would have given the world trash.

It is not unreasonable to believe that there are thousands, perhaps millions, of people in the world today who have not begun to glimpse, let alone develop, their potential for achievement *simply because they are using work habits borrowed from someone else or fallen into by chance or force of circumstance.* Your best approach is not to assume your work habits fit your needs but to experiment a little and find out what really works best for you. What you find may not make a dramatic difference, but even modest improvements in proficiency will continue to pay dividends over the years.

Consider Time

An hour of prime time will often get better results than two or three hours of the wrong time. When are you in the habit of working? Early in the morning? Late at night? At midday? For the next week or two try different times and note the effect on your work.

Consider Place

You can observe students studying in strange places: dormitory lounges, crowded cafeterias filled with people clanging and chattering, and snack bars (often next to a blaring jukebox). You've probably studied in some of these places, too, at one time or another, and for no other reason than that you happened to be there at the time an assignment had to be done. But that is hardly a good reason for being there. If you need quiet to work efficiently, you should seek a quiet place—if not a dormitory room, then an empty classroom, a park bench, or a parked car. Of course, if you find that a busy place actually stimulates your thinking, by all means work there.

Consider Conditions

Thinkers throughout history have occasionally needed some strange stimuli. Poet Johann Schiller needed a desk filled with rotten apples. Novelist Marcel Proust needed a cork-lined workroom. Dr. Samuel Johnson demanded a purring cat, an orange peel, and a cup of tea. But you'd do well not to become dependent on gimmicks or bizarre conditions, if for no other reason than the fact that they're hard to maintain. You're better off trying such approaches as taking a walk or a brisk jog across campus before beginning work, taking a warm bath, or playing music while you work.

A word of caution is in order here. Don't confuse what you like with what works best for you. You may, for example, enjoy being in the dormitory lounge in the early evening watching TV or listening to the stereo blare. But these might hinder more than help your efforts to think or write. Similarly, alcohol and drugs may make you feel good (temporarily, at least), but they are definitely harmful. Although the notion persists that such substances enhance creativity, researchers are almost unanimous in concluding that they have the reverse effect: They cloud and numb the mind.

USING FEELINGS TO ADVANTAGE

Feelings were greatly emphasized in the 1960s and early 1970s. "Do your own thing," "If it feels good, do it," and "Get in touch with your feelings" were the catchphrases of the time. In light of the neglect of feelings in the 1950s, that emphasis was understandable, but it often took the form of a rejection of thought. The proper relationship of thoughts and feelings is harmonious, not mutually exclusive.

The contribution feelings can make to problem solving and decision making is immeasurable. Not only do feelings often yield the hunches, impressions, and intuitions that produce the answers we seek; they also, more importantly, provide the enthusiasm to undertake difficult challenges and persevere in them. Albert Einstein spent 7 years working out his theory of relativity; Thomas Edison spent 13 years perfecting the phonograph; Copernicus devoted more than 30 years to proving that the sun is the center of the solar system. And millions of men and women labor tirelessly to realize the most elusive of goals—victory over disease, poverty, ignorance, and inhumanity. Without deep and abiding feelings about the importance of their work, such people could not sustain their efforts.

The popular notion that only artists feel, that scientists and other practical people approach problems in computerlike fashion, has long been discredited by scholars.[8] Albert Einstein himself affirmed the role of intuition in science. "There is no logical way to the discovery of [complex scientific laws]," he explained. "There is only the way of intuition, which is helped by a feeling for the order lying behind the appearance."[9] And Arthur Koestler, who studied the lives of innumerable great scientists, observed, "In the popular imagination [they] appear as sober ice-cold logicians, electronic brains mounted on dry sticks. But if one were shown an anthology of typical extracts from their letters and autobiographies with no names mentioned, and then asked to guess their profession, the likeliest answer would be: a bunch of poets or musicians of a rather romantically naive kind."[10]

Of course, not all feelings are good. Some direct us in ways good sense would not have us go. From time to time even the mildest individuals may feel like responding violently to people they don't like, experience a strong urge for sexual contact with those who don't share the sentiment, or be overtaken by the impulse to steal something. For this reason, wisdom demands that we refuse to surrender ourselves to our feelings but instead examine them dispassionately and separate the worthy from the unworthy.

As you proceed through this course, try to become more aware of your feelings. Accept the challenge of finding your best and noblest feelings and allowing them to motivate you.

LEARNING TO CONCENTRATE

Many people have the notion that concentration means a constant, unbroken line of thought. They imagine that scientists, writers, inventors, and philosophers start from point A and move smoothly to point B without distraction. That notion is incorrect. Concentration is not so much something done to *prevent* distraction and interruption as it is something done to *overcome* distraction and interruption when they occur. To concentrate means to return our attention to our purpose or problem whenever it wanders.[11]

Concentrating is much like steering a car. When experienced drivers steer, they don't lock their hands on the wheel in one fixed position; they turn it slightly to the right and to the left to keep the car on course. Even on a straight road, the car stays on course only a small percentage of the time. They must make constant adjustments, many of them almost imperceptible. Experienced drivers are not more talented than inexperienced ones; they have simply learned to make subtle corrections at the right time.

Similarly, the secret of efficient thinkers is not that they experience fewer distractions but that they have learned to deal with them more quickly and more effectively than inefficient ones do. There is no magic in what effective thinkers do. You can learn it as they did, by practicing.

COPING WITH FRUSTRATION

All thinkers have their share of frustration: Confusion, mental blocks, false starts, and failures happen to everyone. Good thinkers, however, have learned strategies for dealing with their frustration, while poor thinkers merely lament it—thus allowing themselves to be defeated by it. One important study of students' problem-solving processes revealed some interesting differences between good and poor problem solvers. Among them were the following:[12]

GOOD PROBLEM SOLVERS	POOR PROBLEM SOLVERS
Read a problem and decide how to begin attacking it.	Cannot settle on a way to begin.
Bring their knowledge to bear on a problem.	Convince themselves they lack sufficient knowledge (even when that is not the case).
Go about solving a problem systematically—for example, trying to simplify it, puzzling out key terms, or breaking the problem into subproblems.	Plunge in, jumping haphazardly from one part of the problem to another, trying to justify first impressions instead of testing them.
Tend to trust their reasoning and to have confidence in themselves.	Tend to distrust their reasoning and to lack confidence in themselves.
Maintain a critical attitude throughout the problem-solving process.	Lack a critical attitude, and take too much for granted.

All of these differences are matters of habit. If you have not yet developed the habits of the good thinker, begin practicing. In time they will be yours.

As was noted, Appendix D offers guidance to help get you started doing the exercises at the ends of the chapters. Now, here are two additional tips to help you begin with an extra measure of confidence. Use them whenever you begin working on an exercise or application and encounter a mental block:

1. Reread the directions, this time *aloud.* Let your ear join your eye in determining what you are being asked to do. Two senses are better than one.
2. Refuse to sit passively, staring at the problem. Do something to attack it. If you took a dead-end street by accident, you wouldn't sit in your car staring at the dead-end sign—you'd turn the car around and try moving in another direction.

Let's take an actual problem and see how tip 2 would work. You have three unmarked glasses of different sizes: 3 ounces, 5 ounces, and 8 ounces. The largest glass is full. Your job is to end up with 4 ounces of liquid in each of the larger two glasses.

Let's say you look at the problem and draw a blank. Following step 1, you reread the problem aloud. Now you understand it. But you still don't know how to begin. What can you do to attack it, to get your mind in motion? One approach is to get three appropriate-sized glasses and fill the largest with water; then go through the motions of transferring liquid to see where the difficulty lies. But an easier way is to draw the glasses, however roughly, on a piece of paper, like this:

3 ounce   5 ounce   8 ounce

What next? Pour some liquid into one of the empty glasses (by sketching or by imagining). Which one? It makes no difference. Just get busy *doing.* If you make a mistake, and encounter a dead end, so what? You can always turn around and try another approach. The point is that you will be exerting some initiative on the problem. You'll no longer be at its mercy. If you'd like to pause now and try to solve the problem, do so. (You'll find the answer on page 242.)

Not every problem, of course, can be so easily visualized (or visualized at all). We'll see other approaches in subsequent chapters.

WRITING TO DISCOVER IDEAS

We have seen that it is possible to think without expressing the thought. Nevertheless, expressing our thoughts is a valuable way of clarifying them. And the benefit is reciprocal. In other words, expressing helps thinking, which in turn helps expressing, and so on. You've surely had the experience of believing you have an idea clearly in mind and then trying to express it and finding out it isn't so clear after all. It's a common experience. And it hints at a deeper condition than most of us realize. Ernest Dimnet explains:

> Most men and women die vague about life and death, religion or morals, politics or art. Even about practical issues we are far from being clear. We imagine that other people know definitely their own minds about their children's education, about their own careers, or about the use they should make of their money. The notion helps us to imagine that we ourselves are only separated from decision on these important issues by the lightest curtain of uncertainty. But it is not so. Other people, like ourselves, live in perpetual vagueness. Like us they foolishly imagine they are thinking of some important subject when they are merely *thinking of thinking about it.*[13] [emphasis added]

As a cure for this problem, Dimnet suggests taking a sheet of paper and doing your thinking on it rather than just inside your mind. Then you'll be able to see whether you're really thinking and how well you're thinking. It's a simple enough approach. And it works. You'll find, too, that the very act of recording your thoughts helps to focus them better and improves your concentration.

The activity Dimnet is referring to, and which is recommended by many authorities on thinking and writing, is called *freewriting.* It consists of focusing on a problem or issue and letting your mind produce whatever associations it will, then writing down whatever ideas result, without stopping to evaluate any idea or shutting off the flow of ideas prematurely. This kind of writing is private expression, for your eyes only. Its aim is very different from that of formal writing: It is to stimulate thought rather than to communicate it. Therefore, it can be—indeed, should be—informal, casual, and highly tentative. There's no need, either, for correct spelling or accurate typing. Freewriting can be filled with grammatical blunders. No one else will see it, so you needn't worry whether any of your ideas seem foolish. If you decide an idea is unworthy, you can cross it out later without embarrassment or loss of face.

Another way to discover ideas is *listmaking.* Because it involves single words and brief phrases, listmaking is an even more efficient process than freewriting. You'll find it especially useful in recording thoughts that occur fleetingly at inopportune moments. As you have undoubtedly learned, such thoughts often give you only one chance to capture them; if you fail to do so, you lose them. Keep a pencil and paper handy at all times and whenever a valuable thought occurs, jot it down. If you are in the middle of a conversation, simply say, "Excuse me, I've got to write something down before I forget it." If you are in a group discussion, write while others are speaking.

Many professional authors find listmaking an invaluable strategy. A single page from their notebooks may contain ideas for several books or articles in various stages of completion, as well as ideas for new works. When time permits, they rearrange the lists, then ponder each idea and let it suggest others, then arrange again, and so on, working recursively.

Additional strategies for stimulating your imagination and producing ideas may be found on pages 126–130.

WRITING FOR OTHERS

The other kind of writing, the kind you are probably more familiar with, is writing to be shared with others. This writing is done when you have finished producing and evaluating ideas and are ready to present them for others' consideration. The structure of this writing will vary with the specific nature of the problem, the audience, and the purpose you hope to achieve by writing. All these matters will be discussed in depth in later chapters and in Appendix A. For now we'll discuss only the basics. Use the following approach for all your formal responses to the exercises and applications at the ends of the chapters, unless otherwise directed:

- State what you think in response to the problem.
- Explain the reasoning by which you arrived at your view.
- Add whatever supporting information or reasoning is appropriate and would be helpful to your reader in understanding your view.

There is no specific length required for the responses to most exercises and applications. As a guide for determining whether your responses are satisfactory, use the test of *adequacy*. That is, ask yourself, "Is my response adequate to convey my thoughts clearly and effectively to my readers?"

WARM-UP EXERCISES

Here and in subsequent chapters, the warm-up exercises, as the name implies, provide a chance to "limber up your thinking" before addressing the chapter applications. Unlike those applications, the warm-ups have no special relation to the chapters. They may demand creative thinking, critical thinking, or both. Since they will usually concern matters that are of no great consequence, you should feel free to be as daring and imaginative as you wish in responding to them.

1.1. Decide whether the reasoning that underlies the following statement is sound or unsound. Write a paragraph or two stating and explaining your judgment. (If you have difficulty doing this assignment, consult Appendix D.)

There's a possibility that the price of postage stamps will be raised again soon. I think I'll stock up on them now to avoid paying the higher price.

1.2. Follow the directions for Exercise 1.1.

The sun has always risen in the past; therefore, it will rise tomorrow.

1.3. A young child is convinced that the time between 2 o'clock and 3 o'clock is longer than the time between 1 o'clock and 2 o'clock. Compose a brief explanation, with or without a diagram, that helps the child understand that the time isn't longer.

APPLICATIONS

1.1. For each of the following statements, write a brief response (one or two sentences) stating your position and explaining why you hold it.

    a. Violence is better than reason in dealing with dangerous situations.
    b. Only the good die young.
    c. It's human nature to be greedy.
    d. Capital punishment is a deterrent to crime.
    e. If people are unemployed, they must be lazy. There's a job for everyone who really wants to work.
    f. Everyone has a value system of some kind.
    g. We know ourselves better than others know us.
    h. An unborn fetus is a human being.
    i. If guns are outlawed, only outlaws will have guns.
    j. Truth is an intensely personal matter—what is true for me is not necessarily true for you.
    k. Winning isn't everything—it's the only thing.
    l. Challenging another's opinion is a sign of intolerance.
    m. Atheists are generally moral people.
    n. Censorship is evil.
    o. Black people are better athletes than white people.
    p. The oil companies manipulate gasoline prices.
    q. Getting your feet wet can cause a cold.
    r. Homosexuals are as likely to control their sex urges as are heterosexuals.

1.2. Read the following dialogue carefully, looking for flaws in thinking. If you find a flaw, identify it and explain what is wrong with it in sufficient detail to persuade someone who read the passage without seeing the flaw. If you find two or more flaws, decide which is most serious and limit your discussion to that one. If you find nothing wrong with the thinking in the dialogue, explain why you agree with what is said. (If you have difficulty doing this assignment, consult suggestion 7 in Appendix D.)

    SALLY: Norma, have you begun your composition yet, the one that's due tomorrow?
    NORMA: No, I haven't. But I have done quite a bit of research on the topic. I've got a few very interesting facts I plan to refer to. Have you done any reading?
    SALLY: Not me. I want to do my own thing in my compositions; you know, be original.
    NORMA: Really? Maybe I'd better not use those facts. They could work against me, I guess.

1.3. Follow the directions for Application 1.2.

    HOMER: Excuse me, Professor Collins, may I speak to you for a minute?
    PROF. C.: Sure, Homer. What can I do for you?
    HOMER: It's about the test we had last week. You gave me a 40 on it.
    PROF. C.: That's not a very good grade. Had you read all three chapters carefully?

HOMER: *Carefully?* I read each one four times, underlined every important detail, and then studied them for about 10 hours for three nights before the test. I took No-Doz and stayed up until 4:30 A.M. the night before the test.

PROF. C.: I see. That would surely seem to be more than adequate preparation. What do you think went wrong?

HOMER: I think the test was unfair ... I mean, it's not ... I know you wouldn't make a test unfair on purpose. I think you're a good teacher and all. Sociology is your field and I'm just an amateur, but after all that trying, I wouldn't have gotten a 40 if the test were fair.

1.4. Follow the directions for Application 1.2.

LILLIAN: Do you think parents should be told when their teenage daughters are given birth control devices by doctors?

ROY: Absolutely. Parents are responsible for their children until they become of age. They have a right to be told.

LILLIAN: I'm not as sure as you. I can see how not telling them is a violation of their rights as parents, and the family has been weakened enough today without weakening it further. But on the other hand, teenage girls are not just objects. They're people, and as such they have rights, such as the right to determine how their bodies will be used. And many times they can't talk to their parents about sex.

ROY: Nonsense. Parents care about their kids. They have their interests at heart more than anyone else, particularly some money-grabbing doctor. If kids really want to talk to their parents, there's nothing stopping them—except the possibility that they don't want to hear what their parents will say.

LILLIAN: Another thing bothers me, too. Why does the issue always focus on teenage girls rather than teenage boys?

ROY: Check with your local anatomist.

1.5. Follow the directions for Application 1.2.

GUY: Want to know what makes me sick? The tolerance our society has for transsexuals. I can't think of anything more disgusting than a person changing sexes to act out homosexual fantasies or to get more sexual satisfaction.

DARRELL: You obviously don't know much about transsexualism.

GUY: Don't tell me you excuse their perversion, too.

DARRELL: There's nothing to excuse. And you're mistaken in calling it a perversion. It's not.

GUY: What else can it be but a perversion? A man decides to be a woman, or vice versa. It's a mockery of nature. We are what we're born to be and it's our responsibility to accept that. It ought to be against the law to tamper with nature the way they do.

1.6. The following passage is an excerpt from a student's letter home. Read it carefully. Then decide whether its reasoning is sound or unsound. State and explain your judgment in a paragraph or two, including whatever supporting material you believe will help persuade your reader.

The one thing that really bugs me about my schedule this term is that required course in "Introduction to Literature." Some students may not know what their future career is. I do. It's to help you, Dad, with the business, and someday to take it over. If we sold books I could see the value of such a course. But literature surely isn't going to make me a better furniture store manager.

GROUP DISCUSSION EXERCISE

Discuss the following issue with two or three of your classmates. Observe the guidelines to group discussion presented in Appendix B. Consider all sides of the matter and try to reach consensus. Be prepared to report your group's deliberations to the class, describing how your analysis proceeded, what questions were asked, and what agreements were reached. If differences of viewpoint remain unresolved, be prepared to report them objectively.

> Some people believe that the emphasis on competitive sports such as basketball, softball, and volleyball in physical education classes is a form of discrimination against students who lack athletic ability. They propose that competitive sports be replaced by aerobic exercises, interpretive dancing, and other noncompetitive activities. Do you support this proposal?

COMPOSITION OR SPEECH EXERCISE

Write a composition or, if your instructor specifies, a formal speech, presenting the view your group reached in the preceding group discussion exercise. (If you hold a dissenting view, present that instead.) Be sure to provide evidence that your view is the most reasonable one. Naturally your composition or speech will bear some resemblance to those of the other members of your group—you will have developed ideas as a team, so at least some of your ideas will be similar, even identical, to theirs. Don't be concerned about such similarities. Your composition or speech will be a unique effort if you (a) use supporting material from your own experience, observation, and research; (b) develop your own line of reasoning about that material; (c) employ your own ingenuity in designing an introduction and conclusion and in arranging the material in the body of your composition or speech; and (d) express your thoughts in your own words. For further guidance, consult the appropriate appendix—A for writing, B for speaking.

PART I

Be
Aware

Establish a Foundation

If thinking took place in a mind completely insulated from the outside world, an intellectually germ-free environment, there would be no need for the preliminary work in this chapter. We could just turn to techniques and strategies for thinking and begin practicing them. But that is not the case. We humans are social creatures. We live in an imperfect world, a world of conflicting ideas and values. And these affect us, for good or for ill.

Thus the ideas you have about free will, truth, knowledge, opinion, and the debating of moral issues will make a difference in your development as a thinker. Some ideas will enhance your thinking; others will hinder it. Still others may paralyze it altogether. It is therefore important to examine these matters closely before proceeding, sorting out helpful from harmful notions, and establishing a firm conceptual foundation. First we'll consider the question of free will.

FREE WILL VERSUS DETERMINISM

Are you reading this chapter because you chose to do so or through compulsion? By *compulsion* I don't mean your instructor's direction, "Read Chapter 2 for tomorrow." That is a kind of gentle (and benevolent) pressure, but it is not compulsion. Compulsion is a force you are virtually powerless to resist. Some psychologists would argue that you have no free will and so you are not reading through choice but through compulsion.

"Wait a minute," you say, "I know I have free will because right at this minute there's a party in my friend's room and I had to struggle with my conscience to read this chapter instead of going there." The psychologists smile patiently and say, "Sorry, that struggle was an illusion. There's no choice—just a stimulus-response bond. You've been conditioned to behave in a certain way, and so you behave that way."

"Oh, yeah," you respond, "then watch this." You slam shut the book and head for the door. They yawn and say, "Quite unconvincing. All that your dramatic action shows is that you've been conditioned to be stubborn in the face of a disagreeable idea."

At this point your fists are clenched and you're beginning to grind your teeth. That's a normal reaction. And a lot of scholars and intellectuals—yes, and a lot of other psychologists—react similarly. Many of them have wisely given up arguing with the strict determinists. They realize that it's as impossible to win with someone whose rule is "Anything you say will prove my point" as it is to play cards with someone who stacks the deck.

This is not to say that reasonable people reject the idea of conditioning. On the contrary, they reject only the extreme notion that *all* human action is governed by conditioning. They take the moderate view that though we are all influenced by our surroundings and background, sometimes very strongly, we usually retain a significant measure of free will. Reasonable people would say that it is possible you are reading this chapter because of some compulsion but more likely that you are doing so because you chose to read rather than to attend the party. What role has conditioning in your choice? They would say it increases or decreases the probability of one choice over another. A student who has acquired the habit of putting responsible action before self-indulgence would be more likely to do so in any particular situation.

It is important for you to accept this more moderate view for a number of reasons. First, you can discuss moral issues meaningfully only if you affirm that people have some control over their behavior and to that extent are responsible for it. (There is little point in discussing which of two actions is preferable if no one has the ability to choose between them.) In addition, you can profitably discuss social issues like nuclear disarmament, prison reform, or the treatment of the elderly only if you affirm that individuals or a whole society can change their policies and priorities. Most important, you can become motivated to approach problems creatively and critically only if you affirm that you have control over what you say and do, only if you affirm that careful thinking can make a difference.

WHAT IS TRUTH?

We live in an age that has made the true-false test not only the basis of educational achievement but also the staple of one of our most durable (if lamentable) forms of entertainment, the game show. For this reason, it is ironic that so much confusion exists about truth. Even otherwise intelligent people can be heard saying things such as "Everyone makes his own truth," "One person's truth is another person's error," "Truth is relative," and "Truth is constantly changing." All of these ideas undermine thinking.

If everyone makes his or her own truth, no person's idea can be better than another's. All must be equal. And if all ideas are equal, what is the point in researching any subject? Why dig into the ground for answers to archaeological questions? Why probe the causes of tension in the Middle East? Why search for a cancer cure? Why explore the galaxy? These activities make sense only if some answers are better than others, if truth is something separate from, and unaffected by, individual perspectives.

Consider, for instance, this interesting (though hardly momentous) question: What are the most popular street names in the United States? If the truth here is relative, any answer is as good as any other. One person says, "Maple," another, "Roosevelt," still another, "Grove," and so on. Many people would say, "Broadway" or "Main." (After deciding on your answer, check page 245.)[1] If every answer were equally correct, few people would be interested in the question. Yet progress depends on the curiosity and interest of people, the drive to find the *right* answer, the desire to know the truth.

Truth is *what is so* about something, the reality of the matter, as distinguished from what people wish were so, believe to be so, or assert to be so. From another perspective, in the words of Harvard philosopher Israel Scheffler, truth is the view "which is fated to be ultimately agreed to by all who investigate."[2] The word *ultimately* is important. Investigation may produce a wrong answer for years, even for centuries. *The Man with the Golden Helmet*, a well-known and often-reproduced seventeenth-century painting, was for centuries considered the work of Rembrandt. Only in recent years was it established to be the work of an unknown contemporary of Rembrandt.[3] Though generations of art experts proclaimed the work to be Rembrandt's, the truth remained unaltered.

At various times and places, some very strange ideas were widely accepted as true: for example, the idea that a horsehair turns into a snake when placed in water. (Even Shakespeare believed this one.[4]) The reason people were deceived is obvious to anyone who has observed how refraction of light in water makes any object appear to be moving.

Similarly, many people believed erroneously that small flies, moths, and bees are babies of larger ones.[5] And the history of medicine includes an interesting and often bizarre collection of folk cures—for example, curing a headache by putting a bowl on the head, cutting the hair around the bowl, and then burning the hair; curing an earache by having someone spit tobacco juice in the affected ear; curing pneumonia by cutting a live chicken in two and placing it over the person's lungs; and curing weak vision by piercing the ears.[6]

We laugh at these ideas today, and rightly so. But it is important to realize that our laughter underlines the fact that people do not *create* truth. If they did, how would scientists ever test theories? The very creation of a theory would be documentation of its validity, and every theory would thus be equally acceptable. This, of course, is nonsense. We know from everyday experience that some theories prove accurate and others inaccurate. The test of a theory's validity must lie outside the theory itself.

But if people do not create their own truth, what do they do? They reach out to apprehend it and construct expressions that they hope represent it faithfully. Sometimes they succeed, and sometimes they fail. Novelist H. G. Wells summed up the challenge and the difficulty of the task in a simple metaphor: "The forceps of our minds are clumsy forceps and crush the truth a little in taking hold of it."[7]

Does the truth ever change? No. It may sometimes seem to, but on closer inspection it will be found not to. Some years ago for example, a previously unknown species of fish was accidentally found deep in the Pacific Ocean.[8] We might think that the truth was that no such fish existed at first, and that the truth changed when the fish was discovered. But think of just how foolish that idea is. It asks us to believe that there was no such fish swimming in the water and that someone in a deep-diving machine "looked" it into existence. How much more reasonable it is to believe that the fish existed but we didn't know that it did: in other words, that the truth of the matter was the same before and after the discovery, and only our knowledge of it changed.

Consider another very different example, the case of the authorship of the first book of the Bible, the book of Genesis. For centuries Christians and Jews alike believed that the book had a single author. In time this view was challenged and eventually replaced by the belief that as many as five authors contributed to Genesis. Then the results of a 5-year linguistic analysis of Genesis were published, stating that there is an 82 percent probability of single authorship, as originally thought.[9] Has the truth about the authorship of Genesis changed? No. Only our belief has changed. Perhaps one day we will have final and conclusive proof. On the other hand, perhaps, like an unsolved crime, the matter will never be resolved. The truth will not be changed by our knowledge or by our ignorance.

One easy way to spare yourself any further confusion about truth is to reserve the word *truth* for the final answer to an issue. Get in the habit of using the words *belief, theory,* and *present understanding* more often. This will have the added benefit of making you more willing to revise your views when new evidence appears and casts them in doubt.

WHAT IS KNOWING?

Here's a brief quiz. Don't read ahead until you have completed it:

1. Who said, "I only regret that I have but one life to give for my country"?
2. What was the agreed-upon signal that was to be given Paul Revere from the tower if the British were coming?
3. What was Cinderella's slipper made of in the original story?
4. What is a camel's hair brush made of?

Most people could answer these questions quite readily. But the answers that come quite readily to those who are sure they "know" are often wrong.[10] (See page 246 for the correct answers.) The point is that *thinking we know* is not the same as *knowing*. We can think we know, be certain we know, proclaim loudly that we know, and yet not know at all. Our ideas do not constitute knowledge unless they correspond to reality.

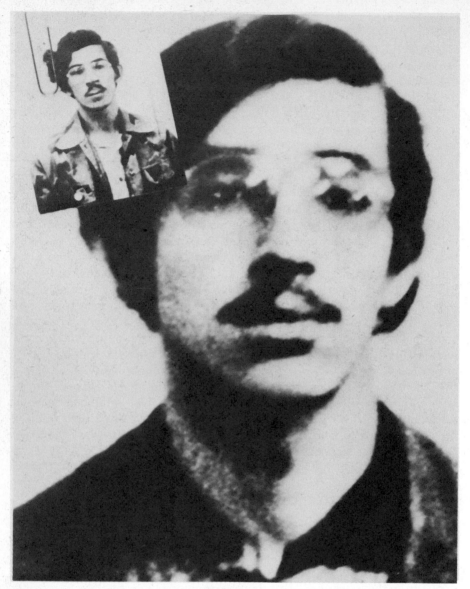

Figure 2.1 Lawrence Berson (inset) and his look-alike, Richard Carbone. Copyright © 1974 by the New York Times Company. Reprinted by permission.

Reality, unfortunately, can be deceptive. In 1972, 17-year-old college student Lawrence Berson was held for more than a week on multiple rape charges . . . until another man, Richard Carbone, 20, confessed to the crime. A glance at photographs of the two (Figure 2.1) will explain why the victims who identified Berson "knew" he was the rapist.[11]

It is obvious that situations in which we believe we know but really *don't* know pose an obstacle to effective thinking. Why should anyone go to the trouble to investigate a matter or listen to opposing testimony if one believes one knows already? It is important, therefore, to understand the dynamics of knowing—how we come to know and what kinds of knowledge are most trustworthy.

WAYS OF KNOWING

We know in one of three ways—*by experiencing situations, by witnessing others' experiences,* or *by report.*° Each way is subject to error.

Direct Experience

Of the three ways of knowing, direct experience is usually the most trustworthy. But even this way is less than perfect. We do not just receive experiences and store them, hermetically sealed, in our minds. We compare them with previous experiences; classify, interpret, and evaluate them; and make assumptions about them. All these processes may occur quite unconsciously, without our being aware of them. And any flaw in them makes our experiences seem different from the reality we encountered.

Consider this situation. Agnes has grown up in a religious family. She went to a parochial school and celebrated all the feasts of her church, including Christmas. She knows that Christmas is a Christian feast, and throughout her lifetime it has always been a sacred time. From her knowledge she unconsciously creates the idea that it has always been so, throughout the history of Christianity. In time, this vague idea becomes a certainty in her mind. She can even imagine herself hearing it expressed in a classroom. Yes, she *knows* that Christmas has always been a major Christian feast.

Alas, she is wrong. In fact, in seventeenth-century England the Puritans forbade the celebration of Christmas. They felt it was a pagan custom. Similarly, it was banned in colonial New England. Christmas was not made a legal holiday in Massachusetts until 1856.

Here is another, even more common, example. All of us have experienced childhood as a stage in our development. Most of us have never conceived of anyone *not* experiencing childhood, so it is easy for us to believe with certainty that childhood always existed. Yet research shows this idea to be false. Historian J. H. Plumb writes,

> The world that we think proper to children—fairy stories, games, toys, special books for learning, even the idea of childhood itself, is a European invention of the past four hundred years. The very words we use for young males—boy, *garçon, Knabe*—were until the seventeenth century used indiscriminately to

---

°Our concern here is with the most commonly discussed kind of knowing, *knowing that*. Its focus is information. (Another, equally important kind of knowing is *knowing how*. Its focus is procedures and strategies. The measure of knowing how, or know-how, is not the possession of a body of content but the performance of a skill.)

mean a male in a dependent position and could refer to men of thirty, forty, or fifty. There was no special word for a young male between the age of seven and sixteen; the word "child" expressed kinship, not an age state.[12]

Because our perceptions are not passively received but are influenced by our emotional states and mental processes, they seldom mirror reality. At times, in fact, they seriously distort reality.

Witnessing Others' Experiences

It is certainly possible to observe accurately, but we often fall short of doing so. We usually see the world through glasses colored by our experiences and beliefs. If we believe that blacks are more athletic than whites, we are likely to "see" a particular black athlete outperforming a white athlete in a basketball game—even if that is not occurring. If we believe that Italians are violent by nature, we are likely to "see" an Italian man making threatening gestures and preparing to strike another person when we observe him in a spirited discussion—even when those gestures are not unfriendly. Exactly how such distortions of observation occur may be explained as follows:

> We are told about the world before we see it. We imagine most things before we experience them. And those preconceptions, unless education has made us acutely aware, govern deeply the whole process of perception. They mark out certain objects as familiar or strange, emphasizing the difference, so that the slightly familiar is seen as very familiar, and the somewhat strange as sharply alien. They are aroused by small signs, which may vary from a true index to a vague analogy. Aroused, they flood fresh vision with older images, and project into the world what has been resurrected in memory.[13]

Report

This source of knowledge covers most of what we are taught by parents and teachers, what we hear reported in the news, and what we read in books and magazines. Most people who present ideas to us are undoubtedly trying to teach accurately and not deliberately misinform us; they themselves believe what they tell us. Yet because they are human and therefore capable of error, it is likely that a fair percentage of what we have been taught is at least partly incorrect.

An interesting example of the extent to which error can creep into news reports was revealed by George Seldes. Here is an original news story, together with the actual facts, as later determined by Seldes:[14]

THE STORY

Belgrade, Oct. 27—A few moments before she should have appeared on the stage at the Lioubliana Theater last

THE FACTS

After the first act. Not at the Lioubliana, but the Klägenfurt. Her name, Ella Beer. Not Slovene, but Viennese. Not in night, Mme. Alla Behr, a Slovene actress, was found hanging dead in her dressing-room. The reason for the suicide is unknown.

her dressing-room, but in her hotel. The reason was known.

How could the reporter make such a total botch of the story? It's really not too difficult to imagine. He probably arrived at the scene late, found the area cordoned off, and got his details from bystanders or police keeping the crowd back—in other words, from people whose only knowledge was the fragments of fact and hearsay that circulated among them.

Errors are sometimes made from simple carelessness. For example, it was reported in an upstate New York daily newspaper that Thomas Simmons was arrested for striking Carl Peterson on the head. A day or two later, a corrected version was published. It seems Peterson had struck Simmons.[15] All those who read the first version but missed the second "knew" what had happened, but they were wrong.

But what of magazine articles and books? These are researched more carefully than newspaper articles and therefore ought to be more accurate. Edwin Clarke writes,

It is well known that secondary sources are likely to be written to harmonize with generally accepted beliefs and prejudices. Most popular histories, for instance . . . make heroes more heroic, villains more wicked, battles bloodier, and peaces more glorious than the best primary sources warrant. In short, they tend to present historical events, not as they were, but as the author likes to think of them, or as he believes his public likes or ought to think of them.[16]

THE PROBLEM OF REMEMBERING

Finally, all three ways of knowing—experience, observation, and report—are subject to another problem, one that occurs days, months, or years later. This problem is the tendency to remember inaccurately. Memory, of course, is a great blessing—the agony of amnesia is evidence enough of this fact. But memory can work tricks on knowledge. When we remember, according to authorities, the first thing that occurs is something like an attitude. Then we reconstruct what we are remembering, largely in conformity with our attitude. It is common to add new details, to condense what happened, and to elaborate and invent things that weren't part of the original experience.[17]

Even eyewitness testimony is subject to this distortion. "It has been found," one report states, "that witnesses have a tendency both to perceive and to remember things, first according to their expectations, second, according to their emotional bias, and third, according to their private notions as to what would be the natural or reasonable way for things to happen."[18]

One simple example, of a kind that everyone has experienced at one time or another, will illustrate the problem. Professor Sage is sitting captive at a faculty meeting as a long-winded administrator drones on and on. Seeking escape, he opens a book and begins to read. Suddenly he hears his name spoken: "Mr. Sage, may I have your attention, please." Caught off guard, he looks up awkwardly, accidentally drops his book, and stammers, "Uh . . . I was listening . . . sort of . . . sorry."

As he is driving home after the meeting, his mind ranges over the responses he could have made to the speaker. Finally, he settles on the best one. He would rise to his feet dramatically and reply in his most withering tone, "Sir, my attendance at this meeting you may require; my attention you must *earn*." Several months later, Professor Sage tells a friend the experience as it exists in his memory. Which version is that? The one he truly believes is the correct one: the one he imagined in his car.

This seems a rather pessimistic view of knowing and remembering, but you shouldn't be discouraged by it. It is not the whole story—only the neglected side. It is possible for you to know accurately and to remember with little distortion. The point is that this seldom happens automatically for anyone. The key to having it happen for you is to be cautious in claiming to know, be ready to update your views, and make an effort to avoid distortion wherever possible.

WHAT ARE OPINIONS?

Opinions are intensely personal, so it is understandable that people have strong feelings about theirs. But many people carry those feelings beyond the boundaries of good sense. They take the valid idea "Everyone has a right to his or her opinion" to the ridiculous extreme of "Everyone's opinion is right." No one can hope to be a good thinker without acquiring a mature understanding of the nature of opinion.

The basic problem with the word *opinion* is that it is too general. It is made to carry a heavier load than it can bear, covering both expressions of taste and expressions of judgment.

Expressions of Taste

Expressions of taste describe internal states and preferences. They say essentially, "I like this" and "I dislike that." For example, one may say, "I find bald men attractive" or "I wouldn't buy any car but a Buick" or "When I look at a painting of a cow, I want to see something resembling a cow, not a swirl of color" or "Yellow and purple go well together." All these statements are expressions of taste. We may share the preferences or find them deplorably vulgar. But we have no business asking someone to defend these statements. No defense is necessary.

Expressions of Judgment

Expressions of judgment are assertions about the truth of things or about the wisdom of a course of action. Thus, if people say, "Bald men get more colds than hirsute men" or "Buicks are more economical cars than Fords" or "Paintings of cows that are unrecognizable as cows are inferior paintings" or "Yellow and purple combinations have never been in style in America," they are not expressing taste (though their taste may be lurking in the background). They are expressing judgment every bit as much as if they had commented on the question of whether the death penalty deters crime or whether the voting age should be raised.

It is not impolite or undemocratic to challenge an expression of judgment. Judgments are only as good as the evidence that supports them. History is filled with examples of judgments based either on insufficient evidence or narrow interpretation of evidence. In many cases they did untold harm because people were timid about challenging them.

For centuries people accepted the idea that the heart rather than the brain is the center of human consciousness. As late as the seventeenth century people believed that the planets were guided in their orbits by angels. (Even the renowned astronomer Johannes Kepler did not question this belief.)[19] Fossils were known to exist long before Charles Darwin's day; in the Middle Ages they were interpreted as relics of plants and animals destroyed by Noah's flood, as creations of Satan to deceive religious people, or as tests of religious faith put in the ground by God.[20]

Similarly, at various times our ancestors believed that disordered behavior was caused by demons and that the most effective cure was either magic, an enema, imprisonment in an asylum, beating, spinning in a rotating machine, or stoning to death.[21] And as late as 1902 books were being written proclaiming that black people were created along with animals to serve Adam, that they possess minds but not souls, that Adam's temptress was a black servant, and that Cain married a black woman and so mixed the blood of men and beasts.[22]

The fact that human judgment can be not only wrong but also ludicrous is the best reason to base your judgments on sufficient evidence, carefully interpreted, rather than on prejudice, whim, or blind faith, and to be quick to reconsider your judgments when new evidence challenges them.

DEBATING MORAL QUESTIONS

Nowhere is modern thinking more muddled than over the question of whether it is proper to debate moral issues. Many argue it is not, saying it is wrong to make "value judgments." This view is shallow. If such judgments were wrong, ethics, philosophy, and theology would be unacceptable in a college curriculum—an idea that is obviously silly. As the following cases illustrate, it is impossible to avoid making value judgments.

Raoul Wallenberg was a young Swedish aristocrat. In 1944 he left the safety of his country and entered Budapest. Over the next year he outwitted the Nazis and saved as many as 100,000 Jews from the death camps (he was not himself Jewish). In 1945 he was arrested by the Russians, charged with spying, and imprisoned in a Russian labor camp. He undoubtedly perished there.[23] Now, if we regard him as a hero (as there is excellent reason to do), we are making a value judgment. Yet if we regard him neutrally, as no different from anyone else, we are also making a value judgment. We are judging him to be neither hero nor villain, only unexceptional.

Consider another case. A 20-year-old mother left her three infant sons unattended in a garbage-strewn tenement in New York City.[24] Police found them there, starving, the youngest child lodged between a mattress and a wall, covered with flies and cockroaches, the eldest playing on the second-floor window ledge. The police judged the mother negligent, and the court agreed. Was it wrong for them to judge? No. Refusing to judge would have been a judgment in the mother's favor.

No matter how difficult it may be to judge such moral issues, we *must* judge them. Value judgment is the basis not only of our social code but also of our legal system. The quality of our laws is directly affected by the quality of our moral judgments. A society that judges blacks inferior is not likely to accord blacks equal treatment. A society that believes a woman's place is in the home is not likely to guarantee women equal employment opportunity.

Other people accept value judgments as long as they are made *within* a culture and not about other cultures. Right and wrong, they believe, vary from one culture to another. It is true that an act frowned on in one culture may be tolerated in another, but the degree of difference has often been grossly exaggerated. When we first encounter an unfamiliar moral view, we are inclined to focus on the difference so much that we miss the similarity.

For example, in medieval Europe animals were tried for crimes and often formally executed. In fact, cockroaches and other bugs were sometimes excommunicated from the church.[25] Sounds absurd, doesn't it? But when we penetrate beneath the absurdity, we realize that the basic view—that some actions are reprehensible and ought to be punished—is not so strange. The core idea that a person bitten by, say, a dog, has been wronged and requires justice is very much the same. The only difference is our rejection of the idea that animals are responsible for their behavior.

Is it legitimate, then, for us to pass judgment on the moral standards of another culture? Yes, if we do so thoughtfully, not simply conclude that whatever differs from our view is necessarily wrong. We can say, for example, that a culture that treats women as property or places less value on their lives than on the lives of men is acting immorally by denying women their human rights. Consider the following cases.

In nineteenth-century Rio de Janeiro, Brazil, a theatrical producer shot and killed his wife because she insisted on taking a walk in the botanical gardens against his wishes. He was formally charged with her murder, but the judge dismissed the charge. The producer was carried through the streets in triumph. The moral perspective of his culture condoned the taking of a woman's life if she disobeyed her husband, even in a relatively small matter. A century later that perspective had changed little. In the same city, in 1976, a wealthy playboy, angry at his lover for flirting with others, fired four shots into her face at point-blank range, killing her. He was given a 2-year suspended sentence in light of the fact that he had been "defending his honor."[26]

Surely it is irresponsible for us to withhold judgment on the morality of these cases merely because they occurred in a different culture. It is obvious that in both cases the men's response—murder—was out of all proportion to the women's "offenses" and therefore demonstrated a wanton disregard for the women's human rights. Their response is thus properly judged immoral. And this judgment implies another: that the culture condoning such behavior is guilty of moral insensitivity.

THE BASIS OF MORAL JUDGMENT

On what basis should moral judgment be made? Certainly not the majority view—that is too unreliable. In the 1976 murder in Rio, for example, a radio poll revealed that 90 percent of the people surveyed agreed with the verdict. Hitler enjoyed the support of a majority of the German people. The American people at one time supported slavery. And more recently, the majority first opposed abortion, then approved it. Nor should the basis of moral judgments be feelings, desires, or preferences. If it were, then we would be forced to conclude that every rapist, every murderer, every robber is acting morally. Conscience provides a better basis for judgment, but it too can be uninformed or insensitive. (After all, the most vicious criminals sometimes feel no remorse.)

The most reliable basis for moral judgment, the basis that underlies most ethical systems, is the principle that people have rights existing independently of any government or culture. The most fundamental is the right to be treated with respect and left undisturbed as long as one does not infringe on others' rights. Other rights—such as "life, liberty, and the pursuit of happiness"—extend from that right.

The basic principle, of course, is not itself adequate to judge complex moral questions. Additional working principles are needed. The following four are found in most ethical systems and provide common ground for the discussion of issues, even among people of very different ethical perspectives.

1. Relationships with other people create *obligations* of various kinds, and these should be honored unless there is compelling reason not to do so. There are, for example, formal agreements or contracts, obligations of family membership (parent to child, child to parent, husband to wife, and vice versa), obligations of friendship, employer-employee obligations, and business and professional obligations.
2. Certain *ideals* enhance human life and assist people in fulfilling their obligations to one another. These should be served whenever possible.

Among the most important ideals are tolerance, compassion, loyalty, forgiveness, peace, brotherhood, justice (giving people their due), and fairness (being impartial, as opposed to favoring selected people).

3. The *consequences* of some actions benefit people, whereas those of other actions harm people. The former actions should be preferred over the latter. Consequences, of course, can be emotional as well as physical, momentary as well as lasting, and subtle as well as obvious.

4. Circumstances alter cases. Generalizations have their place, but too often they are used as a substitute for careful judgment. "Taking a human life is wrong" is useful as a general moral outlook, but it provides little help in deciding real cases. It blurs important distinctions. A contract killer for the mob takes a life when completing a contract. So does a police officer who kills a robber in self-defense. And so does a small child who mistakes a real pistol for a toy and accidentally shoots a sibling. But all three acts are very different from one another. Good thinking about issues means getting beyond generalizations and examining the particulars of the case.

To achieve depth in your examination of moral issues and wisdom in your judgment, you must deal effectively with complexities. The presence of two or more conflicting obligations or ideals creates complexity. So does the likelihood of multiple consequences, some beneficial and some harmful. Here is an easy-to-follow guide for dealing with such complexities.

1. Where two or more obligations are in conflict, decide which is the most serious obligation or which existed first.
2. Where two or more ideals are in conflict, ask which is the highest or most important ideal.
3. Where multiple consequences exist, some good and some bad, ask which are most significant, and whether the good effects outweigh the bad, or the reverse.

Let's look at an actual moral issue and see how these considerations apply. Ralph is a middle-aged man. In his youth he was a good athlete, and his son Mark grew up sharing his father's enthusiasm for sports. In seventh grade Mark went out for three sports but was rather poor in two of them. Basketball was his best sport; in that he was fair but not outstanding. Ralph decided that Mark could only be a first-string player if he received some assistance. So Ralph struck up a friendship with the junior varsity and varsity basketball coaches. He invited them to his house for dinner, opened his personal sports library to them, and got them tickets to professional games through his business contacts.

Through his friendship with the coaches, Ralph was able to help his son. He spoke to them often about Mark's intense desire to excel in basketball and asked whether they would mind giving Mark some tips to improve his game. The coaches were happy to help Mark; their help was an expression of their friendship with Ralph. They opened the gym to him on weekends and took personal responsibility for developing his skills.

Soon Mark was playing junior varsity basketball. Ralph took every opportunity not only to remind the coach of Mark's dedication but also to point out other players' weaknesses and apparent lack of dedication. Mark received more playing time in each game than his skills alone justified, and in time he became the team's scoring leader. When he moved up to varsity, Mark received further special treatment. He was almost never benched, even when his team was far ahead; instead, he was kept in to raise his point total. During his senior year, most of the team's plays were designed for him. And Ralph persuaded the coaches to write letters praising Mark's playing to a number of college coaches.

Did Ralph behave morally? Let's apply the principles we discussed earlier and see.

There are three important obligations involved in this case: Ralph's obligation to guide his son responsibly to manhood, through teaching and example; obligations of friendship between Ralph and the coaches; and the coaches' obligation to help all their players develop their potential and learn the values associated with sports.

The ideals that should be considered are sensitivity to others' needs, justice, and fairness. The first applies to Ralph: He should have appreciated the other players' needs for encouragement, support, and equal opportunity. The other two ideals, justice and fairness, apply to the coaches: They should have considered giving each player on the team the attention and help he deserved, rather than concentrating their attention on one player. (This, of course, does not mean that it would be an injustice to give special attention to an outstanding player; Mark, remember, was only a fair player at the outset.) And the coaches should have considered treating players impartially (fairly). One way they could have done this was by opening the gym on weekends to all players who wished to practice, instead of only to one.

The clearest and most certain consequence was that Mark's skills were developed and the other players were shortchanged because they did not have the same opportunities. Other probable consequences were that Mark's teammates developed a feeling of bitterness and cynicism over the coaches' favoritism and that Mark acquired the attitude that it was permissible, even desirable, for him to disregard other people's rights and needs to achieve his own goals.

It is clear that though Ralph's actions achieved some good (the development of his son's skills), they also caused a great deal of harm to a number of people. The obvious harm was to the players. But they also caused the coaches to put friendship over responsibility to their players and to violate the ideals of justice and fairness. (The main responsibility for the coaches' actions is, of course, their own. They could have resisted Ralph's influence.) Moreover, Ralph's actions probably even harmed his son. The self-serving attitude created in him far outweighs the development of his modest athletic skill.

In light of these considerations, we would find Ralph's actions morally wrong. Further, the fact that he knew what he was doing and actually *planned* it makes him even more blameworthy.

DEALING WITH DILEMMAS

Moral issues frequently pose dilemmas, situations in which a number of choices are available, but no choice is completely satisfactory. Such situations are frustrating. No matter what choice we consider, it seems the wrong one. "It's impossible to decide," we tell ourselves. Such situations are best approached with a clear strategy in mind. The following strategy will help you get beyond confusion and indecision:

1. Remember that you needn't classify your choices into simple good-versus-bad terms. It is possible to view them in a more sophisticated way. To do so, ask where each choice fits on the following scale.

| Best | Better | Good | Bad | Worse | Worst |

Note: This approach will help you to distinguish between choices that at first glance seem equally moral.
2. In situations where the choices are all good, decide which is the *greater good*. In situations where none of the choices is really good, decide which is the *lesser evil*.

WARM-UP EXERCISES

Remember that the warm-up exercises have no special relation to the chapter and generally concern matters of less consequence than the applications. They are intended mainly to "limber up" your thinking, so be as daring and imaginative as you wish in responding to them.

2.1. Your niece, a preschooler, asks you the following question: "Is it possible to remember the future?" Compose an answer simple and clear enough for her to understand.

2.2. If I say, "I'll see you tomorrow," three days in a row, am I saying the same thing each time? Explain your answer thoroughly.

2.3. A man is walking up on the down escalator, and it is moving down faster than he is moving up. Is he going upstairs or downstairs? Explain thoroughly.

APPLICATIONS

2.1. Read the following dialogue carefully, looking for flaws in thinking. If you find a flaw, identify it and explain the fault in sufficient detail to persuade someone who has read the passage without seeing the flaw. (If you find two or more flaws, identify and explain your thinking about each.)

> CLEM: Can you believe that stuff Chapter 2 says about truth and opinion? I mean, it's a lot of garbage.

CLYDE: I don't know . . . it sort of made sense to me.

CLEM: Come on, man, you've got to be kidding. How can some egghead textbook writer tell *me* what truth is for me? He's himself, not me. How can he see through my eyes or make up my mind? Only I can do that.

CLYDE: But wait a minute. . . .

CLEM: Wait, nothing. You're taken in by all the words, man. Like that stuff about opinion. This is a democracy, isn't it? In a dictatorship, the governement can say which opinion is right, but not here. My opinion is as good as anyone else's. It says so right in the Constitution.

2.2. In November 1914 the German army invaded and captured the city of Antwerp, Belgium. The German press reported that the occasion was celebrated in Germany. Other European newspapers noted the German report and wrote their own news releases. Here are the texts of the original German statement and four subsequent accounts.[27]

When the fall of Antwerp became known, the church bells were rung [meaning in Germany]. *(Kölnische Zeitung)*

According to the *Kölnische Zeitung,* the clergy of Antwerp were compelled to ring the church bells when the fortress was taken. *(Le Matin)*

According to what *Le Matin* has heard from Cologne, the Belgian priests who refused to ring the church bells when Antwerp was taken have been driven away from their positions. *(The Times)*

According to what the *Times* [London] has heard from Cologne via Paris, the unfortunate priests who refused to ring the church bells when Antwerp was taken have been sentenced to hard labor. *(Corriere della Sera)*

According to information to the *Corriere della Sera* from Cologne via London, it is confirmed that the barbaric conquerors of Antwerp punished the unfortunate Belgian priests for their heroic refusal to ring the church bells by hanging them as living clappers to the bells with their heads down. *(Le Matin)*

In a paragraph or two explain how such distortion could have occurred. Draw on what you learned in this chapter or in Chapter 1 to write your response.

2.3. When jazz musician Billy Tipton died at age 74, it was learned that "he" was a woman. Tipton apparently had begun the deception early in life to enhance "his" chances of success as a musician. Virtually everyone who knew, or knew of, Tipton (including "his" three adopted sons) was certain "he" was a man. Did the fact that millions of people believed Tipton was a man change the truth of the matter? Does your answer support or challenge the popular notion that people create their own truth?

2.4. Turn back to Application 1.1. Select one of the statements there (a–r) and recall your response to it. Examine that response in light of what you learned in this chapter about knowledge and opinion. That is, determine the source(s) of your view and its soundness.

2.5. In a small Central American village some years ago, a visiting American student witnessed the following incident. A homosexual was dragged through the street by the police after being found in a compromising situation with his lover. When they got him in front of the police station, they made him take off his pants and bend over. The police chief proceeded to beat him on the buttocks with a riding crop until blood flowed from his wounds. Then the chief made the man repeat, "I am a man and will behave like a man." Finally, he was taken inside the jail and forced to have intercourse with a prostitute. Discuss the moral considerations in this case and judge the moral quality of the police's treatment of the man.

2.6. The quotation that follows is by a famous American politician. Does it challenge any idea you read in this chapter? If so, identify the idea it challenges and decide which view is more reasonable. If it does not challenge anything, identify the part of the chapter it is most in agreement with.

It is a great and dangerous error to suppose that all people are entitled to liberty. It is a reward to be earned, not a blessing to be gratuitously lavished on all alike;—a reward reserved for the intelligent, the patriotic, the virtuous and deserving;—and not a boon to be bestowed on a people too ignorant, degraded and vicious, to be capable either of appreciating or of enjoying it. (John C. Calhoun)[28]

2.7. Each of the following cases involves a moral question. (Some also involve legal questions that do not concern us here.) Identify the important moral considerations in each and then judge the morality of the action that was taken (or is proposed). Be sure to explain your reasoning carefully.

a. A 9-year-old Depew, New York, boy turned his mother in to the authorities for using drugs. Do you believe his action was morally acceptable? (The boy's mother and father are separated and he lives with his father, who explained that the boy acted out of "concern and love.")[29]

b. Terrorists often perform random acts of violence in public places, maiming or killing dozens of innocent people. They argue that such acts are justifiable because they call attention to the causes they represent, such as the liberation of their homeland. "Our cause," they reason, "is sacred and therefore must be regarded more important than human lives, our own as well as others'."

c. A doctor in Waltham, Massachusetts, was convicted of raping a nurse at the hospital where he was employed. While free pending appeal of his conviction, he applied for a position at a Buffalo, New York, hospital. The Waltham hospital administration reportedly wrote him a strong letter of recommendation and did not mention the rape case. (Buffalo hospital officials learned of his conviction only when a new rape charge, involving patients, was filed against him in Waltham.)[30] Did the Waltham officials behave morally in withholding information concerning his rape conviction?

d. Dahlia Reyna, 17, was a victim of a rare disease that attacks the central nervous system and destroys brain cells. The doctors in Edinburgh, Texas, gave her no chance for survival: She had no brain waves and only her respirator kept her heart pumping. Her parents requested that the respirator be unplugged so that she could die. The hospital complied and Dahlia expired.[31] Was it morally right to unplug the respirator?

e. In Montpelier, Vermont, 11-year-old Ana Sola was struck by a car and rushed to the hospital. When her father, a Jehovah's Witness, denied permission for the blood transfusion that the doctors felt was imperative, a judge revoked the parents' custody of the girl and gave it to the state so the transfusion could be administered.[32] The judge's behavior was within legal limits, but was it moral?

f.   In Bartow, Florida, a defense attorney doubted that prosecution witnesses could identify his client in an assault case. So he asked a young man he saw in the courthouse corridor to sit in place of his client at the defense table. The young man did so, and the witnesses identified him as the man who had committed the assault and thereby lost their credibility with the jury. As a result of the defense attorney's trick, the defendant eventually went free.[33] Did the attorney behave morally?

g.   Brian and Louise have been dating steadily for 3 years. Although they do not live together, they often stay at each other's apartment for several days at a time. Now Louise has met an attractive man at work and isn't sure about her feelings for Brian. She would like to tell Brian that she believes she no longer loves him and wants to date someone else, but she is afraid of losing him and then having the other relationship fail to develop. So she begins seeing the other man without telling Brian. Is Louise behaving morally?

h.   The law tends to oppose sterilization of retarded people unless they understand the nature of the operation and freely consent to it. But some years ago the parents of three severely retarded girls brought court action to gain the legal right to make the decision for their daughters.[34] Is their position morally acceptable?

i.   A Cedar Rapids, Iowa, high school junior invited a 35-year-old neighbor, the married mother of four children, to the school prom. Even though the woman's husband approved, the school board ruled that the situation was unacceptable.[35] Is such a "date" ever morally acceptable?

GROUP DISCUSSION EXERCISE

Discuss the following issue with two or three of your classmates. Observe the guidelines to group discussion presented in Appendix B. Consider all sides of the matter and try to reach consensus. Be prepared to report your group's deliberations to the class, describing how your analysis proceeded, what questions were asked, and what agreements were reached. If differences of viewpoint remain unresolved, be prepared to report them objectively.

> Dr. Elizabeth Loftus believes that many memories of childhood sexual abuse may have been unwittingly created by therapists. "I've been able to find evidence for a massive amount of suggestion going on in therapy, for things like someone coming in, and a therapist saying, 'Everyone I've seen with your symptoms was sexually abused. Were you?'" Loftus has had a personal experience with the tricks memory can play. An uncle told her that when she was 14, she had found her mother's drowned body. She didn't remember doing so and wondered whether she had repressed the painful memory. Within a couple of days she developed vivid pictures of herself finding the body. Moreover, she began to see the traumatic event as a logical explanation of certain of her personality traits. Then she learned that her uncle had been mistaken—she had not found the body. Thus her vivid pictures of finding the body were *unconsciously manufactured*.[36]

What serious crimes other than sexual molestation depend on the memories of victims or witnesses? How can society ensure that innocent people are not wrongly accused and punished because of manufactured memories?

COMPOSITION OR SPEECH EXERCISE

Write a composition or, if your instructor specifies, a formal speech, presenting the view your group reached in the preceding group discussion exercise. (If you hold a dissenting view, present that instead.) Be sure to provide evidence that your view is the most reasonable one. Naturally your composition or speech will bear some resemblance to those of the other members of your group—you will have developed ideas as a team, so at least some of your ideas will be similar, even identical, to theirs. Don't be concerned about such similarities. Your composition or speech will be a unique effort if you (a) use supporting material from your own experience, observation, and research; (b) develop your own line of reasoning about that material; (c) employ your own ingenuity in designing an introduction and conclusion and in arranging the material in the body of your composition or speech; and (d) express your thoughts in your own words. For further guidance, consult the appropriate appendix—A for writing, B for speaking.

3

Broaden Your Perspective

Do you know the story of the six blind men and the elephant? Able to rely only on their sense of touch, they reached out and touched an elephant to learn about it. One touched its side and decided that an elephant was like a wall. The second touched its trunk and decided—a snake. The third, its tail—a rope; the fourth, its ear—a fan; the fifth, its leg—a tree; the last, its tusk—a spear. Now each had a clear picture of the elephant in mind. But because all the pictures were based on a limited perspective, all were wrong.[1]

All too often we are like the six blind men in our perspective on the world. We see narrowly, and our thinking suffers as a result. The first and perhaps saddest way we are victimized by narrow perspectives is in our view of our own potential. Most of us never come to know ourselves fully. We see only what we are and never realize the larger part of us: *what we have the capacity to be.* We never appreciate just how much of what we are is the result of accident.

Our development, for example, and our degree of success are strongly influenced by the way others regard us. In one experiment, researchers administered an intelligence test to an entire elementary school. The researchers told the faculty that the test would identify students who were ready to undergo a "learning spurt." Actually, the test did no such thing: The testers merely selected some students at random and identified them as the ones whose learning would enjoy a spurt. Teachers were subsequently observed using the same materials and methods for these students as for others. Nevertheless, at the end of the year, when the researchers again tested the student body, they found that the students that had been singled out had gained twice as many IQ points as the other students.

What was responsible for this gain? Obviously the teachers had formed favorable attitudes toward these students and unconsciously transmitted their attitudes to the students. The students' self-images, in turn, were ultimately changed.[2]

If that experiment seems surprising, the following one, similar in its design, will seem astounding. Laboratory assistants were assigned the task of teaching rats to run a maze. They were told the rats were in two groups, fast learners and slow learners. Actually, all the rats were identical. After the test period, the rats that had been designated fast learners were found to have learned the maze better than the other rats. Like the schoolteachers, the lab assistants had formed preconceived notions about the rats, and those notions had not only affected the degree of patience and the amount of attention and encouragement the assistants displayed with the rats but also actually influenced the rats' performance.[3]

Studies show that confused, defeatist, helpless reactions are not inborn in us. They are *learned*. In one study people were given problems they were told could be solved but which in fact could not be. As their efforts to solve the problems failed, the subjects experienced increasing frustration, until they finally accepted their helplessness and gave up. The real point of the study, though, came later. When the same people were given solvable problems, they continued to act helpless and to give up without really trying.[4]

What do these studies suggest about everyday life? That parents who are inconsistent in their demands and unpredictable in their reactions, teachers who focus on the negative rather than the positive, and coaches and activity leaders who ignore actual performance or contribution can rob us of our confidence, lead us into the habit of failure, and blind us to our real potential.

One of the distinguishing marks of many successful people is their refusal to define themselves by other people's assessments. Winston Churchill was branded a slow learner. Martha Graham was told that she did not have the right kind of body to become a dancer. Thomas Edison was urged to quit school because he was considered hopelessly stupid. Later, on his first job, working for the railroad, he set a train on fire with one of his experiments and was dismissed. And Albert Einstein's early record was even worse. Here are some of the details:

- He was not only an unimpressive student; he was told flatly by one teacher, "You will never amount to anything."
- At age 15 he was asked to leave school.
- When he took his first entrance exam to Zurich Polytechnic School, he failed it and was required to spend a year in a Swiss high school before he could be admitted.
- At Zurich he did mediocre work and was so unimpressive to his professors that he was rejected as a postgraduate assistant and denied a recommendation for employment.
- He eventually obtained a job as tutor at a boarding school but was soon fired.
- He submitted a thesis on thermodynamics for a doctoral degree at Zurich. The thesis was rejected.
- Four years later, he submitted his special theory of relativity for a doctoral dissertation at the university at Bern. It was rejected.

"Wait," you may be saying, "Churchill, Graham, Edison, and Einstein were very special people. The question is whether the average person can overcome negative assessments." The answer is yes. To cite just one example, a teacher noticed that when students saw themselves as stupid in a particular subject, they unconsciously conformed to that image. They believed they were stupid, so they behaved stupidly. He set about to change their self-image. And when that change occurred, they no longer behaved stupidly.[5]

The lesson here is not that legitimate criticism or advice should be ignored, nor that one can achieve competency in any field merely by belief. It is that you should not sell yourself short; your potential is undoubtedly much greater than you have ever realized. So when you catch yourself saying, "I'll never be able to do this" or "I don't have the talent to do that," remember that the past does not dictate the future. What people call talent is often nothing more than knowing the knack. And *that* can be learned.

BECOMING AN INDIVIDUAL

All the philosophers and sages of the ages tell us that individuals are rare. Yet the curious thing is that virtually all people consider themselves individuals. (Think about it—have you ever met anyone who admitted, "I am *not* an individual"?) If the philosophers are right, then most people are wrong in their self-assessment. The source of the error lies in the assumption that having unique genes and a unique collection of experiences guarantees individuality. If that were the case, no one could be a conformist. But there *are* conformists. Therefore, the assumption is unwarranted. We are not individuals automatically; rather, we *become* individuals by our willingness to realize our potential and our effort to be "self-aware, self-critical, self-enhancing."[6]

Acknowledging our lack of individuality is the key to becoming an individual. We must make an investment before claiming a profit, an investment of courage—the courage to take a long look at ourselves and to separate fact from fancy. That, of course, can be painful. It means giving up some cherished illusions.

How serious is *your* lack of individuality? Let's see. Ever since you lay helpless and gurgling in your crib, you have been learning. The moment you were able to use your senses, impressions rushed in on you. You received literally millions of impressions before you could interpret them with any sophistication. By the time you were able to interpret effectively, you had long since acquired a large repertoire of actions and reactions—by imitation. You endlessly practiced speaking and walking and, yes, *thinking* as your parents and siblings did.

Later, you attended school, and accepted your teachers' information and beliefs, often imitating their habits and attitudes. You learned, too, from your friends and classmates, and in time (when peer acceptance became more important) you said and did many things, not because they seemed appropriate or mature or because you especially wanted to, but because those things

promised the crowd's acceptance. If you are like most people, you are still selecting your words and actions at least in part by what others want or expect
from you.

But the greatest shaper of your attitudes, habits, and values has probably
not been your parents, siblings, teachers, or friends. It had very likely been
popular culture: the message radio, magazines, books, newspapers, music,
and especially television. By the time the average American graduates from
high school, it is estimated that she or he has spent 11,000 hours in school and
more than 22,000 hours watching television.[7]

How does popular culture affect people? By placing viewers in the role of
spectators, television tends to promote passivity. By bombarding people with
print advertisements and commercials (an estimated 750,000 by age 18), advertising encourages people to be gullible and to accept biased testimony as
fact. By building frequent scene shifts and commercial breaks into programs,
television prevents one's attention span from developing. By urging self-indulgence, impulsiveness, and instant gratification, advertising undermines self-
discipline. By devoting forests of newspaper and magazine space to entertain-
ers and providing them with talk-show platforms to parade their opinions, the
media make it difficult for people to distinguish between excellence and
mediocrity.

The process of being exposed to society—home, neighborhood, church,
school, and so on—sociologists call acculturation. Essentially, it involves set-
tling into our culture. The way we settle in, the way the culture shapes us, can
be powerfully affected by our families' socioeconomic condition, their religious and political views, and the quality of the nutrition and health care they
give us.

Acculturation can occur subtly, creating the illusion that our values, attitudes, and ideas were formed independently of other people and circumstances. Erich Fromm was referring to this kind of illusion when he noted that
much of the time when we say we think something, we really ought to say, "It
thinks in me."[8]

It's not hard to understand how we are deceived about our independence.
We are much more acutely aware of having ideas than of the circumstances in
which we received them. What we feel and believe are current experiences
for us, so we tend to forget their origins. What we think, moreover, seems as
much a part of us as the beating of our heart. The idea that our thoughts are
borrowed is foreign and offensive.

To be an individual means more than claiming independence. It means
achieving it. Here are three steps that will help you begin to achieve your individuality:

1. Acknowledge the influences that have shaped your thinking. Say to
   yourself, "My mind is full of other people's ideas and attitudes, which I
   received uncritically and accepted because I was young and trusting.
   Many of those ideas and attitudes are now hardened into principles and
   convictions. Yet some of them are surely erroneous or unworthy." Iden-

tify the people you have especially admired or been close to: your mother and father, an aunt or uncle, a coach or teacher, a celebrity. Consider each person's convictions and actions. Decide exactly how those convictions and actions contributed to your ideas and attitudes.

2. Sort out and evaluate your ideas and attitudes. Put your realization of influence to work for you in a practical way. Examine your ideas and attitudes, even your most cherished ones. Ask, for example, what your political philosophy is. (That question, of course, means more than "Are you a Democrat or a Republican?" It includes your views on the proper role of government and citizens' responsibility in a democracy.) Ask, as well, about your views on religion, race, nationality, marriage, morality, and law. Compare your ideas and attitudes with others. Make your beliefs prove themselves, not on the basis of their familiarity or their compatibility with other ideas, but on their reasonableness in light of the evidence.

3. Choose the best ones. Decide as objectively as you can which ideas deserve your endorsement and which attitudes are worth striving to acquire. Remember that you are never being more an individual than when you resist the pressure of habit and change the way you think about a subject or issue because the evidence prompts you to do so.

Real individuality, of course, cannot be attained in a single sitting, or even in a hundred sittings. It is an ongoing task, the occupation of a lifetime. But it is a task that everyone who wants to be a good thinker must undertake.

HABITS THAT HINDER THINKING

In your effort to become more of an individual, it is important to identify any habits of mind interfering with clear thinking. Some of these habits will be peculiar to your own situation and depend on your unique background and experience. But there are a number of habits that victimize everyone to some extent. The most significant deserve close attention. They are the mine-is-better habit, face saving, resistance to change, conformity, stereotyping, and self-deception.

The Mine-Is-Better Habit

This habit is natural enough. It begins in early childhood. As children we all said, "My bike is better than your bike"; "My dad is stronger than your dad"; "My mom is prettier than your mom." We believed what we said, too. Whatever we associated with was an extension of ourselves. Asserting its superiority was an expression of ego.

The habit does not go away easily as we grow up. "In later life," writes Rowland Jepson, "we are apt to think that the world in which we grew up was the best of all possible worlds, and to regard the customs and notions which helped to mould our own selves as the acme of wisdom and sound sense, never reached before or since."[9] And we tend to regard our present ideas, values, groups, and political and religious affiliations as superior, too.

Mine-is-better is undoubtedly as old as mankind. Primitive societies tend to regard those who are different—foreigners, criminals, the mentally deranged, the physically or emotionally handicapped, other races, other religions, and other social classes—as lesser beings. "The creature who does not 'belong' to the tribe, clan, caste or parish," they reason, "is not really human; he only aspires or pretends to be 'like us.'"[10] From that, it is only a short step to the decision that such "different people," being subhuman, have no human rights, as some cultures have decided.[11]

We are appalled at such a view, yet our mine-is-better habit leads us to similar (if considerably less extreme) thinking and acting. If a friend proposes a change, we call her a reformer; if an enemy proposes a change, we call him a troublemaker or a fanatic. Likewise, the differences between a traitor and a defector, a religious denomination and a cult, a politician and a statesman depend on how close the person or subject is to us and our view.

The mine-is-better habit hinders our thinking. It destroys objectivity and prompts us to prefer self-flattering errors to unpleasant realities. If you wish to be a good thinker, you must learn to control this habit and keep your ego from interfering with your search for truth.

Face Saving

Like the mine-is-better habit, face saving is a natural tendency arising from our ego. Unlike mine-is-better, it occurs *after* we have said or done something that threatens to disturb our self-image or the image others have of us. Psychologists call face saving a defense mechanism, meaning it is a strategy we use to protect our image.

One common form of face saving is the excuse most children (and many adults) employ at one time or another: "It wasn't my fault—he [or she] made me do it" or "It wasn't my fault—I had no alternative." This excuse, though an obstacle to good thinking, at least has the virtue of acknowledging that something wrong or undesirable has occurred. The dishonesty lies in pointing the finger away from oneself.

A more dangerous form of face saving is called rationalizing. Rationalizing is a dishonest substitute for reasoning whereby we set out "to defend our ideas rather than to find out the truth about the matters concerned."[12] Let's say, for example, that you are a heavy smoker. As the evidence linking smoking to serious diseases mounts, you begin to realize that your habit harms you. You feel like a fool. But instead of admitting that smoking is harmful or at least examining the evidence and deciding whether it is valid, you say, "The case against smoking isn't conclusive" and "The relaxation of tension smoking achieves for me more than balances any minor harm it may cause me." That's rationalizing.

Although rationalizing sometimes resembles honest reasoning, there is a simple way to tell the difference between them. You are reasoning if your belief follows the evidence—that is, if you examine the evidence first and then make up your mind. You are rationalizing if the evidence follows your belief—if you first decide what you'll believe and then select and interpret evidence to justify it.[13]

The process of face saving and its effect on thinking are effectively summed up by Rowland Jepson:

> When we have once adopted an opinion, our pride makes us [reluctant] to admit that we are wrong. When objections are made to our views, we are more concerned with discovering how to combat them than how much truth or sound sense there may be in them; we are at pains rather to find fresh support for our own views, than to face frankly any new facts that appear to contradict them. We all know how easy it is to become annoyed at the suggestion that we have made a mistake; that our first feeling is that we would rather do anything than admit it, and our first thought is "How can I explain it away?"[14]

To control your face-saving tendency, be alert for occasions when your ego is threatened and remember this adage: A person who makes a mistake and refuses to admit it is thereby making another mistake.

Resistance to Change

Resistance to change is the tendency to reject new ideas and new ways of seeing or doing without examining them fairly. It has been the recurrent reaction to creativity throughout the ages. Galileo came close to losing his life when he suggested the sun, not the earth, was the center of the solar system. The inventors of the plow, the umbrella, the automobile, and the airplane were scoffed at, as were the individuals who first advocated using anesthetics during surgery, performing autopsies to determine the cause of death, and extending voting rights to women. Even the ending of child labor, which we now regard as eminently reasonable, was initially scorned: Critics called it a Bolshevik attempt to nationalize children.

One cause of our tendency to resist change is simple laziness. Having gotten used to things one way, we resent being asked to regard them another way; doing so makes us break our routine. Another reason is excessive regard for tradition. The old ways must be best, we believe, because our parents and grandparents used them. New ideas and approaches seem an affront to our ancestors.

But what is tradition, really? Is it the best way of seeing or doing? In some cases it surely is. But in others, it is more like the path in the following verse by Sam Walter Foss:

> One day through the primeval wood
> A calf walked home as good calves should;
> But made a trail all bent askew,
> A crooked trail as all calves do.
>
> Since then three hundred years have fled,
> And I infer the calf is dead.
> But still he left behind his trail,

And thereby hangs my moral tale.
The trail was taken up next day
By a lone dog that passed that way;
And then a wise bellwether sheep
Pursued the trail o'er hill and glade
Through those old woods a path was made.

And many men wound in and out
And dodged and turned and bent about
And uttered words of righteous wrath
Because 'twas such a crooked path;
But still they followed—do not laugh—
The first migrations of that calf,
And through this winding wood-way stalked
Because he wobbled when he walked.

This forest path became a lane
That bent and turned and turned again;
This crooked lane became a road,
Where many a poor horse with his load
Toiled on beneath the burning sun,
And traveled some three miles in one.
And thus a century and a half
They trod the footsteps of that calf.

The years passed on in swiftness fleet,
The road became a village street;
And thus, before men were aware,
A city's crowded thoroughfare.
And soon the central street was this
Of a renowned metropolis;
And men two centuries and a half
Trod in the footsteps of that calf.
Each day a hundred thousand rout
Followed this zigzag calf about
And o'er his crooked journey went
The traffic of a continent.

A hundred thousand men were led
By one calf near three centuries dead.
They followed still his crooked way,
And lost one hundred years a day;
For thus such reverence is lent
To well-established precedent.[15]

In situations where tradition is nothing more than "well-established precedent," or following in the footsteps of those who have gone before, it is more of an insult to our ancestors to follow than to explore new paths.

Another, more significant, reason for resisting change is fear. Each of has developed habits of thinking and acting. These habits, like old shoes, are comfortable. The very idea of trading them for something new is frightening: "How could I ever cope with daily situations?" Our imagination conjures up a hundred apprehensions, all of them intensified by being nameless. So we choose to resist, rather than welcome, the new. Sometimes we avoid feeling ashamed by pretending we are really being honorable and acting on principle.

Unfortunately, if we are resistant to change, we are resistant to discovery, invention, creativity, progress. Each of these, after all, first comes to the world as a new idea. *To resist change is to set our minds against our own best and most worthwhile ideas.*

Being open to change does not mean embracing every new idea uncritically; many new ideas prove, on examination, to be worthless or unworkable. Rather, it means being willing to suspend judgment long enough to give every new idea, no matter how strange it seems, a fair chance to prove itself.

Conformity

Not all conformity is bad. We put our out-of-town letters in the out-of-town post office slot, say hello instead of goodbye when we answer the phone, try to spell correctly and not violate the rules of grammar, and stop for red lights when driving. Such actions, and thousands of others like them, are a sensible kind of conformity. If we were to try nonconformity in such matters, we would waste valuable time, confuse or annoy those around us, or threaten the safety of ourselves and others.

Harmful conformity is what we do instead of thinking in order to belong to a group or to avoid the risk of being different. Such conformity is an act of cowardice, a sacrifice of independence for a lesser good. In time it makes us more concerned about what others think than about what is right and true and sensible. Once we begin to conform, we quickly find ourselves saying and doing not what we believe is best but what we believe others want or expect us to say and do. That focus dulls our ability to think creatively and critically.

It's not always easy to avoid conforming. Our friends, families, and associates may exert considerable pressure on us. It takes courage to say, "I disagree" or "That's wrong," when the group is firm in its view. If you've ever tried it, you know how painful that why-must-you-be-such-a-traitor look can be. That's why so many people give in again and again until they have completely surrendered their individuality. One widely repeated laboratory experiment documented this surrender dramatically. The experiment involved two subjects, who were told they were participating in a memory test. One assumed the role of teacher; the other, the role of student. When the student gave a wrong answer, the teacher was supposed to deliver an electric shock. With each wrong answer the shock increased.

The situation, of course, was rigged. There was really no electric shock, and the "student" was really an actor instructed to say he had a heart condition, to plead with the teacher to stop, and even to claim chest pains. At the highest level of shock, he remained silent, and since he was in another room, the "teacher" must have considered the possibility that the shock had killed him.

The result of the experiment? Fully 65 percent of the "teachers" administered the shocks up to the highest level. Most protested to the experimenter that they didn't want to inflict pain on the student, but when the experimenter insisted, they obeyed.[16]

Perhaps we would behave differently in that experiment. Perhaps not. In any case, the effects of conformity are all around us. Abraham Maslow observed,

> Too many people do not make up their own minds, but have their minds made up for them by salesmen, advertisers, parents, propagandists, TV, newspapers and so on. They are pawns to be moved by others rather than self-determining individuals. Therefore they are apt to feel helpless, weak, and totally determined; they are prey for predators, flabby whiners rather than self-determining persons.[17]

It would be a mistake to fight conformity by refusing to believe and act as others do, to be different for the sake of being different. That is no more thoughtful than mindless conformity. The right way to fight conformity is to think for yourself and not worry about whether or not others agree with you.

Stereotyping

Stereotyping is an extreme form of generalizing. Generalizations classify people, places, and ideas according to their common elements. Thus we may say that most basketball players are tall, that medical doctors study for years before being licensed to practice, that Honda Civics get better gas mileage than Corvettes. These are fair and reasonable generalizations. Some generalizations go beyond the boundaries of reasonableness; these are called *over*generalizations. The beliefs that, for example, city residents are less friendly than rural folk and that athletes don't do well in their studies are overgeneralizations.

Stereotyping, however, is a deeper and more serious problem than overgeneralization. A stereotype is a fixed, unbending generalization, irrationally maintained. As Walter Lippmann explains,

> Stereotypes are loaded with preference, suffused with affection or dislike, attached to fears, lusts, strong wishes, pride, hope. Whatever invokes the stereotype is judged with the appropriate sentiment. Except where we deliberately keep prejudice in suspense, we do not study a man and judge him to be bad. We see a bad man. We see a . . . sainted priest, a humorless Englishman, a dangerous [communist], a carefree Bohemian, a lazy Hindu, a wily Oriental, a dreaming Slav, a volatile Irishman, a greedy Jew, a 100% American. . . . Neither justice, nor mercy, nor truth, enter into such a judgment, for the judgment has preceded the evidence.[18]

The most common stereotypes are racial, religious, and ethnic. There is the stereotype of the black, the fundamentalist Christian, the Italian. But there are many other types, as well, no less firm for being less common. There are stereotypes of homosexuals, the clergy, college dropouts, feminists, male chauvinists, New York City, singles' bars, motherhood—even God.

Stereotyping sets up a nice, neat mental warehouse for ideas. Everything has its own compartment. There is no comparing, no sorting, weighing, or selecting, just storage. Everything is presorted, predetermined, prejudged. Thus stereotyping impedes the mind's dynamic activity, forcing life's infinite variety, the myriad people and circumstances around us, into ready-made categories.

It is difficult for many people to overcome stereotypes because they tend to see them as accurate descriptions of the world, even as insights. Yet it is important to make the effort to expose them, for they distort your view of reality.

Self-Deception

A boy once went fishing with several friends. Someone suggested they all share whatever fish were caught. It seemed a reasonable idea, so the boy agreed. Then, as the day wore on and he caught more fish than his friends, his attitude began to change. By the end of the day, he was violently opposed to sharing, and objected loudly, arguing that good anglers shouldn't be penalized for others' incompetence.[19]

That boy engaged in one of the many kinds of self-deception that tempt us all. "One of the most disturbing habits of the human mind," Katherine Anne Porter observed, "is its willful and destructive forgetting of whatever in its past does not flatter or confirm its present point of view."[20]

One of my colleagues often begins his classes in informal logic by asking students to answer this exercise: "Think of the guy or girl you most resented in high school. In a couple of sentences explain why you resented him or her." He has read hundreds of students' answers and has found that the great majority say, "That guy had the terrible habit of . . . " or "That girl lacked. . . ." Only one or two out of ten will say, "*I* was jealous (or immature or insecure)." In other words, any resentment is clearly the other's fault and not one's own. A similar kind of self-deception occurs when students who get low grades because of missing class, failing to hand in homework, or refusing to prepare for examinations accuse their teachers of favoritism and prejudice.

People with symptoms of serious diseases—cancer, for example—sometimes lie to themselves that the matter is not serious enough for them to see a doctor. Many divorced people deceive themselves about the reasons for the breakup of their marriages. Most alcoholics lie to themselves about their alcohol dependence—"I can stop any time I want" is the common lie. And most marijuana or crack smokers deceive themselves that they smoke because they want to, rather than as a means of escape from unpleasant experiences and frustrations. If they smoke heavily, they may also persuade themselves that they are not getting burned out, even when their symptoms—loss of memory, listlessness, and confusion, among others—are obvious to everyone around them.

In addition, many people deceive themselves about their competency, first pretending to others that they are knowledgeable and then coming to believe the pretense themselves. Edwin Clarke describes their behavior this way:

> Persons who, for instance, would consider it the height of presumption to advise an engineer how to plan a simple culvert, have no hesitation in speaking with an air of authority on far more complex questions such as Portuguese immigration or the nature of a desirable currency, subjects on which their knowledge is very superficial and only too often derived from inaccurate and biased sources.[21]

To be a good thinker you must be able to decide honestly what information you need to solve a problem and then, after acquiring that information, to evaluate it fairly. You will be able to do these things only if you have learned to be honest with yourself.

All six of the habits that hinder thinking—the mine-is-better habit, face saving, resistance to change, conformity, stereotyping, and self-deception—can become deeply ingrained and therefore difficult to overcome. Nevertheless, they can all be overcome with desire and effort. The following section explains how to attack them.

OVERCOMING BAD HABITS

We saw in Chapter 1 how feelings are part blessing and part curse. On the one hand, they can offer intuition and insight and can motivate us to persevere in difficult work. On the other hand, they can mislead us. Having examined the habits that hinder thinking, you should appreciate more fully just how vulnerable we all are to the latter tendency.

The key to overcoming the bad habits we have been discussing is to examine your initial feelings about problems and issues, particularly strong feelings prompting you to take a stand immediately, without examining the evidence or weighing competing arguments. By closely examining such feelings you will often be able to determine that a particular bad habit—resistance to change, for example, or stereotyping—is interfering with your thinking, and thereby realize the importance of suspending that feeling until you have examined the evidence.

Marvin and Martha both read the same magazine article, which discusses a scientific book on the subject of life after death.[22] The article explains that the book is a study of 116 people's near-death experiences and their subsequent memories of floating out of their bodies and, in some cases, traveling down a dark tunnel toward a bright light. It also points out that the author is a medical professor who began his study as a skeptic and conducted his investigations in a thoroughly scientific manner. Finally, it notes that although the author personally believes in life after death, he neither claims that his studies prove it exists nor offers his findings in support of any particular religious perspective.

As Marvin begins reading the article, a strong feeling rises in him: "Here it is—proof that there's life after death—just what we need to show the skeptics, the doubters, those of little faith." Because he merely yields to the feeling without examining it, Marvin fails to realize that it is a mixture of mine-is-better thinking, stereotyping, and conformity. Later that day, he may be heard in the snack bar proclaiming that the book's author is a champion of Marvin's own religion and that the "entire scientific community" has now "conceded" that Marvin's view of an afterlife is "unquestionably true."

A very different, but equally strong feeling rises in Martha as she reads the article: "More nonsense from mindless religious quacks who can't face the reality of oblivion." She, too, yields to the feeling unquestioningly and so fails to realize that it is a mixture of the same errors: mine-is-better thinking, stereotyping, and conformity. At lunch the next day she tells her friends that the book says nothing of value, calling it a "pathetic attempt" to brainwash people.

Marvin's and Martha's self-deception may seem laughable, but it is really sad. Without realizing it, each has read without profit, remaining in a state of self-flattering ignorance instead of learning and growing. Each has substituted what Henshaw Ward termed *thobbing* for considering and evaluating ideas. The term combines the *th* from *thinking,* the *o* from *opinion,* and the *b* from *believing.* Whenever people think the opinion that pleases them and then believe it, they are thobbing.[23]

Your best protection against thobbing is to develop the habit of thinking about your thinking. (The technical name for this activity is *metacognition.*) More specifically, be aware of your initial feelings about problems and issues, particularly those feelings that prompt you to take a stand immediately, without examining the evidence or weighing competing views. When such feelings arise, control them instead of yielding to them, and force yourself to be objective.

WARM-UP EXERCISES

Remember that unlike the applications, the warm-up exercises have no special relation to the chapter contents. They may demand creative thinking, critical thinking, or both.

3.1. As soon as you enter the room, your roommate challenges you: "You're taking a course in thinking, so answer this—if perfection in anything is beyond human attainment, what's the point in striving to be better in anything?" What do you reply?

3.2. Your little niece looks puzzled. You ask her what's wrong and she says, "It doesn't make sense—we blow on our hands to warm them when they're cold, but we blow on our food to cool it when it's hot. How can blowing make things both hot and cold?" Construct a clear and meaningful reply.

3.3. In a dorm gripe session, Bertram advances the following argument. Decide whether it is a reasonable one and explain your view thoroughly.

. I could understand the teacher failing me in the course if I didn't hand in my homework. But I did hand it in, faithfully. Therefore, I didn't deserve to fail.

APPLICATIONS

3.1. Read the following dialogue carefully, looking for flaws in thinking. If you find one, identify it and explain what is wrong in sufficient detail to persuade someone who has read the passage but sees no flaw. If you find two or more flaws, identify each and explain your thinking about it.

> EDNA: Professor, I don't like to complain, but I don't feel I'm getting as much out of this composition course as I should be getting.
> PROFESSOR: Really? Where do you think the problem lies?
> EDNA: Well, you've got us writing just about every other day if we include the brief responses to the readings as well as the longer compositions. Yet so much of the writing seems wasted: You only correct about half the assignments.

3.2. Look back at the exercises for Chapters 1 and 2. Recall your responses. Decide whether those responses were influenced by any of the bad habits discussed in this chapter. Discuss your findings. (Note: In doing this assignment you should expect yourself to resist admitting such influences. Overcoming that resistance is a mark of thinking effectively.)

3.3. Reread the paragraph beginning "How does popular culture affect people. . . " (page 40). Then examine television programs, commercials and print advertisements, and magazines to determine the extent of the influences specified in that paragraph. Be prepared to share your findings with the class.

Note: In doing the following applications, your first objective should be to examine the ideas that occur to you and to decide whether they are the most reasonable responses to the problem or issue. Modify flawed ideas; where appropriate, change your mind completely. The more carefully you conduct this examination process, the more impressive your written and spoken contributions will be.

3.4. Some people argue that the increase in drug use, teenage pregnancy, and crimes of violence is attributable to the attitudes and values promoted by popular culture. Reflect on your findings in Application 3.3 and decide whether this argument has merit.

3.5. In the interest of highway safety a number of states raised their legal drinking age, and others are considering doing so. Evaluate the idea of having a uniform legal drinking age in all states.

3.6. In Pompano Beach, Florida, undercover police agents borrowed a warehouse and stored a large quantity of confiscated marijuana there. Then they passed the word that the supply was available for sale to dealers. When dealers arrived and purchased the marijuana, they were arrested for marijuana conspiracy and trafficking.[24] Do you approve of the police agents' behavior in this case? Explain your position.

3.7. When Rae Landau and Isaac Perlstein were divorced, Ms. Landau won custody of their 8-year-old son. The boy's observance of Jewish dietary laws was one provision of the divorce agreement. Ms. Landau admittedly failed to honor that provision for a period of 5 years. As a result, a New York Supreme Court justice ruled that Ms. Landau had to surrender custody of the boy to his father.[25] Do you agree with the judge's ruling? Explain your position.

3.8. In Skokie, Illinois, a federal judge decided that the community had no right to prohibit the American Nazi party from holding a parade and rally in Skokie's streets and public square. The community, which numbers many former Nazi concentration camp inmates among its citizens, had objected to the march because it represented advocacy of a dangerous and antidemocratic philosophy.[26] Do you agree with the judge's ruling? Explain your position.

3.9. A homosexual minister was granted permanent adoption of a 13-year-old boy by a family court judge in Catskill, New York. The boy was to live with the minister and his male companion.[27] Do you believe the judge should have disapproved the adoption because of the minister's homosexuality? Explain your thinking.

3.10. An 18-year-old San Francisco resident sued the high school from which he graduated, contending that the faculty were responsible for his inability to read and write adequately.[28] Do you think such a suit is reasonable? What factors would you consider if you were responsible for judging its merits?

3.11. It is common for high school coaches to forbid their players to drink alcohol. If a coach has such a rule and catches a player drinking, is it reasonable for the coach to dismiss the player from the team for the rest of the season? Should the coach treat the team's star player differently from a bench-warmer?

3.12. Apparently a sizable number of Americans believe in astrology and think the stars govern their lives. How reasonable is this view? Explain your thinking.

3.13. Some years ago a San Francisco publisher paid two Jewish businesspeople $1500 in an out-of-court settlement. Their lawsuit had charged him with discriminatory business practices. He published *The Christian Yellow Pages,* a directory of businesses operated by born-again Christians. (The publisher required advertisers to sign a pledge that they accepted Jesus as their savior.)[29] Do you believe the publisher was guilty of discrimination? Explain.

3.14. A minister in Pontiac, Michigan, was arrested and charged with practicing medicine without a license—a felony—after he sprinkled blood from a freshly killed rooster on an ailing person. The minister said the authorities were stifling his constitutional rights. Do you agree with him? Explain your position.[30]

GROUP DISCUSSION EXERCISE

Discuss the following issue with two or three of your classmates. Observe the guidelines to group discussion presented in Appendix B. Consider all sides of the matter and try to reach consensus. Be prepared to report your group's deliberations to the class, describing how your analysis proceeded, what questions were asked, and what agreements were reached. If differences of viewpoint remain unresolved, be prepared to report them objectively.

Many schools already distribute condoms to students in their health clinics. Now some schools propose to offer Norplant, a surgically implanted contraceptive, as well. Both approaches are controversial, raising ethical, medical, and legal questions, not least of which is whether the school is the appropriate agency to offer such services. Evaluate this and related issues, and decide which schools (elementary, middle, high), if any, should offer such services. In deciding, be sure to address the major concerns of people on both sides of the argument.

COMPOSITION OR SPEECH EXERCISE

Write a composition or, if your instructor specifies, a formal speech, presenting the view your group reached in the preceding group discussion exercise. (If you hold a dissenting view, present that instead.) Be sure to provide evidence that your view is the most reasonable one. Naturally your composition or speech will bear some resemblance to those of the other members of your group—you will have developed ideas as a team, so at least some of your ideas will be similar, even identical, to theirs. Don't be concerned about such similarities. Your composition or speech will be a unique effort if you (a) use supporting material from your own experience, observation, and research; (b) develop your own line of reasoning about that material; (c) employ your own ingenuity in designing an introduction and conclusion and in arranging the material in the body of your composition or speech; and (d) express your thoughts in your own words. For further guidance, consult the appropriate appendix—A for writing, B for speaking.

4

Sharpen Your
Analytical Skills

A lively curiosity, as we have seen, can help you become a better thinker by revealing the challenges and opportunities around you. To be successful in meeting those challenges, however, you need more than curiosity. You need analytical skills. These skills enable you to understand and evaluate any ideas you encounter. Undoubtedly you have some of them already. (If you did not have at least rudimentary analytical skill, your education would not have proceeded this far.) But since analysis is not usually taught systematically in American education, you probably learned it haphazardly and use it sporadically, unconsciously, and inefficiently. This chapter will help you improve your analytical skills.

IMPROVING YOUR READING

The term *reading* is used here in the broad sense, covering not only printed material but also all received ideas, including those you get from listening. Almost 400 years ago, Francis Bacon warned about the danger of reading improperly. He advised people as they read not to dispute the author's view nor to accept it uncritically, but to "weigh and consider" it. In the nineteenth century, British statesman Edmund Burke expressed the same view in more dramatic terms: "To read without reflection," he said, "is like eating without digesting."

The definition of reading these men had in mind is best explained as follows:

> There is one key idea which contains, in itself, the very essence of effective reading, and on which the improvement of reading depends: *Reading is reasoning.* When you read properly, you are not merely assimilating. You are not automatically transferring into your head what your eyes pick up on the page. What you

see on the page sets your mind at work, collating, criticizing, interpreting, questioning, comprehending, comparing. When this process goes on well, you read well. When it goes on ill, you read badly.[1]

Reading with the mind, and not just with the eyes, is not equally intense during every reading occasion. A bus schedule or a menu, for example, can be read well with little or no reasoning. But even the smallest reading challenges involve considerably more reasoning than we realize at the time. Consider the following sentences:

He who hesitates is lost. (Proverb)

We never step into the same river twice. (Heraclitus)

The girl who can't dance says the band can't play. (Yiddish proverb)

The first one, of course, is so familiar that you may be unaware you ever had to reason out its meaning. But consider the first time you encountered it, probably as a small child. You undoubtedly wondered, "Just who does *he* refer to in this sentence? And what does *lost* mean here?" In time, when you considered and tested some possible meanings, you reasoned out the meaning.

The other two sentences are even more challenging. The key to Heraclitus's line is the relationship between *same* and *river*. Only when you perceive that, and grasp the idea that the river is constantly changing, can you be said to have read the line. And you can understand the Yiddish proverb only when you see that the message is not just about girls and bands but about anyone who can't do something and resorts to face saving.

The kind of reading Bacon and Burke had in mind, and which concerns us here, is not a passive process but an active, dynamic one. It consists of examining ideas and deciding what they mean and whether they make sense, rather than merely receiving and accepting them. If your education has not given you much experience in evaluating ideas, you may be a little apprehensive about trying the approaches detailed in this chapter. If that is the case, reassure yourself that everyone has the capacity to master the art of thinking. Practice is the key to mastery.

MAKING IMPORTANT DISTINCTIONS

One of the best ways to overcome confusion about ideas is to make important distinctions; that is, to avoid lumping all considerations together indiscriminately. The following distinctions are those most often overlooked. Keep them in mind whenever you are reading (or listening).

Distinctions Between the Person and the Idea

Your reaction to a sentence beginning "Adolf Hitler said. . . " would probably be very different from your reaction to one beginning "Winston Churchill said. . . ." In the first instance you might not even continue reading. At the very least you would read with great suspicion: You'd be ready to reject what was said. There's nothing strange about that. You've learned things about Hitler and Churchill, and it's difficult to set them aside. In one sense, you *shouldn't* set them aside. Yet in another sense, you *must* set them aside to be a good thinker. After all, even a lunatic can have a good idea, and a genius will, on occasion, be wrong.

If you do not control your tendency to accept or reject ideas on the basis of who expresses them, your analysis of everything you read and hear is certain to be distorted. You will judge arguments on whether the speaker is of your race, religion, or political affiliation or whether you like his or her hairstyle. And so you might embrace nonsense and reject wisdom. Aristotle's contemporaries tell us he had very thin legs and small eyes, favored conspicuous dress and jewelry, and was fastidious in the way he combed his hair.[2] It's not hard to imagine some Athenian ignoramus muttering to friends the ancient Greek equivalent of "Don't pay any attention to what Aristotle says—he's a wimp."

To guard against confusing the person and the idea, be aware of your reactions to people and try compensating for them. That is, listen very carefully to people you are inclined to dislike and very critically to people you are inclined to like. Judge the arguments as harshly as you wish, but only on their merits as arguments.

Distinctions Between Matters of Taste and Matters of Judgment

In Chapter 2 we saw that there are two broad types of opinion: taste and judgment. They differ significantly. In matters of taste we may express our personal preferences without defending them. In matters of judgment, however, we have an obligation to provide evidence.

Many people confuse taste and judgment. They believe their right to hold an opinion is a guarantee of the opinion's rightness. This confusion often causes them to offer inadequate support (or no support at all) for views that demand support. For example, they express judgments on such controversial issues as abortion, capital punishment, the teaching of evolution in the schools, mercy killing, hiring discrimination, and laws concerning rape as if they were matters of taste rather than matters of judgment.

Keep in mind that whenever someone presents an opinion about the truth of an issue or the wisdom of an action—that is, whenever someone presents a judgment—you not only have a right to judge his or her view by the evidence. To be a careful thinker, you *must* do so.

Distinctions Between Fact and Interpretation

A fact is something known with certainty, something either objectively verifiable or demonstrable. An interpretation is an explanation of meaning or significance. In much writing, facts and interpretations are intertwined. It is not always obvious where one leaves off and the other begins. Here is an example of such intertwining:

The writer's interpretation (Note that merely callinginter- pretation fact does not make it so.)

People don't seem to care much about family life any more. At least one study has made that unfortunate fact very clear. The study, in which 1596 Americans were surveyed, was conducted for *Psychology Today* magazine in March, 1982, by Potomac Associates.[3] It revealed that Americans are more concerned about the standard of living, personal health, economic stability, and employment than about family concerns. William Watts, president of Potomac Associates, commented as follows: "Traditionally, when asked to talk about their most important hopes and fears, Americans have ranked family concerns near the top of the list. . . . Americans now talk less . . . in interviews about the happiness and health of their families." The cause of this moral decline is without question the emphasis on the self that has dominated our culture for the past two decades.

Fact

The writer's interpretation (Both the classification of the trend as a "moral decline" and the assertion about its cause are interpretive.)

The danger in failing to distinguish between fact and interpretation is that you will regard uncritically statements that ought to be questioned and contrasted with other views. If the habit of confusing the two is strong enough, it can paralyze your critical sense.

Distinctions Between Literal and Ironic Statements

Not everything a writer says is intended literally. Sometimes a writer makes a point by saying the exact opposite of what is meant—that is, by using irony or satire. Suppose, for example, you encountered this passage in your reading:

Congress is right in reducing the taxes of the wealthy more than those of the working classes. After all, wealthy people not only pay more into the treasury, but they also have a higher standard of living to maintain. If the cost of soybeans has risen, so also has the cost of caviar; if the subway fare has increased, so has the maintenance cost of a Rolls-Royce and a Lear jet. If the government listens to the minor grumbling and whining of the unemployed, it surely should be responsive to the plight of the affluent.

On the surface, this certainly looks like a plea on behalf of the rich. But on closer inspection it will be seen as a mockery of that plea. The clues are subtle, to be sure, but undeniable—the reference to the higher standard of living, the comparison of travel by Rolls-Royce or jet with travel by subway, the reference to the "plight" of the rich. Such tongue-in-cheek writing can be more biting and therefore more effective than a direct attack. Yet you must be alert to the subtlety and not misread it, or the message you receive will be very different from the message that has been expressed.

Distinctions Between an Idea's Validity and the Quality of Its Expression

The way an idea is expressed can influence people's reactions. This is why a mad leader like Hitler won a large popular following even among intelligent and responsible people and why Jim Jones's followers killed their children and committed suicide in Guyana. Impassioned, eloquent expression tends to excite a favorable response, just as lifeless, inarticulate, error-filled expression prompts a negative response. Compare these two passages:

> Ain't right to treat some folks good and others bad. If a man don't treat all equal, he ain't much of a man.

> To achieve success in a competitive world, you must honor the first principle of success: Treat well those people who can benefit you, and ignore the others.

The first passage may seem less appealing than the second. And yet it contains an idea most philosophers would enthusiastically endorse, whereas the second contains an idea most would find reprehensible. Careful thinkers are able to appraise the passages correctly because they are aware that expression can deceive. Such thinkers make a special effort to separate form from content before judging. Thus they are able to say, "This idea is poorly expressed but profound" and "This idea is well expressed but shallow."

Distinctions Between Language and Reality

Language is our principal means of understanding reality and communicating that understanding to others. Words come so naturally and become so closely associated with what they represent that we may unconsciously regard them as synonymous with reality. That can be a costly mistake. A people's language develops according to their insights and observations, and since no people have equal insights into all dimensions of reality, no language is perfectly suited to express all realities. For example, Eskimos have many words for snow, each word denoting a certain kind of snow (heavy and wet versus light and fluffy, small and fine versus large and dense, and so on), so they can speak with much greater precision about snow than can English-speaking peoples. Similarly, the ancient Greeks had a number of words for love, each representing a distinct type of love (love of God, love of family, romantic or sexual love, and so forth), whereas we require our word *love* to bear an excessive burden and create confusion in our discourse. Remembering that the words you and others use are merely the imperfect means of describing reality will help you approach communication with appropriate care and humility.

EVALUATING AN ARGUMENT

Analyzing a long piece of writing line by line may seem a formidable task. You picture yourself gathering dust while scrutinizing each word and pondering its relationship with every other word. "If that's what analytical thinking is all about," you may say, "count me out." Here's some good news: Most scholars feel the same way. They know that such an approach would not only be boring; it would also be inefficient. They'd never get anything done if they worked that way. And so they develop shortcuts.

Particular shortcuts, of course, vary from scholar to scholar. But one common approach is reducing a book or article to manageable proportions before beginning one's analysis. In other words, scholars analyze in miniature. By applying three simple steps, you can master this approach quickly and easily.

Step 1: After reading the book or article carefully, summarize its essential argument and the evidence presented in support of that argument.

Step 2: Evaluate the essential argument and evidence. (In cases where you are not qualified to evaluate, postpone your evaluation until you do the necessary research.)

Step 3: Draw your conclusion about the validity of the argument. In other words, decide whether you accept it, accept it in part, or reject it.

We'll discuss each of these steps more closely and see how they apply in an actual case, but first let's clarify the terms *essential argument* and *evidence*.

Essential Argument   The essential argument is the central or controlling idea in persuasive writing, the idea the writer wishes to present as the most reasonable conclusion. In any well-written article or book, the essential argument is expressed directly and given prominence. (Not every article or book, unfortunately, is well written. Whenever you encounter an essential argument not expressed directly or expressed unclearly, you must construct the argument on the basis of probability; that is, you must decide what essential argument is suggested by the overall presentation.) The argument may be expressed in one place: in an article, usually right after the introduction. Or if the argument is complex, it may be expressed in several parts at different points in the presentation. In any case, it is usually kept in clear focus throughout the work and reinforced in the conclusion, so it will be clear and recognizable to the careful reader.

Evidence   Evidence is any material used to support the essential argument, thereby demonstrating the validity of the writer's judgment. There are four broad categories of evidence: confirmed details or statistics, the writer's own experience and observation, the judgment of authorities, and other people's experience and observation. Evidence may take a variety of forms; for example, factual details, statistics, examples, cases in point, anecdotes, quotations, comparisons, descriptions, and definitions. The author's reasoning about supporting material is also evidence.

There is a difference between evidence and *proof.* It is proper to speak of proof only when the evidence is sufficient in amount and kind to remove all reasonable doubt and establish certainty. Such a situation is rare, even though all good thinkers strive for it (and sometimes decide prematurely that they have it).

With these important terms clarified, let's return to the three steps in evaluating an argument and look at them more closely.

Step 1: Summarizing

After you've read the article or book carefully, look back at the author's divisions of the work. In an article, look at the subheadings; in a book, at the chapter titles and the subheadings. These will provide valuable clues to the relationships the author sees among his or her ideas. Next, underline the key sentences or paragraphs in the work.* For an article, limit yourself to one sentence in every few paragraphs; for a book, to a few sentences in every chapter.

When you have finished underlining key sentences, review your work and consider how many sentences can be combined without changing the author's meaning. Using the underlined sentences as a guide, write the essential argument in complete sentences, keeping to the original phrasing and the original order of presentation as much as possible to avoid distortion. Then briefly list the kind and amount of evidence offered in support of the writer's argument. (Do not attempt to write the evidence as the author presented it—it will make your summary too long to be manageable.)

If you've summarized effectively, you should now have a brief version of the original work that is faithful in content yet much easier to analyze. A whole book can be reduced to several paragraphs in this way; a full-length magazine article, to seven or eight sentences; a short article, to two or three sentences. Whenever you summarize, however, keep in mind the danger of distortion and oversimplification. It is not only unfair but pointless to criticize an author for something he or she did *not* say.

---

*It is a common practice to underline while reading. The problem is that you may tend to underline too much, which defeats your purpose in summarizing. Unless you can restrict your underlining to key passages only, it is better to underline *after* you have read.

Step 2: Evaluating

Read over your summary of the essential argument several times, asking these questions:

- How clear is the author's position? Is any important part of it vague or ambiguous; that is, open to more than one meaning? If you identify any vagueness or ambiguity, consider all reasonable interpretations.
- What challenges would a critic raise about the author's ideas? Go through each sentence of your summary, asking all the questions you can think of and noting all the responses a critic would probably offer.

Next, look over your list of evidence, asking these questions:

- Is all the evidence relevant to the issue? If any isn't, note it and be prepared to explain why it is not.
- Are the sources cited still current? There is nothing necessarily wrong with old sources. Something written in 1800 may still be valid today. But later findings may have discredited older views.
- Are the sources cited authoritative and reliable? The fact of being well known does not make anyone an authority. A Nobel Prize winner in physics may be totally incompetent in psychology or government. And even if a person is an authority in the field in question, his or her view is open to question if he or she has been guilty of unreliability (professional dishonesty, for example) in the past.
- Are the examples and cases offered as evidence typical and comprehensive? The author's citation of some examples and cases does not necessarily establish the argument's validity. If the cases are extraordinary (exceptions rather than typical instances), they are worth very little. Similarly, if they represent one narrow aspect of the issue rather than all aspects, they may not adequately support the argument.
- Is any significant evidence omitted? Often the weakness in an argument lies in what the author does *not* say. For example, let's say someone told you that several years ago an American engineer and his wife visited the Congo, trying to find evidence of a dinosaurlike creature reportedly living there. They returned with a picture that documented their sighting of the creature. Everything the person told you is correct.[4] However, one important detail is missing: The picture was severely underexposed and therefore worthless as documentation. The only defense against such omissions is to be as well informed as you can about the issue.

Step 3: Judging

The final step in analyzing an argument is to decide whether you agree with it, and if so, to what extent. If you have performed the second step carefully and evaluated your evidence thoughtfully, this step should pose little difficulty. You will simply decide whether the author's view is more reasonable than any other in light of the evidence presented and any additional evidence you considered. In some cases, you will find the author's argument to be most reasonable in every detail; in other cases, completely unreasonable. Far more often, however, you will accept some parts of an author's argument, reject others, and perhaps be uncertain about still others. In such cases, follow these guidelines:

- If you agree in part and disagree in part, explain exactly what your position is, and support it carefully. Remember that good thinkers judge your arguments as closely as you judge other people's.
- If some vagueness or ambiguity in the author's argument prevents you from giving a flat answer, don't attempt one. Rather, say, "it depends," and go on to explain. The if-then approach is very helpful in such cases. Here's how it works. Suppose someone had written, "A human being is an animal." You might respond as follows:

  It <u>depends</u> on what you mean by *animal*. <u>If</u> you mean human being is included in the broad classification *animal*, as opposed to *vegetable* or *mineral*, <u>then</u> I agree. But <u>if</u> you mean a human being has nothing more than animal nature, no intellect and will that distinguish him or her from other members of the animal kingdom, <u>then</u> I disagree. I believe that. . . .

- If you must deal with conflicting testimony and cannot decide your position with certainty, identify the conflict and explain why you cannot be certain. If you believe that circumstances seem somewhat in favor of one side, explain those circumstances and why you are inclined to judge them as you do.

One example of conflicting testimony occurred in the highly publicized trial of Jack Henry Abbott. Abbott, who had spent 24 of his 37 years behind prison bars, was paroled after Norman Mailer arranged for Abbott's book, *In the Belly of the Beast*, to be published. Six weeks after his parole, Abbott stabbed a waiter in a dispute over the use of a restroom. Abbott testified that he thought the waiter had pulled a knife first and that he lunged forward with his knife in self-protection. A passerby, however, witnessed the incident and testified that the waiter had made what appeared to be a "conciliatory gesture" and turned to walk away when Abbott raced after him, reached over his shoulder, and stabbed him with "terrible ferocity," then taunted him as he lay dying.[5]

In this case, you might reasonably say that although you cannot be certain which testimony is correct, circumstances seem to favor the witness's testimony. You would go on to explain that Abbott's testimony was more likely to be colored by emotion and self-interest than the witness's.

These guidelines for dealing with ambiguity and conflicting testimony may seem to encourage evasion, straddling the fence. They are not intended to do so and should not be used for that purpose. Apply them when reasonableness demands a qualified answer, not in situations in which timidity prompts you to avoid answering.

A SAMPLE ARGUMENT

Let's see how this approach works in an actual case. You read a magazine article arguing that "inferior" people should be sterilized at puberty. You summarize it as follows (for reference purposes, the sentences and items of evidence
are numbered):

> (1) A serious world population problem exists today. (2) The ideal solution is for
> everyone to be responsible in deciding whether he or she should reproduce. (3)
> However, few people make that decision rationally—emotion overwhelms logic.
> (4) Moreover, the least talented and least intelligent are likely to have the most
> children. (5) In time, this tendency may set the process of evolution in reverse. (6)
> The best and most practical solution is to identify inferior people and force them
> to be sterilized at puberty.

> Evidence presented in support of the argument:

> 7. UN statistics on world population
> 8. Selected UN statistics on world poverty, illiteracy, and disease
> 9. A research study showing that more-affluent, better educated, higher-
>   IQ couples tend to have fewer children
> 10. Quotations from geneticists showing the favorable genetic effects that
>   would occur if only higher-IQ individuals were to reproduce
> 11. Quotations from medical authorities showing the benefit that would ac-
>   crue to world health if people with hereditary diseases did not reproduce.

Your evaluation of the argument and evidence would probably look like
this (parenthetical numbers refer to the preceding statements and evidence):

> *Concerning the clarity of the argument:* Several terms are ambiguous. Do
> *talented* and *intelligent* refer to the broad range of abilities or to some
> specific ones? Mildly retarded people often possess considerable talent
> and intelligence, measured by a broad definition of the terms. Does
> "the process of evolution" (5) mean survival of the physically fit or the
> perpetuation of culture as we know it? And does "inferior people" (6)
> mean those with hereditary diseases, the mentally retarded, neurotics,
> nonconformists, or all of these?

> *Concerning the questions critics might raise:* These are the most probable
> ones: Isn't it possible forcible sterilization might pose even worse dan-
> gers to civilization than a reversing of evolution (5)? Might it not lead
> to totalitarianism? Wouldn't a better and more practical solution (6) be
> to improve the distribution of wealth among nations, to find cures for
> disease, to share technology, and to expand educational opportunity
> (including education in birth control methods)?

> *Concerning the kind and quality of the evidence presented:* One signifi-
> cant question about some of the evidence (10,11) concerns how typical
> and comprehensive it is. Is the view expressed in the quotations one
> that is shared by most geneticists and medical authorities, or is it a mi-

nority position? An even more important question concerns the evidence that is omitted. Surely psychologists, sociologists, and historians must contribute to this issue. Some of the questions they could answer are these: What psychological effects would forced sterilization have in those subjected to it? A feeling of worthlessness, perhaps, or rage? What social behavior would be likely to result from such effects? Violence? Revolution? What historical precedents are there to help us measure the probable effects?

In light of these considerations, you might conclude that although the world population problem and the related concerns of poverty, illiteracy, and disease are serious and should be addressed, the idea of forced sterilization should be opposed—at least until its advocates clarify their terms and answer the important critical questions. If you were to make a formal response to the argument in an analytical paper or article, you would develop your ideas thoroughly, meeting the same standards you expect of others. (For a discussion of the principles and approaches used in analytical writing, see Appendix A.)

WARM-UP EXERCISES

4.1. Make up as many new words—*non* words like *garrumptive*—as you can to reflect people's moods. In each case, indicate the specific mood each word reflects. Be sure to list many possible words before choosing the best one.

4.2. Make up a new name for yourself (both first name and last), one that fits the special qualities you have or are striving for. Be sure to consider unusual names (Honor Trueblood, Rick Decent) and list many possibilities before choosing the best one.

4.3. Your young nephew is confused. He has learned that "he who hesitates is lost" and that "haste makes waste." The sayings seem to oppose each other and he wants to know which is right. Answer in a way he will understand.

APPLICATIONS

4.1. Read the following dialogue carefully. Decide which statements are reasonable and which are not. Provide a brief explanation of why you consider any statement unreasonable.

[Scene: a college dormitory room. A bull session is in progress. George and Ed, freshmen at Proudly Tech, are discussing academic affairs with their sophomore roommate, Jake.]

GEORGE: When I arrived on campus last month, I went to see my advisor to get my freshman English course waived. I didn't get to first base with him. "Everyone takes freshman English," he said. "Everyone!" I'll bet he's got that line taped and just plays it whenever a student raises the question. It really burns me having to take that course. I can see it as a requirement for most students. But I earned straight B's in high school English. Why should I spend more time on that stuff in college?

ED: You're right, George. This place is like home—everybody's on your back making you do things you don't want to do. I should have gone to Bloomville State instead of to this dump.

JAKE: What's so great about Bloomville State?

ED: They let you take whatever courses you want. No required courses at all.

JAKE: Look, my uncle went there after the Korean War. He told me a lot about his college days. But he never mentioned that.

ED: It's true. Listen, there was this guy I was talking to at the bar in the train station when I was coming up here. He goes to Bloomville and he told me they had no required courses.

GEORGE: That really bugs me. Straight B's. And still I've got to take this crappy course. . . .

JAKE: Listen, pal. You're lucky you were born talented in writing. I wish I had that gift. For me, nothing but D's and F's. Hopeless.

ED: Who'd you have for English, Jake?

JAKE: Crawford. An OK guy, I guess, but sort of scholarly. Talks over everybody's head, always quoting some writer or other.

ED: I've got Mr. Schwartz. What's the word on him?

JAKE: You've lucked out, boy. Three of my friends had him last year and two got B's and one a B+. A guy who grades like that has got to be a winner.

GEORGE: I'm glad somebody's luck held. Mine certainly didn't. For the two comps I've written so far, I've gotten a D+ and a C−.

JAKE: Who have you got?

GEORGE: Mr. Stiletto.

JAKE: He wasn't here last year.

GEORGE: I'll bet he's just out of graduate school. Or maybe he never went. At any rate, he sure has it in for me. Maybe he's prejudiced against Germans.

ED: Maybe you picked the wrong side of the issue to write on—you know, the one he disagrees with.

GEORGE: Hey, you may be right. The first topic was birth control and I'm sure he's Catholic because I saw a little statue of Jesus on his car dashboard when his wife dropped him off outside the building last week. I wrote in favor of birth control. Wow. What a jerk I am. Hey, and come to think of it, that second comp. . . .

JAKE: I should have taken him for comp. I'm Catholic.

GEORGE: That second comp was on civil rights. And I know he's against blacks. The guy who sits next to me is black and Stiletto really cut him down just because he was late a few times. And there's a black girl he always calls on for the tough questions. No wonder I got a C−.

JAKE: Wait till you guys take psych next year. I don't know if I'll be able to last till the end of the term. It's the boringest subject ever thought up by man. Professor Clifford walks in, opens his book, and begins reading from his notes in a low mumble. "mmmm . . . Freud says . . . mmmmmm . . . Oedipus complex . . . repression . . .

mmmmm." Deadliest stuff you ever heard. I'm glad I don't need another social science course. Those guys are really out of it.

ED: Doesn't he ever let you discuss what you read?

JAKE: Yeah, once in a while. Yesterday, for example, we were talking about some guy named Frankl and Clifford said that according to this Frankl, boredom causes people more problems than distress does. Some kids in the class gave examples of how that's so—you know, there are always some guys looking to agree with the prof to make some points. . . .

ED AND GEORGE: Yeah.

JAKE: . . . And so I raised my hand and said that that guy Frankl was all wet, that everybody knows that distress causes more problems than boredom. I told him that my own experience proved it because five years ago when my father lost his job, my family really had to struggle for more than a year. We had problems, believe me; and they weren't caused by *boredom!*

GEORGE: What did he say to that?

JAKE: Well, he mumbled something about Frankl not meaning that. And then he started tossing around a lot of statistics and examples to try to get me confused. He couldn't corner me, though. I finally said, "Frankl's entitled to his opinion; I've got my own."

GEORGE: Hey, that's great. I bet he cursed you out under his breath. You really socked it to him.

JAKE: Yeah, I guess I did. When I get mad, I can argue pretty good. Now I've just got to be careful he doesn't take it out on me in my grade.

ED: Say, fellas, I've got to cut out. I'm going to the library and prepare for tomorrow's English class.

GEORGE: What's your assignment?

ED: Oh, a piece by Orwell. We just have to read it and be ready to discuss it. I've read it five times already, but I can't find anything wrong with it, nothing to disagree with. I'll just have to read it again. Be seeing you.

4.2. Follow the directions for Application 4.1. In addition, decide what action you would recommend if you were a school board member. Explain why you think that action best.

[Scene: The Alertia, Indiana, town hall. The members of the Alertia school board are meeting with a group of parents concerned about the school's new sex education program for seventh- and eighth-graders.]

CHAIR: I'd like to welcome the guests of the board to our regular meeting. As you all know, the board agreed to Ms. Jackson's request for an opportunity for those who wished to present their views on the school's new program in sex education. As we know, sex was around for quite a while before this program began, heh, heh . . . [silence].

MS. SCHULTZ: It's exactly that sort of levity about this dangerous program that worries me.

CHAIR: I'm sorry, Ms. Schultz. I only meant that as a little joke.

MS. SCHULTZ: Well, there's nothing funny about a program that introduces raw sex into the minds of innocent young children.

MS. JACKSON: The reason we asked for this meeting is that we feel what is taking place in sex education class goes beyond the bounds of decency.

CHAIR: Could you be more specific please. Just what is taking place?

MS. JACKSON: Someone told me that Ms. Babette encouraged the students to touch each other freely to overcome any inhibitions they might have about sex. Can you deny that such encouragement goes beyond the bounds of decency?

CHAIR: No, I certainly wouldn't deny that. But. . . .

MS. BROWN: I heard that last week she asked two students to come to the front of the room and demonstrate what petting means.

MS. GREEN: That doesn't surprise me a bit. She *does* have a sluttish manner, you know. Those miniskirts, that long hair. The way she talks to men is most provocative. Positively lewd. If my daughter dressed and acted like that, I'd feel I had failed as a parent.

CHAIR: Ladies, please. We've got to have a little more order. Mr. Lessrow has had his hand up for some time.

MR. LESSROW: Thank you. Of course, I agree with the good ladies who have spoken thus far. But with all respect to them, I think they may be missing the real nature of this threat to the morals of our young people. We must not forget that those young people are the United States citizens of tomorrow. And let me ask you, just who will stand to profit if they are corrupted, if their preoccupation with the flesh stays them from their duties and obligations as citizens? Let me ask. . . .

MEMBER 1: Who *will* stand to profit, Mr. Lessrow?

MR. LESSROW: I was getting to that point, sir. Who else but the communists.

MEMBER 1: Are you suggesting that the communists are in some way responsible for sex education in American schools, for the course in our school?

MR. LESSROW: I am saying precisely that. Sex education is a plot to lure our children into lives of lustful hedonism. It is a plot designed and supported by the international communist conspiracy. All a person needs to do is a little reading, have a little concern for the truth, and not be like these hothouse liberals who believe the communists are our "brothers." The charges have been made, clearly and forcefully, against the national organization that publishes the filth used in these courses—at best, they're a lot of misguided, uninformed dupes; at worst, conscious agents of the conspiracy.

MEMBER 2: Now that's surely a very extreme interpretation of. . . .

MR. LESSROW: It's an extreme plot! Extreme situations demand extreme responses.

MEMBER 2: As I started to say, it's an extreme interpretation of a very complex issue. Surely we should be a little less quick to jump at every charge we read in the newspapers, be a little more open-minded.

MS. SCHULTZ: A person should be open-minded while searching for the truth but not after finding it.

MS. JACKSON: I just can't understand how people can resist common sense. It should be clear enough to everybody—even to the teachers of this school—that when you bring sex into the classroom, you dignify it.

When you encourage the young to talk about it openly in school, they'll talk about it openly out of school. And talking is a very short step away from acting. I for one don't want my teenagers to become promiscuous just because some so-called educators in this town persist in denying the obvious.

MS. OVERLOOK: I don't see the need for a sex education course in the first place. Surely if parents know enough to raise their children in other respects, they are qualified to teach them about sex. Sex is a moral matter—and the school has no business butting into the moral upbringing of the young. The school should stick to the three R's and leave moral and spiritual matters to the home and church.

MS. SCHULTZ: If the school were as anxious to guard the innocence of the young as it is to fill their heads with sex ideas, perhaps our society wouldn't be slipping so badly today.

MEMBER 2: I'd like to go back to something Ms. Jackson said a few minutes ago, about promiscuity. Ms. Jackson, no one wants to make teenagers promiscuous. The whole effect of the program in sex education, as I understand it, may be to prevent just that development. There is a great deal of emphasis on sex in advertising today, and an increasing tendency toward frankness in the arts. The board had only a brief explanation of the objectives and approaches of this course, but we were told by the principal that the faculty committee that developed the course consulted numerous statistical studies, and every one showed that most young people receive very little direct, honest, and accurate information about sex. Despite appearances, he said, they're woefully ignorant, in many cases, about the facts of life. That is what the course and its teacher, Ms. Babette, are trying to overcome: misinformation and ignorance.

MS. GREEN: [Turning to Ms. Brown and whispering] It's obvious why he speaks that way. I've seen the way he looks at Ms. Babette. Those bachelors and their filthy minds.

MS. SCHULTZ: A course in sex education is a strange way of decreasing promiscuity. How come since courses like this have been added to curricula around the country, the incidence of rape, out-of-wedlock pregnancy, and venereal disease has risen so dramatically?

MEMBER 2: I'm not sure I understand the point you are making. Are you suggesting that. . . .

MS. SCHULTZ: I'm suggesting that I'm in favor of ridding our society of its preoccupation with sex. I confess I don't know quite how to do that. But I do know where to start. Right here in Alertia—by ridding our school of that course.

MR. LESSROW: [Applauding vigorously] My sentiments exactly. If we're not going to defeat the communists abroad or in Washington, at least we can stop their insidious campaign against our youth at home. I voted for you for the school board—probably most of us in this room did. We had confidence in your ability to act wisely, do the right thing. You now know the facts in this matter. It's time to act on them. You can justify our confidence in you by demanding that that course be discontinued immediately.

CHAIR: [After a minute or two of silence] Well, I believe the board has a good idea of the nature of your concern about this course. If there are no more comments at this time, I'd like to thank you ladies and gentlemen for coming out tonight, and to assure you that we will give your position our careful consideration. If the board members will remain, we'll continue with our meeting in a few minutes.

4.3. Read the following dialogue carefully. Then evaluate both Pia's and Mort's positions. Decide with whom you agree or whether you disagree with both. State your judgment and support it thoroughly. (Note: In 1982 the New York State Legislature dropped the requirement that rape victims must offer "earnest resistance" to the rapist in order for prosecution to take place but added the provision that the force used by the rapist must cause in the victim "fear of immediate death or serious physical injury."[6])

PIA: In other words, those lawmakers were saying that no crime takes place when a woman is raped unless she fears death or serious injury.

MORT: In the technical sense, that's right.

PIA: Are those lawmakers for real? When a woman doesn't want to have sex and a man makes her do so anyway, that's rape. It shouldn't matter whether he threatens her with a submachine gun or simply overpowers her. It's still a violation of her body and should be treated as a crime.

MORT: You're oversimplifying. There are cases where the woman says no and really means yes, and cases where the woman says yes and then later decides she really should have said no. There are even cases where a woman is excited by the rapist's advances and, though she initially protests, actually derives sexual pleasure from the act. There has to be some test the courts can apply to separate those cases from real rapes. I believe the "earnest resistance" approach is the best test, but if that's unacceptable, then the "fear" test will do.

PIA: With that kind of thinking you qualify for a seat in the state legislature.

4.4. Evaluate the argument in the following letter to the editor using the approach explained in this chapter. State your judgment and support it thoroughly.

Dear Editor:
I enjoyed your recent series of articles on religious views. I believe religious values occupy the central place in one's being. Today an increasing number of young people are giving up their religion because of the vocal skepticism of those who find religious values too restrictive. If more of us who do believe were as vocal, the young would surely see the relevance of religion and not be so easily deceived by those who wish to mislead them.

It is fashionable today among so-called humanists to place people's reason above religious faith. They say a person must follow his or her own lights, affirm what he or she believes is true. But are they really so open-minded and humble as that view makes them seem? I think not. For underneath that view lies the fact that they exalt their own judgment. When they accept the word of an authority, it is only because they agree with that authority. And they do not accept one authority without, by that very acceptance, rejecting other authorities. In short, they are superegotists who refuse to accept what transcends their understanding and who try to fit God into their understanding. Their efforts are in vain; for God will not fit into the finite mind. A god who can be understood by human beings is no God at all, but a poor imitation.

I do not believe that any intelligent, honest person can place his or her confidence in human intelligence and reason. Human learning is too sparse and fragmentary to warrant such trust. Human knowledge and understanding change all too quickly. Yesterday's theories gather dust in the attics of libraries. And history judges all things mercilessly. But the Bible, God's own word, remains. It stands as an immutable beacon to all who love the truth. One need only put aside his or her probing and questioning and doubting, become like the little children, and accept it.

Sincerely yours,
Mrs. Joan Truly

4.5. The following letter appeared in the *New York Times Magazine*.[7] Evaluate the argument it presents by using the approach explained in the chapter. State your judgment and support it thoroughly.

To the Editor:

As a man whose past is considerably peppered with the buckshot of imprisonment including four years at Attica prison I am in a position to state that William R. Coons's article, "An Attica Graduate Tells His Story" (Oct. 10), is equipped with built-in blinders. The reader can look in only one direction: at the brutal guards, the butcher doctors, the unfeeling, unconscionable warden, etc. A cartoon, therefore, forms in the mind of the reader. He sees a huge, hairy monster, frothing fangs bared, labeled "Penal System" and crushing the life out of a ragged, pity-evoking figure labeled "Defenseless Convict."

I wonder why Mr. Coons omitted the worst handicap facing the inmate who is sincerely interested in rehabilitation—his own "brothers" in gray?

Contrary to what Mr. Coons would have the reader believe, prison populations are not made up solely of misunderstood, slightly tarnished angels unjustly sentenced to hundreds of years for merely stealing wormy apples.

Many—let me lean on that word—*many* convicts are incorrigible scum whose sole purpose in life closely parallels that of a demented crocodile. They wouldn't lead an honest life if guaranteed a thousand dollars per week and half of God's throne in the hereafter.

They are the ones who steal from their fellow inmates, who collect "protection money" from the weak and frightened, who force others with "shanks" pressed to their throats to commit homosexual acts, whose roaring animal voices fill the cell blocks until your brains vibrate from the obscene cacaphony and you couldn't write your own name without misspelling it. They are the ones who will grip prison reform by the throat and choke it, exploit it, mangle and tramp on it until, in disgust, the administration rescinds it.

The first step toward *lasting* prison reform is to collect all the incorrigible scum, the human cockroaches who infest prison populations and place them in separate institutions. Let them prey on each other. Let them, if it comes to it, kill each other off . . . incurable cancers devouring each other.

Unless this step is taken, prison reform, however great and shining, will fade into the limbo of things that might have worked.

Name Withheld

4.6. Evaluate the argument presented in the following brief essay by using the approach explained in this chapter. State your judgment and support it thoroughly.

Each year hundreds of thousands of animals are killed in research experiments. These include not only rats and mice, but also rabbits, monkeys, dogs, cats, and birds. The deaths are considered justified because the research is necessary to save human lives. But this reasoning reflects a complete disregard of animals' rights.

Animals' rights? The idea may seem strange if you've never heard it before. But it is not a new idea. Eighteenth-century French philosopher Voltaire reasoned that because animals have feelings and can understand, at least in a primitive way, they therefore have rights. Albert Schweitzer, the famous jungle doctor and humanitarian, believed that "reverence for life" applied not just to humans, but to all living creatures.

More recently Dr. Thomas Regan, professor of philosophy at North Carolina State University, argues persuasively for such rights in his book *Animal Rights and Human Obligations*. He believes that people resist the idea that animals have rights largely because they think of the world as belonging exclusively to humans. They see dogs and cats and even more exotic animals like dolphins and apes as objects rather than creatures, as things to be *owned* and *used*. He concludes that "it's not crazy to believe, as some Eastern cultures do, that animals have rights. Our aim is to break some standard patterns of thought about animals that are held in Western society."

A number of people have begun to speak out on this issue. For example, the group that organized a petition-signing drive in Ann Arbor to save the lives of six gorillas scheduled to be used (and probably maimed or killed) in a University of Michigan automobile accident research project. And the man in Honolulu who freed two dolphins from a University of Hawaii laboratory where, though they were not being harmed, they were wrongfully imprisoned. Such people may be scorned and derided as fanatics today, but they will one day be regarded as heroes.

Such praiseworthy actions, unfortunately, are too limited to make much of a difference. What is desperately needed is legislation that will grant animals exactly the same rights that humans enjoy, and that will prohibit the use of any animal in any research experiment that will cause it suffering, regardless of the supposed value of the research. All sensitive and caring people will support such legislation and urge their legislators to enact it without delay.

GROUP DISCUSSION EXERCISE

Discuss the following issue with two or three of your classmates. Observe the guidelines to group discussion presented in Appendix B. Consider all sides of the matter and try to reach consensus. Be prepared to report your group's deliberations to the class, describing how your analysis proceeded, what questions were asked, and what agreements were reached. If differences of viewpoint remain unresolved, be prepared to report them objectively.

> Fifty years ago parents told their children if they worked hard, they would achieve, and their achievement would make them feel good about themselves. Today the self-esteem movement argues that the opposite is true—that only if people first feel good about themselves will they be able to achieve. (This argument underlies the often-expressed idea that lack of self-esteem causes a variety of conditions from academic underachievement to criminal behavior.) Which of these ideas is better supported by everyday experience?

COMPOSITION OR SPEECH EXERCISE

Write a composition or, if your instructor specifies, a formal speech, presenting the view your group reached in the preceding group discussion exercise. (If you hold a dissenting view, present that instead.) Be sure to provide evidence that your view is the most reasonable one. Naturally your composition or speech will bear some resemblance to those of the other members of your group—you will have developed ideas as a team, so at least some of your ideas will be similar, even identical, to theirs. Don't be concerned about such similarities. Your composition or speech will be a unique effort if you (a) use supporting material from your own experience, observation, and research; (b) develop your own line of reasoning about that material; (c) employ your own ingenuity in designing an introduction and conclusion and in arranging the material in the body of your composition or speech; and (d) express your thoughts in your own words. For further guidance, consult the appropriate appendix—A for writing, B for speaking.

PART 2

Be Creative

The Creative Process

The human mind, as we have seen, has two phases. It both produces ideas and judges them. These phases are intertwined; that is, we move back and forth between them many times in the course of dealing with a problem, sometimes several times in the span of a few seconds. To study the art of thinking in its most dynamic form would be difficult at best. It is much easier to study each part separately. For this reason, we will focus first on the production of ideas (Chapters 5 through 9), and then turn to the judgment of ideas.*

Although everyone produces and judges ideas, the quality of the effort varies greatly from person to person. One individual produces a single common or shallow idea for each problem or issue and approves it uncritically, whereas another produces an assortment of ideas, some of them original and profound, and examines them critically, refining the best ones to make them even better. The terms *creative thinking* and *critical thinking*, as we will use them throughout the remaining chapters, refer to the latter kind of effort.

KEY FACTS ABOUT CREATIVITY

Before the mid-1950s, creativity received little scholarly interest. Then one researcher examined more than 121,000 listings of articles recorded in *Psychological Abstracts* during the previous 23 years. He found that only 186 articles—less than two-tenths of 1 percent of the total—had any direct concern with creativity.[1] Since that finding, however, interest in creativity has increased considerably, and many books have been published on the subject.[2] Researchers have examined the lives of creative achievers, probed the creative process, and tested creative performance in every conceivable circumstance and at every age level.

Researchers' efforts have helped deepen our understanding of creativity and overcome the many misconceptions that for so long went unchallenged.

---

*Because it is impossible to separate the two completely, minor elements on judging will be included in our treatment of creativity, and vice versa.

You have undoubtedly been exposed to some of these misconceptions and therefore have developed some false impressions about what creativity is and how it works. Replacing those false impressions with facts is an important first step in developing your creative potential. The facts that follow are the most important ones. Some we mentioned in passing in Chapter 1; all are worth returning to and reflecting on from time to time.

"Doing your own thing" is not necessarily a mark of creativity. "For many people," George Kneller observes, "being creative seems to imply nothing more than releasing impulses or relaxing tensions. . . . Yet an uninhibited swiveling at the hips is hardly creative dancing, nor is hurling colors at a canvas creative painting."[3] Creativity does involve a willingness to break away from established patterns and try new directions, but it does not mean being different for the sake of being different or as an exercise in self-indulgence. It is as much a mistake to ignore the accumulated knowledge of the past as it is to be limited by it. As Alfred North Whitehead warned, "Fools act on imagination without knowledge; pedants act on knowledge without imagination."[4] Being creative means *combining* knowledge and imagination.

Creativity does not require special intellectual talent or a high IQ. The idea that highly creative people have some special intellectual ability lacking in the general population has enjoyed popularity for centuries. When the IQ test was devised, that idea was given new currency, and anyone who achieved less than a genius-level score (135 and above) was considered to have little or no chance for creative intellectual achievement.

However, when researchers began studying the lives of creative people and comparing IQ test performance with creativity test performance, they made two discoveries. They found that creativity depends not on the possession of special talents but on the *use* of talents that virtually everyone has but most never learned to use. In addition, they found that the IQ test was not designed to measure creativity, so a high score is no indication of creative ability and a low score no indication of its absence. In fact, they found the great majority of creative achievers fell significantly below the genius level.[5]

The use of drugs hinders creativity. Although many people seem determined to resist this fact, it has long been acknowledged by those who have studied creativity. If liquor and other drugs have been such a boon to original thought, one researcher asks, why hasn't the corner saloon produced more creative achievers? No one, as yet, has answered this question satisfactorily. Nor is anyone likely to. The reason drugs harm creativity, Brewster Ghiselin explains, is that "their action reduces judgment, and the activities they provoke are hallucinatory rather than illuminating." What is needed, he argues, is not artificial stimulation of the mind but increased control and direction.[6]

The use of drugs and liquor as stimulants is sometimes part of a larger misconception that might be termed the *bohemian mystique.* This misconception is the notion that a dissipated life-style somehow casts off intellectual restraints and opens the mind to new ideas. Eliot Hutchinson offers an assessment that most researchers would endorse: "Narrow streets, shabby studios, undisciplined living, and artistic ballyhoo about local color may all have their place in pseudo artistry, but they have little to do with genuine creation. Nor is the necessary creative freedom clearly associated with them at all. . . . Bohemianism squanders its freedom, returns from its hours of dissipation less effective. Creative discipline capitalizes its leisure, returns refreshed, reinvigorated, eager."[7]

Creativity is an expression of mental health. One common image of the creative person is reinforced by a number of low-budget horror films. That image depicts a wild-eyed mad scientist, shuffling nervously around a laboratory (pronounced *lab-or´-a-try* in an ominous tone of voice), rubbing hands together evilly and drooling. Many people really believe the image—they view *creative person* and *lunatic* as near synonyms. They are wrong.

Harold Anderson summarizes in the following passage a leading psychological view concerning the relative sanity of creative people. (Endorsers include such respected thinkers as Erich Fromm, Rollo May, Carl Rogers, Abraham Maslow, J. P. Guilford, and Ernest Hilgard.)

> The consensus of these authors is that creativity is an expression of a mentally or psychologically healthy person, that creativity is associated with wholeness, unity, honesty, integrity, personal involvement, enthusiasm, high motivation, and action.
>
> There is also agreement that neurosis either accompanies or causes a degraded quality of one's creativity. For neurotic persons and persons with other forms of mental disease [who are, at the same time, creative] such assumptions as the following are offered: that these persons are creative in spite of their disease; that they are producing below the achievements they would show without the disease; that they are on the downgrade, or that they are pseudo creative, that is, they may have brilliant original ideas which, because of the neurosis, they do not communicate.[8]

CHARACTERISTICS OF CREATIVE PEOPLE

Studies of people who have developed their creative potential have identified a number of characteristics they share.[9] The following characteristics are among the most prominent.

Creative People Are Dynamic

Unlike most people, creative people do not allow their minds to become passive, accepting, unquestioning. They manage to keep their curiosity burning, or at least to rekindle it. One aspect of this intellectual dynamism is *playfulness*. Like little children with building blocks, creative people love to toy with ideas, arranging them in new combinations, looking at them from different perspectives. It was such activity that Isaac Newton was referring to when he wrote, "I do not know what I may appear to the world; but to myself I seem to have been only like a boy playing on the seashore, and diverting myself in now and then finding . . . a smoother pebble or a prettier shell than ordinary whilst the great ocean of truth lay all undiscovered before me."[10]

Einstein was willing to speculate further. He saw such playfulness as "the essential feature in productive thought."[11] But whatever the place of playfulness among the characteristics of creative people, one thing is certain: It, and the dynamism it is a part of, provide those people a richer and more varied assortment of ideas than the average person enjoys.

Creative People Are Daring

For the creative, thinking is an adventure. And they go about it with what Carl Rogers calls "openness to experience," which is the very opposite of defensiveness.[12] Free of preconceived notions and prejudiced views, creative people are less inclined to accept prevailing views, less narrow in their perspectives, less likely to conform with the thinking of those around them. They are bold in their conceptions, willing to entertain unpopular ideas and zany, even outrageous, possibilities. Therefore, like Galieo and Columbus, Edison and the Wright brothers, they are more open than others to creative ideas.

Their daring has an additional benefit. It makes them less susceptible to face saving than others. They are willing to face unpleasant experiences, apply their curiosity, and learn from those experiences. As a result, they are less likely than others to repeat the same failure over and over.

Creative People Are Resourceful

Resourcefulness is the ability to act effectively and conceptualize the approach that solves the problem—even when the problem stymies others and even when the resources at hand are meager. This ability is not measured by IQ tests, yet it is one of the most important aspects of practical intelligence. One dramatic example of this quality was reported in *Scientific American* half a century ago. A prisoner in a western state penitentiary escaped but was recaptured after a few weeks. The prison officials grilled him for days. "Where did you get the saw to cut through the bars?" they demanded. In time he broke down and confessed how he had managed to cut the bars. He claimed he had picked up bits of twine in the machine shop, dipped them in glue and then in emory, and smuggled them back to his cell. Night after night for three months he had "sawed" the 1-inch-thick steel bars. They accepted his explanation, locked him up, and made sure he never visited the machine shop again.

That, however, is not the end of the story. One dark night about three and a half years later, the man escaped again, and the prison officials found the bars cut in exactly the same manner. Though he was never recaptured, the way he escaped is legendary in the underworld. He'd lied about using material from the machine shop either time. He had been much more resourceful than that. He had used woolen strings from his socks, moistened them with spit, and rubbed them in dirt on his cell floor.[13]

Creative People Are Hardworking

"All problems," states William Gordon, "present themselves to the mind as threats of failure." Only people who are unwilling to be intimidated by the prospect of failure, and who are determined to succeed no matter what effort is required, have a chance to succeed. (Even for them, of course, there is no guarantee of success.) Creative people are willing to make the necessary commitment. It was that commitment Thomas Edison had in mind when he said, "Genius is 99 percent perspiration and 1 percent inspiration"; so did George Bernard Shaw when he explained, "When I was a young man I observed that nine out of ten things I did were failures. I didn't want to be a failure, so I did ten times more work."

Part of creative people's industriousness is attributable to their ability to be absorbed in a problem thoroughly and to give it their undivided attention. But it is derived, as well, from their competitiveness, which is unlike most people's in that it is not directed toward other people but toward ideas. They take the challenge of ideas *personally*. Lester Pfister was such a person. He got the idea of inbreeding stalks of corn to eliminate weaker strains. He began with 50,000 stalks and worked by hand, season after season. After five years he had only four stalks left, and he was destitute. But he had perfected the strain.[14] Where others would have succumbed to frustration and disappointment, he persevered because he was unwilling to accept defeat.

Creative People Are Independent

Every new idea we think of separates us from others, and expressing the idea increases the separation tenfold. Such separation is frightening, especially to those who draw their strength from association with others and who depend on others for their identity. Such people are not likely to feel comfortable entertaining, let alone expressing, new ideas. They fear rejection too much.

Creative people are different. This is not to say that they don't enjoy having the acceptance and support of others or that the possibility of losing friends doesn't bother them. It means that, however much they may want acceptance and support and friendship, they don't need them the way others do. Instead of looking to others for approval of their ideas, they look within themselves.[15] For this reason they are less afraid of appearing eccentric or odd, are more self-confident, and are more free to speak and act independently.

Knowing these five characteristics can help you develop your creative potential if you are willing to make the effort to acquire them—or if you already possess them, to reinforce them. It is never an easy task; old habits resist replacement. But even modest progress will make a difference in the quality of your thinking.

APPLYING CREATIVITY TO PROBLEMS AND ISSUES

The two broad applications of creativity that are of special concern to us are solving problems and resolving controversial issues. The terms *problem* and *issue* overlap considerably. Both refer to disagreeable situations that challenge our ingenuity, situations that have no readily apparent, satisfactory remedy. But an *issue* has an additional characteristic. It tends to divide people into opposing camps, each sure that it is right and the opposition wrong.

The most important ways to apply creativity to problems and issues include taking a novel approach, devising or modifying a process or system, inventing a new product or service, finding new uses for existing things, improving things, and inventing or redefining a concept. Let's see some examples of each.

Taking a Novel Approach

D. B. Kaplan's, a Chicago delicatessen, approaches menu writing with its tongue well in cheek (and in some cases, in the sandwich). Items include Tongue Fu, The Italian Scallion, Chive Turkey, Ike and Tina Tuna, Dr. Pepperoni, The Breadless Horseman, Annette Spinachello, and Quiche and Tell. The ingredients are as creative as the names.

Humane Society inspectors who found two dogs in a closed car in brutal 92-degree heat used a novel approach in dealing with the dogs' owners. They offered them an alternative to being charged with cruelty to animals: spend an hour inside the closed car themselves in the same heat the dogs endured, while the dogs spent the hour in the air-conditioned Humane Society building.[16]

A judge in a Michigan divorce court took a novel approach to the issues of custody and the right to live in the family home. He awarded the house to the *children* until the youngest reached 18. The parents would take turns living in the house and paying the bills. (Since both parents lived in the area, their housing was no problem during the time they were not occupying the children's house.)[17]

To instill in students a sense of obligation to help those in need, Tulane University Law School set the unusual graduation requirement of performing at least 20 hours of volunteer legal work for the poor.[18]

The City of Venice, Italy, long subject to periodic flooding that threatens artistic and architectural treasures, has begun a novel and ambitious project to hold off high water. From 60 to 70 giant water-filled sea gates, each weighing 200 tons, will be sunk in the Venice lagoon. When a storm approaches, they will be pumped out to become a floating barrier that breaks the force of waves.[19]

Devising or Modifying a Process or System

The Dewey decimal system and the Library of Congress system are two techniques that were invented for classifying books. (Even more basic to learning, of course, is the invention known as the alphabet.)

In recent decades a new surgical procedure has been devised for combating periodontal disease and making it possible for people to keep their teeth throughout their lives. The procedure involves cutting back diseased gum tissue and scraping accumulated plaque from the teeth. (Left untreated, periodontal disease can cause teeth to loosen and fall out.)

Over the years several procedures have been developed for determining the health of a fetus. Both amniocentesis and chorionic villus sampling involve the extraction of amniotic fluid; ultrasound involves the bouncing of sound waves off the fetus to form an image.

London police pioneered the use of a novel scientific technique called genetic fingerprinting to identify a rapist or killer. The technique involves the examination of the genetic structure of blood, saliva, and/or semen, which are said to be as individually distinctive as fingerprints.[20]

Reacting to widespread criticism of the 1988 presidential campaign as superficial, Indiana Congressman Lee Hamilton proposed a change in the traditional debating format. His idea was to have each candidate speak alone for an hour, presenting his ideas on a single issue and responding to in-depth questioning by a panel of experts. The presentations would be videotaped simultaneously for sequential televising at a later time.[21] (Unfortunately, the idea was not implemented in 1992.)

Inventing a New Product or Service

In 1845 a man needed money quickly to pay a debt. "What can I invent to raise some money?" he thought. Three hours later he had invented the safety pin. He later sold the idea for $400. Virtually all the products we use every day have similar, though perhaps less dramatic, stories. The hammer, the fork, the alarm clock, the electric blanket, the toothpaste tube, the matchbook—these and thousands of other products first occurred as ideas in a creative mind. And new ideas are occurring every day. Two relatively recent ones you may not have heard of are Graffiti Gobbler, a chemical compound that can remove ink or paint from wood, brick, or steel,[22] and the Moto-Stand, a three-wheeled, upholstered, motorized truck invented by a man paralyzed from the chest down. The vehicle permits him to maneuver around the house in a standing position.[23]

The laundromat, the car wash, and the rent-a-car agency are examples of successful services that have been invented. When the rent-a-car service became quite expensive, some enterprising people invented rental services providing older, high-mileage cars in good working condition. (One such agency is called Rent-a-Wreck; another, Rent-a-Heap.) A public-spirited psychiatrist invented a service for insomniacs; called Sleepline, it offers an 8-minute recorded message ("Sleep is coming . . . slower . . . deeper . . . ") to help people sleep.[24]

Finding New Uses for Existing Things

No matter how old something is, there are always new uses that can be devised for it. Consider how many kinds of nails, nuts, bolts, and brushes have been developed from the original ideas. Even the water bed, a relatively new variation on the bed, has been given a new use: to simulate the warmth and protection of the womb for premature babies.[25] In some cases, apparently useless objects can be put to good use. For example, a St. Louis barber combines hair clippings with peat and other substances to form an unusually rich potting soil that he believes may help restore drought-ravaged soil in parts of Asia and Africa. And at least one college student devised a use for empty beer and soda cans: He punched holes in the top and bottom, ran heavy cord through them, and hung the cans in close rows as window curtains.

Agricultural crops have long been used for unusual purposes. Cotton lint, for example, is used to manufacture explosives, and ground-up tobacco is used for insecticide. Now scientists have found new uses for our nation's largest surplus crop: corn. These uses include deicing materials, adhesives, disposable bottles, and biodegradable garbage bags. Such creative ideas promise to reduce our dependency on oil imports and to reduce pollution.[26]

New uses for the computer and the laser continue to multiply. Here is one that combines the two. A Cleveland firm is marketing a computer device that measures a person for a suit of clothing and then telephones the information to a factory where lasers cut the fabric.[27]

Improving Things

Far more patents are issued each year for improvements in existing things than for new inventions. There is a very good reason for this. Nothing of human invention is perfect; everything can be made better. Consider the development of the light, from the prehistoric torch to the latest flashlight, or that of the camera and the automobile.

Recent developments in the telephone, for example, include call block, call trace, priority call, return call, repeat call, and caller ID. Each of these features was developed in response to a particular need that was not being met by existing equipment.

The use of creativity to improve things is nowhere more evident than in the computer industry. Every few months a significant breakthrough is announced in hardware or software, and minor improvements are constantly being made.

Inventing or Redefining a Concept

We tend to regard the many concepts that help us think and deal with reality as fixed and eternal. Yet that is not so. Concepts are invented, just as products and services are. The concepts of taxation and punishing criminals, for example, may be very old, but they were once new. Numerous other concepts are relatively recent. It is hard to imagine how mathematics could even be used without the concept of zero. Yet that concept was invented by a Hindu around A.D. 500. Similarly, the concept of a corporation originated in the sixteenth century, and our ideas of progress and worldly success in the seventeenth. The concept of the zip code is very recent.

STAGES IN THE CREATIVE PROCESS

Being creative means more than *having* certain traits. It means *behaving creatively,* addressing the challenges we encounter with imagination and originality. In short, it means demonstrating skill in applying the creative process. Although authorities disagree over the number of stages in this process—some say three; others, four, five, or seven—the disagreement is not over substantive matters. It is merely over whether to combine activities under one heading or several. There is no real disagreement about the basic activities involved.[28]

For ease in remembering and convenience of application, we will view the creative process as having four stages: searching for challenges, expressing the particular problem or issue, investigating it, and producing a range of ideas. Each of these stages will be the subject of a separate chapter, but a brief overview of the process will enable you to begin using it right away.

The First Stage: Searching for Challenges

The essence of creativity is meeting challenges in an imaginative, original, and effective way. Often challenges need not be sought out; they come to you in the form of obvious problems and issues. For example, if your roommate comes home night after night at 2:00 or 3:00 A.M., crashes into the room, and begins talking to you when you are trying to asleep, you needn't be very perceptive to know you have a problem. Or if you find yourself in the middle of a raging argument over whether abortion is murder, no one will have to tell you that you are addressing an issue.

However, not all challenges are so obvious. Sometimes, the problems and issues are so small or subtle that few people notice them; at other times, there are no problems and issues at all, only *opportunities to improve existing conditions.* Such challenges arouse no strong emotion in you, so you will not find them by sitting and waiting—you must look for them.

This first stage of the creative process represents the habit of searching for challenges, not at one specific time, but constantly. Its importance is reflected in the fact that you can be creative only in response to those challenges that you perceive.

The Second Stage: Expressing the Problem or Issue

The objective in this stage is to find the best expression of the problem or issue, the one that will yield the most helpful ideas.* "A problem properly stated," noted Henry Hazlitt, "is partly solved." Because different expressions open different avenues of thought, it is best to consider as many expressions as possible. One of the most common mistakes made in addressing problems and

---

*In the case where there is no real problem or issue but only an opportunity to improve an existing condition, you would treat the situation *as if it were* problematic, saying, for example, "How can I make this process work even more efficiently?"

issues is to see them from one perspective only and thus to close off many fruitful avenues of thought.

Consider the prisoner deciding how to escape from prison. His first formulation of the problem was probably something such as "How can I get a gun and shoot my way out of here?" or "How can I trick the guards into opening my cell so I can overpower them?" If he had settled for that formulation, he would still be there (where he belonged). His ingenious escape plan could only have been devised as a response to the question "How can I cut through those bars without a hacksaw?"

Often, after expressing the problem or issue in a number of ways, you will be unable to decide which expression is best. When that happens, postpone deciding until your work in later stages of the process enables you to decide.

The Third Stage: Investigating the Problem or Issue

The objective of this stage is to obtain the information necessary to deal effectively with the problem or issue. In some cases this will mean merely searching your past experience and observation for appropriate material and bringing it to bear on the current problem. In others, it will mean obtaining new information through fresh experience and observation, interviews with knowledgeable people, or research. (In the case of the prisoner, it meant closely observing all the accessible places and items in the prison.)

The Fourth Stage: Producing Ideas

The objective in this stage is to generate enough ideas to decide what action to take or what belief to embrace. Two obstacles are common in this stage. The first is the often unconscious tendency to limit your ideas to common, familiar, habitual responses and to block out uncommon, unfamiliar ones. Fight that tendency by keeping in mind that however alien and inappropriate the latter kinds of responses may seem, it is precisely in those responses that creativity is to be found.

The second obstacle is the temptation to stop producing ideas too soon. As we will see in a later chapter, research has documented that the longer you continue producing ideas, the greater your chances of producing worthwhile ideas. Or as one writer puts it, "The more you fish, the more likely you are to get a strike."

There is one final matter to be clarified before you will be ready to begin practicing the creative process: How will you know when you get a creative idea? By what characteristics will you be able to distinguish it from other ideas? A creative idea is an idea that is both imaginative and effective. That second quality is as important as the first. It's not enough for an idea to be unusual. If it were, then the weirdest, most bizarre ideas would be the most creative. No, to be creative an idea must work, must solve the problem or illuminate the issue it responds to. A creative idea must not just be uncommon: It must be *uncommonly good*.

WARM-UP EXERCISES

5.1. Four friends have a large garden in the following shape. They want to divide it into four little gardens the same size and shape, but they don't know quite how to. Show them.

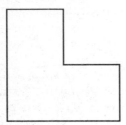

5.2. How many uses can you think of for old socks, stockings, or panty hose? Be sure to guard against setting unconscious restrictions on your thinking and to resist the temptation to settle for too few ideas.

5.3. Every change of season brings a new clothing fashion for men, women, and children. Invent as many new fashions as you can. (If you wish, you may include out-of-date fashions in your list, as long as they have not been popular in recent years.) Observe the cautions mentioned in Exercise 5.2.

APPLICATIONS

5.1. For each of the following problems, apply stages 2 through 4 of the creative process. Record all your thoughts as they occur, and be prepared to submit them to your instructor. When you have finished with the last stage, state which of your solutions is best and briefly explain why.

a. Barney has early classes five days a week. Yet he has attended few of them because he just can't seem to wake up in the morning. If he doesn't find a solution to his problem soon, he'll surely flunk out of college.

b. Olaf was recently in a motorcycle accident that gashed the calf of his right leg and required 10 stitches. The doctor told him not to get the wound wet for at least a week. "Do you mean I can't bathe for a week?" Olaf asked. The doctor shrugged her shoulders.

c. The campus library has been losing articles from magazines and even pages from expensive books. Irresponsible students just tear them out, hide them in their book bags, and walk out of the library. But yesterday a student was caught leaving with ripped-out pages. Some of the library staff favor making an example of her by expelling her from school and pressing criminal charges against her. Others favor merely charging her for the mutilated books.

d. "What do you do with a frozen elephant?" may sound like a joke, but it wasn't when Jackson Township, New Jersey, officials asked it. A 5-ton elephant that was being kept in a drafty barn by a former circus employee had caught pneumonia and died. And so it lay in the barn, frozen solid.[29]

e. Virtually every building with a public bathroom has a graffiti problem. Even when the messages are not offensive, they create maintenance problems.

f. The cost of arresting crime suspects and trying their cases in court is high. The financial burden of the police and court system, unfortunately, is carried by the taxpayers, most of whom are law abiding. In these financially troubled times, many communities are unable to bear this burden.

g. Arnold is the president of a small toy-manufacturing company. His business has been declining over the past few years. Traditional toys and games just don't seem to be as attractive to the public as they used to be.

h. Shoplifting cuts deeply into store owners' profits. Owners and managers would welcome a solution to this problem.

i. Many elderly and handicapped people live lonely lives. No longer active in careers, they are often forgotten by former associates and neglected by family and friends. Many lack transportation to community affairs.

j. In recent years sports stadium and arena crowds in this country and abroad have grown increasingly rowdy, often engaging in acts of violence and destruction of property. (In one such incident, at a soccer match in Belgium, 38 spectators were killed.) Alcohol consumption is often a factor in such incidents.

k. Many college women still assume that the typical rape involves a stranger hiding in a dark area of campus and assaulting an unsuspecting passerby. Though such rapes do occur, in many cases rapes occur on dates when men ignore women's protests and force themselves on the women.

5.2. Think of the most unpleasant task you ever had to do. Use your creativity to make it more pleasant. Follow the directions given at the beginning of Application 5.1.

5.3. Think of your biggest pet peeve about other people, the thing they do that aggravates you most. Use your creativity to reduce or eliminate that aggravation. Follow the directions given at the beginning of Application 5.1.

GROUP DISCUSSION EXERCISE

Discuss the following issue with two or three of your classmates. Observe the guidelines to group discussion presented in Appendix B. Consider all sides of the matter and try to reach consensus. Be prepared to report your group's deliberations to the class, describing how your analysis proceeded, what questions were asked, and what agreements were reached. If differences of viewpoint remain unresolved, be prepared to report them objectively.

Cloning, copying an organism's DNA and making one or more identical organisms, was the subject of the fiction book and film *Jurassic Park*. But experiments done by Dr. Gerry Hall and his colleagues at George Washington University have shown that the cloning of humans is a *definite scientific possibility*. Hall took a fertilized human egg and, once it had divided into a two-cell embryo, separated the cells and demonstrated that they would continue to grow into two separate, identical fetuses.[30] Consider the impact human cloning would have on society and, in light of that impact, decide whether cloning should be regulated or banned outright. If you favor regulation, specify what form it should take and what agency should be responsible for it. (Begin this exercise by identifying the wide variety of situations that would be complicated by the practice of cloning.)

COMPOSITION OR SPEECH EXERCISE

Write a composition or, if your instructor specifies, a formal speech, presenting the view your group reached in the preceding group discussion exercise. (If you hold a dissenting view, present that instead.) Be sure to provide evidence that your view is the most reasonable one. Naturally your composition or speech will bear some resemblance to those of the other members of your group—you will have developed ideas as a team, so at least some of your ideas will be similar, even identical, to theirs. Don't be concerned about such similarities. Your composition or speech will be a unique effort if you (a) use supporting material from your own experience, observation, and research; (b) develop your own line of reasoning about that material; (c) employ your own ingenuity in designing an introduction and conclusion and in arranging the material in the body of your composition or speech; and (d) express your thoughts in your own words. For further guidance, consult the appropriate appendix—A for writing, B for speaking.

6

Search for Challenges

Dennis was sitting at the breakfast table reading the morning paper when he first noticed that the pictures and descriptions of two missing children were printed on the side of the milk carton. A public service organization employee, Dennis was impressed with the idea. "Such an obvious idea," he thought, "using the milk carton for a public service advertisement. Now why didn't I think of that?" He asked the question rhetorically, assuming it was unanswerable, and returned to reading his newspaper.

The question, however, is answerable. People fail to think of new ideas because they are mentally *re*active rather than active. That is, they go through each day unimaginatively, oblivious of problems and issues until someone else solves them, unaware of opportunities until other people transform them into achievements. At that point they spend a few moments envying the other person for his "luck" and slip back into their daily routine, never realizing that, as Robert P. Crawford observed, "Luck is often simply a sensing of an opportunity—an opportunity that is there for all of us to see."

It is one thing to possess thinking skills and quite another to use them in everyday situations. By the end of this course, you will undoubtedly have mastered the various skills of creative and critical thinking. Yet that mastery will benefit you little if you have not also developed the desire to use those skills and a heightened sensitivity to the challenges and opportunities that surround you. This chapter will assist you in this development.

THE IMPORTANCE OF CURIOSITY

Curiosity, useful in every stage of thinking, is indispensable in the first stage, searching for challenges. Curiosity is not a quality reserved for the gifted few; virtually every child is boundlessly curious. A researcher once recorded all the *why* questions asked by a child slightly under 5 years of age over a 4-day period. Read the following transcript of that recording carefully; it will help you recall your own childhood and the state of mind you felt so comfortable with then. (One asterisk indicates no answer was given; two asterisks, no answer and the question was not repeated. Italics are used for the mother's responses.)

1. Why do you have this box for your feet?
2. Why did they bring the bed down from the attic?
3. *Take your dollies in now, Joyce!* Why?
4. *Fix the rug! You caught your feet under the edge of it!* Why? Why did I?
5. Why did you take two cookies?
6. Why does the watering pot have two handles?
7. Why did he put the solder in so many places?
8. *The song sparrow isn't pretty to look at*—Why isn't he pretty?
9. *The bobolink has a brown coat in winter.* Why?* Why?
10. *It was careless of you to lose your shovel.* Why?* Why?
11. *This is your orange juice.* Why?**
12. *You are to sit here, in Daddy's place.* Why?*—Please, Mother, tell me why.
13. Do we have bangs at the back of our heads? *No!* Why?* Why, Mother?
14. *And then he made a mast for his little boat.* Why? Please tell me why he made a mast.
15. Why do you wash the hair off (the razor)?
16. (Putting on bathrobe without putting her arms in the sleeves) Is this good? *No.* Why?*—(impatiently) *Why? Speak out!* (but then without waiting for an answer) *Because it wouldn't stay on. There, you thought it out for yourself, didn't you?*
17. Why did you stub your toe? *Because I wasn't watching out.* Why?
18. *I will tell you a story about this willow plate*—Why?**
19. *Please hurry, Joyce!* Why?*—*Because you want me to wash?* Why didn't you wash first? *Because you knew I wanted to go with Daddy?*
20. See the little tea things! Why did we buy them? *Why do you think?* Because we might use the others all up.
21. Why did you use both a fork and a spoon in making that cake?
22. Why did you sit in that chair, Mother?
23. *Please don't climb in that chair!* Why?**
24. Why are you putting up that screen?**
25. Why are you opening that window?**
26. Why does the little chicken grow in the shell?
27. *You can't win by jumping up and down!* Why?
28. Jeremiah, Jeremiah. He got into a pit, didn't he? Why did they put him into a pit?
29. *Please be careful not to break the bean plants.* Why?
30. I saw your blue apron through a crack in the door. I thought it was a spider. *A spider isn't blue, dear!* Why?*—Please, Mother, tell me why a spider isn't blue.
31. *You shouldn't talk about a visitor's beard, Joyce, until he has gone!* Why?* Please tell me why.
32. Why don't you have a beard, Mother?

33. I want to cut my eyebrows in half! *Oh! You wouldn't want to do that!* Why? Because I would look funny?
34. Why do we have eyebrows?
35. Why must I hurry?
36. Why should I wait for candy until after supper?
37. Why did you speak to that man?
38. *Please don't bang the car door!* Why?*
39. Why did the chickens walk in front of the car?
40. *It is time to go home for dinner now!* Why?*[1]

Some of the questions, of course, are merely designed to get her mother's attention. But judging from both the content of the question and the child's expression when asking it, the researcher concluded that 13 of the 40 questions were genuine expressions of curiosity. Considering that the list contains only *why* questions, and omits *how, where, who,* and *when* questions (which also express curiosity), it is clear how marvelous a child's curiosity is.

HOW CURIOSITY IS LOST

Unfortunately, children who at 4 are bombarding parents with questions often lose their curiosity by 14. How this happens is clear enough, at least in broad overview. Their parents grow weary of answering and begin to discourage questions. "Don't ask so many questions," they scold. And they warn, "Curiosity killed the cat." Then the children enter school and find the teacher has little time to answer. There are too many other boys and girls in the room, there is a schedule to be followed and material to be covered, and time is short.

Nor are parents and teachers the only agents suppressing curiosity. The various media contribute to the problem. Most television programming aims to entertain the audience rather than inform them or explore complex issues with them, thereby fostering a passive spectator mentality. (Curiosity is, by definition, an *active* response to life.)

The publishing industry seldom serves curiosity much better. Popular magazines stimulate morbid curiosity about intimate details of celebrities' lives rather than healthy curiosity about the challenges of life. And book publishers tend to be more interested in fiction than in nonfiction and in physical rather than intellectual development. Diet and bodybuilding books are marketed with an enthusiasm that used to be reserved for the great books of the Western world. Even so-called self-improvement books, which might be expected to emphasize developing important qualities of mind, frequently offer little more than advice on dressing well or playing office politics or inflicting oneself on others.

Thus the suppression of curiosity begins in childhood and continues indefinitely. The result is that most people lose the habit of raising meaningful questions about the world around them.

REGAINING YOUR CURIOSITY

At first thought it may seem impossible to regain your childhood curiosity. Yet it is possible. Many people have done so. In fact, without realizing it, you have already taken the first important step in regaining yours. You have learned that disinterest and the tendency to take everything for granted are not natural, but acquired, characteristics and that lack of curiosity is a bad habit that can and should be broken.

A number of years ago, as a young industrial engineer, I had the privilege of working for a man who realized this and shared his realization with his subordinates. The first day I arrived on the job, this man, the chief industrial engineer, gave me these instructions: "For the next week I want you to do nothing but walk around the plant (a large mail-order company), question everything you see, and keep a record of your questions. Screen nothing out; record even the silliest and most obvious questions. At the end of each day I'd like to meet with you for half an hour and have you share those questions with me." At first I thought the direction strange. "What good can come from this?" I wondered. But I obeyed. I walked through the various departments—shipping and receiving, accounting, merchandising, order filling. And I wrote down my questions.

As the week passed my list grew, and each day's conversation with the chief engineer increased my understanding of my assignment. He wanted me (and every new engineer) to develop a special work style: to see things with heightened curiosity as if through a child's eyes, so that I might think more effectively about what I saw. "What is being done in this operation? Is it all necessary? If so, in what other ways might it be done? Are any of those ways simpler, quicker, safer, more economical? Who is doing it? Could a less highly paid employee do it? How might the work of several people be reduced to the work of one? Is it done at the right time, in the best place, with the most appropriate materials and equipment?" The four years I spent as an engineer were filled with such questions. (And the answers saved the company tens of thousands of dollars.) Yet they all proceeded from that first strange lesson in regaining my curiosity.

You can regain your curiosity, too. It will take effort, just as it takes time and practice to rebuild muscles that have fallen into disuse. But whatever the effort, the payoff in effective thinking is worth it. That payoff will not be only in personal satisfaction but also in increased career effectiveness. Whatever your field of study, the habit of curiosity will enable you to find and address challenges before others do.

SIX HELPFUL TECHNIQUES

Fortunately, it isn't necessary to pretend you are a child again and go about asking a child's kind of questions. (If you were to try it, your friends would probably report you to the campus psychologist.) Nor is it necessary to adopt an industrial engineer's approach; though it works well in that context, it might not fit your situation. There is a better approach. This approach, which fits a wide variety of situations, has six specific techniques:

1. Be observant.
2. Look for the imperfections in things.
3. Note your own and others' dissatisfactions.
4. Search for causes.
5. Be sensitive to implications.
6. Recognize the opportunity in controversy.

Be Observant

Some people are oblivious to what is going on around them. They are so involved in their own internal reverie that they miss much of what is happening. Subtle hints are wasted on them; they never really learn much from experience. How can they? They aren't really in touch with it.

Even if you are not such a person, chances are your powers of observation can stand improvement. Here's a little test to help you decide how observant you are.

1. Does your instructor wear a wedding band?
2. What color are your mother's eyes?
3. How many gas stations are there in your hometown (or neighborhood)?
4. How many steps are there on your front porch at home (or on the stairway to your apartment)?
5. How many churches are there in your hometown (or neighborhood)? What denominations are they?
6. Are there any trees in your best friend's yard? If so, how many? Are there any flowers? If so, what kind?
7. What color are the walls in your old high school hangout?
8. Can you describe your high school's band uniforms in detail? Can you describe the athletic uniforms (any sport)?

Most people are surprised at how little they know about supposedly familiar people, places, and things. You've probably heard the stories about people who have lived in a city or town all their lives, yet can't give directions to a stranger. It's because they travel the same route over and over in a daze, automatically, like robots.

Begin looking at and listening to people, places, and things more closely. Try to pick up details you'd usually miss. See how people behave. For example, next time you are in the cafeteria or dining hall, watch people's actions. Note how many enter alone. Compare the way those alone and those with others behave. How at ease do those alone seem? Do they seem more or less relaxed? Do they seem nervous as they look for a table? What clues do they give about their feelings?

When you are sitting in a group of people discussing something, note the mannerisms of the group. What speech patterns are repeated? How do they look at each other? Do certain people tend to dominate? If so, in what ways? How does their behavior affect the others?

What clues do you get from people you pass in the hall (students, professors, administrators) about their states of mind? How courteous are people to one another? Do people look and speak differently to those they especially like? What manner betrays their attitude?

What excuses do people give for their behavior? How many of your friends accept responsibility as easily as they give it to others? When your friends go to parties, do their personalities seem to change in any way? Do they behave very differently from when they are in the company of professors? What are your friends' prejudices? How do they reveal them (other than by telling you directly)?

The types of observations you can make about people could be extended indefinitely. But remember, too, not just to be observant about other people. Observe yourself as well, the way you act, the broad or subtle clues you give about your attitudes and values.

Look for Imperfections

This advice will seem at first to contradict what most parents teach their children. "Don't expect things to be perfect," they say. "Learn to accept things as they are and be happy they aren't worse." But there is no real contradiction. Seeking imperfections does not mean being chronically dissatisfied, a complainer about life. It means realizing where improvements can be made.

Research suggests that productive thinkers and creative people have a keen sense of imperfection and that this sense is one of the sources of their achievement. They recognize that all ideas, systems, processes, concepts, and tools are inventions and therefore open to improvement.[2]

In some cases, creative people go out of their way to find imperfections. Walter Chrysler, for example, the mechanical genius who founded Chrysler Corporation, was just a young railroad mechanic on a meager salary when he saved enough money to buy a Pierce Arrow automobile. It cost $5000 (at that time a huge sum of money). His purpose was not to drive around and play the big shot but to take the car apart bolt by bolt—to see what parts and assembly design he could improve.[3]

Look around you at any manufactured object: the classroom blackboard and desks, your bed, your clothes, your car, the library's cataloging system, the rules governing your favorite sport, our democratic system of government. All of these in their present form evolved from earlier inventions. And every step in their evolution was an attempt to overcome imperfection. Consider the broad development of two inventions.

ARTIFICIAL LIGHTING	WRITING IMPLEMENTS
The torch	The hammer and chisel
The candle	The stylus

The oil lamp	The quill pen
The electric lamp	The fountain pen
The battery-powered lamp	The ballpoint pen
The fluorescent lamp	The felt-tip pen
The flashlight	The hard-point flowing pen

More important than the evolution to the present is evolution beyond the present. Everything is still imperfect. One authority estimates that fully 80 percent of the patents issued by the U.S. Patent Office are not for new inventions but for improvements in existing ones.[4] There is literally no need to curse the darkness: You can invent a new kind of light.

Note Your Own and Others' Dissatisfactions

Each day brings its share of disappointments and frustrations. There's no way to avoid them. But there is a way to capitalize on them. The common response to such experiences, of course, is anger, resentment, and anxiety. Though that response is understandable, many people wallow in it, letting dissatisfaction ruin their days.

Starting today, take note of the dissatisfactions you feel, like your resentment when your professor's sneak quizzes catch you unaware or when your younger sister orders you around to make herself look important. Notice, too, your disgust when your car refuses to start at the most inopportune moment and your impatience at having to stand in line at the supermarket. Also, when you converse with other people, listen carefully for their expressions of dissatisfaction, even the minor ones that are mentioned only briefly in passing.

Instead of surrendering yourself to your own feelings of dissatisfaction or plunging into other people's laments, pause and remind yourself that viewed positively, every dissatisfaction is a signal that some need is not being met. In other words, regard the situation not merely as an aggravation but also as a challenge to your ingenuity, and consider how the situation can best be improved.

A good example of how dissatisfaction can be used to produce creative ideas is consumer activist Ralph Nader's proposal for a new measure of the state of the economy. Disturbed over the fact that the gross national product focuses on things (notably production) instead of on people, Nader has proposed recording how many people are being fed rather than how much food is being produced and how many people have shelter rather than how many houses are being constructed.[5]

Search for Causes

The people who make breakthroughs and achieve insights are those who wonder. And their wondering extends to the *causes* of things, how they got to be the way they are, how they work.

For example, it was known for years that the disease called anthrax remained in the soil indefinitely. However, that process was a puzzle to scientists. Then one day, while visiting a farm, Louis Pasteur's curiosity was aroused. He observed that one patch of soil was a different color than the soil around it. When he asked the farmer about it, the farmer explained that he buried some sick sheep there the previous year. Pasteur wondered why that should that make a difference. So he examined the soil more closely, noticed worm castings, and theorized that worms bored deep into the earth and carried the anthrax spores up with them. His later laboratory experiments proved him right.[6]

Similarly, diabetes might still be a mystery if it weren't for the curiosity of a research assistant engaged in unrelated research. When he noticed flies gathering around the urine of one dog used in an experiment, he wondered what about that dog's urine would attract flies. His search for the cause ultimately led to the understanding and control of diabetes.[7]

The key to searching for causes is to be alert to any significant situation or event you cannot explain satisfactorily. One especially good time to practice this alertness is while reading the news or watching it on television. For example, if you read the report of the man who killed his wife in a dispute over a penny on Valentine's Day, your curiosity would be aroused. (Legally separated, they were meeting to discuss their property division. She refused to give him a valuable Indian-head penny and he shot her to death.)[8] "What makes a person lose his or her sense of priorities?" you might wonder and thus identify a challenging problem about human behavior.

Be Sensitive to Implications

As a child you probably enjoyed throwing pebbles in a still pond and watching the ripples reach out farther and farther until they touched the shore. Through those ripples the tiniest pebble exerts an influence out of all proportion to its size. So it is with ideas. Every discovery, every invention, every new perspective or interpretation makes an impact whose extent is seldom fully realized at first. Good thinkers usually recognize that impact before others because they are sensitive to implications. Several examples will illustrate this sensitivity.

In August 1981 the Kinsey Institute released a study of homosexuality that challenged the traditional theories about its cause. The researchers concluded that homosexuality seemed to derive from a deep-seated predisposition that may be biological.[9] The report immediately stirred controversy, so no careful thinker would leap to the conclusion that it was the final word in the matter. Yet a person sensitive to implications would quickly realize that if the report proves correct—if homosexuality is determined by biology—homosexuality cannot fairly be considered immoral behavior because homosexuals have little or no choice in the matter.

Some years ago research suggested that in about one-third of all cases, shyness is caused by a genetic predisposition rather than by environmental factors, and that in those cases it is especially difficult to overcome.[10] The person sensitive to implications would consider how shyness affects performance and immediately think of school and career. That would raise, among other questions, the question of whether it is fair to judge students on class participation and whether career guidance should be offered at much earlier ages than at present.

At about the same time, another study demonstrated that some people have a genetic predisposition to commit crimes and that measurements of brain waves, heart rates, and the skin's electrical properties can predict the onset of criminal behavior as early as 10 years in advance. (The study also made clear that it is possible to overcome such a predisposition and avoid criminal behavior.)[11] One serious implication was immediately recognized by the legal profession: whether testing for evidence of criminal tendencies (in the schools, for example) would constitute a violation of the test subjects' rights.

One final example: The Georgia Supreme Court decided a convicted murderer engaging in a hunger strike while in prison had a legal right to starve himself to death.[12] One interesting, if subtle, implication of this decision concerns the question of suicide. Traditionally, suicide has been considered a crime. (Technically, a person attempting suicide and failing can be legally charged for the attempt.) The Georgia decision implies that one has a right to take one's own life, thereby challenging the tradition.

Recognize the Opportunity in Controversy

Many people do little more than rant and rave when a controversial issue is mentioned, rambling on about the wisdom of their side and damning those who disagree. They miss the real opportunity in controversy: the opportunity to be adventurous, explore new perspectives, and enrich their understanding.

What, after all, is a controversial issue? It is a matter about which informed people disagree. Not just any people, mind you, but *informed* people. If such people disagree, there must be some basis for disagreement. Either the facts are open to more than a single interpretation or there are two or more competing values, each making a persuasive demand for endorsement.

In light of this, *it is probable that neither side in a controversy possesses the total truth, that each side has a part of it.* Is each side 50 percent right or is the ratio 51:49, 60:40, or perhaps 99:1? What does the latest evidence suggest? Have I perhaps been mistaken in my views? In these questions lie the challenge and the opportunity.

Mistakes, after all, are common, even about issues regarded as once and for all settled. For example, until recently most scientists agreed that the age of the universe is 20 million years. Available data supported that view and the matter was considered closed. Then in 1982 a team of astronomers produced new data that suggested that the universe is really closer to 10 billion years old.[13] The controversy was alive again—and with it the adventure.

WARM-UP EXERCISES

6.1. Most high school athletic teams have rather predictable, uncreative and sometimes offensive names—Bulldogs, Indians, Warriors, and so on. Think of as many creative names as you can for high school teams, names you have never heard used before. Be sure to guard against setting unconscious restrictions on your thinking and to resist the temptation to settle for too few ideas.

6.2. List as many ideas as you can for new products or services; that is, products or services that do not presently exist but for which there is a need.

6.3. Divide the circle below into as many parts as you can, using four straight lines.

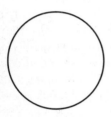

APPLICATIONS

6.1. Spend some time in the dining hall, snack bar, or some other place where people congregate, and listen carefully to their conversations. (Do the same with conversations you are participating in and with conversations you hear on the radio or see on television.) Note all the things people complain about, including procedures, policies, people's actions, tools, and machines (cars, washing machines, and so on); note, too, the nature of their complaints. Keep a record of your findings.

6.2. Visit a general department store (K-Mart, for example) and browse in every department, looking for items whose design could be improved. Make a list of those items. Add to that list any items, from a shoehorn to a toaster, whose imperfections you have had personal experience with.

6.3. Think of as many experiences as you can that caused you to be dissatisfied or frustrated, experiences that posed a challenge to your ingenuity but that you were too aggravated to see. Describe the experiences and state the challenges you now see.

Note: To make seeking out challenges a habit you use every day, continue to do applications 6.1, 6.2, and 6.3 each day for the rest of the term, in addition to your other assignments. Set aside a special notebook for this use and make your daily entries in journal fashion. (Consult your instructor for special format directions.)

6.4. In each of the following situations the causes of behavior are not self-evident. Speculate about those causes, first listing as many possible explanations as you can think of and then deciding which explanation seems most reasonable in each case. Explain your choices.

a. Many athletes who use anabolic steroids reportedly do so with full realization that such use may result in serious physical injury and even death.

b. Many people who decided their parents' Jewish, Protestant, or Catholic faith is irrelevant to this age of science and technology have become devotees of belief systems that science long ago rejected as sheer superstition, systems such as astrology, tarot cards, and channeling (giving over one's body to beings from other spheres to receive enlightenment).

c. In Tampa, Florida, a 30-year-old man threw a 6-week-old cocker spaniel 30 feet out into a lake. (A photographer caught the incident on film and the Associated Press wired the sad picture to newspapers around the country.)[14] The puppy drowned trying to swim back to shore.

d. Four hundred employers of young people in five major cities were studied. The study drew this conclusion: "When recruiting young employees, employers consider in order of importance: appearance and dress, language and speech mannerisms, references and previous work experience. They rely primarily on appearance even though lack of reliability, not lack of proper appearance, is their major complaint about youthful employees."[15] Why would employers place so much importance on dress?

e. Three high school students doing research on shoplifting entered a large drugstore in an upper-middle-class neighborhood and (with the knowledge of the owner) walked up and down aisles stuffing their pockets with large and small items—candy, magazines, watchbands, perfume, a hair dryer, and more. More than 100 shoppers were in the store, and at least 50 of them saw what was happening. Yet every one of the shoppers either walked away or turned his or her head.[16] How do you explain their reaction?

f. Thirty-eight apartment dwellers in Kew Gardens, New York, watched out their windows while a killer stabbed a woman, was frightened away, returned again, was frightened away again, and returned a third time, finally killing her. The attacks took place over a 35-minute period, yet not one of the 38 people either went to the woman's aid or even called the police.[17]

6.5. Each of the following cases is (or could be viewed as) a controversy as defined in the chapter. Examine each carefully, decide whether you agree or disagree with the decision reached or action taken, and explain your view. In addition, identify any implications suggested by each case and any connections with other issues.

a. Female employees of the National Broadcasting Company (NBC) have long been eligible for six months of maternity leave with job and seniority guarantees. However, when a male engineer with the company applied for *paternity* leave with the same guarantees (so that he could care for his baby and ease his wife's return to work), he was turned down.[18]

b. An Illinois minister proposed that convicted murderers be executed publicly on prime-time television. The shock of seeing such executions, he reasoned, would deter others from crime.[19]

c. Through most of their 10-year marriage, Mark Sullivan was training to be a doctor, and Janet Sullivan was working to support them. Shortly after he got his degree and set up practice, they were divorced. As part of the divorce settlement, Janet claimed a partial financial interest in Mark's medical degree.

The court agreed that her investment in his education entitled her to part of its value (the exact amount was not decided by the court, but was scheduled for later determination).[20] Some people argue that the decision is unfair, that she really has no right to any part of his medical degree's value. Others say her share should be at least half. And still others say she should merely be repaid for the money she spent supporting Mark while he was in medical school.

d. Fire raged through the Cicero, New York, home of Richard and Meloni Galavotti, taking the lives of the couple and two of their four children. Investigation revealed that a faulty heat-dispersal fireplace caused the blaze; there were at least six flaws in its installation. Because of these flaws, the installing contractor was charged with criminally negligent homicide. The case is unusual because faulty workmanship had previously been the basis of civil lawsuits, but never of *criminal* charges. In effect, the faulty fireplace unit was regarded as a deadly weapon.[21] Many feel that criminal charges are inappropriate in this case.

e. Kathy York Rodriquez was convicted of severely beating her 8-year-old daughter in what police believe was an attempt to exorcise the devil. At her trial in Bartow, Florida, the judge sentenced Rodriquez to 10 years' probation, then added the stipulation that she not become pregnant during that time or marry a man with children. (If she ignored the stipulation, her probation could be revoked and she could be jailed.) Her attorney believed such a stipulation is improper.[22]

f. There has been a tendency in recent years for unmarried pregnant teenagers to have and keep their babies rather than give them up for adoption. Some people believe the decision to raise a child alone is a sign of maturity and responsibility. Others believe otherwise and argue that it creates many problems.

g. Robert L. Race of Toddsville, New York, believes the state has no authority to require that everyone have a driver's license, so he turned in his license and publicly announced his intention to drive without it. In his view driving is not a privilege but a right.[23] Many would disagree with his view.

h. Anthony Broussard raped and murdered his girl friend, then threw her body into a ravine. Later, before the crime was discovered by authorities, he bragged about it to friends and took some of them to the ravine to see the body. One friend, 16-year-old Kirk Rasmussen, kicked leaves over the body. After the crime was discovered and Broussard was arrested, Rasmussen was charged with being an accessory after the fact. He was found guilty and sentenced to 3 years in a reformatory.[24] Many would argue that Rasmussen's sentence was excessive. Some would say he shouldn't even have been charged.

i. A resident of Washington State name Colbard asked his friend Churches for permission to drive his car to a drinking party with another friend. Churches knew that Colbard was in the habit of getting drunk. Later that night Colbard, drunk, drove the car at a reckless speed and collided with Mitchell's car. Mitchell sued both Colbard and Churches for damages and won. Churches appealed the jury's verdict to the Washington Supreme Court. That court upheld the lower court's verdict.[25] Some would hold that Churches was done an injustice; a person should not be held responsible for an act he did not himself commit.

GROUP DISCUSSION EXERCISE

Discuss the following issue with two or three of your classmates. Observe the guidelines to group discussion presented in Appendix B. Consider all sides of the matter and try to reach consensus. Be prepared to report your group's deliberations to the class, describing how your analysis proceeded, what questions were asked, and what agreements were reached. If differences of viewpoint remain unresolved, be prepared to report them objectively.

> A survey of almost 9000 high school and college students and other young adults revealed that many are willing to lie, cheat, and steal to get what they want. (The research group, the Josephson Institute of Ethics, noted that dishonesty and other unethical behavior is less prevalent among those over age 30.)[26] Why is it that young people have this attitude? What can be done to prevent future generations from developing it?

COMPOSITION OR SPEECH EXERCISE

Write a compostion or, if your instructor specifies, a formal speech, presenting the view your group reached in the preceding group discussion exercise. (If you hold a dissenting view, present that instead.) Be sure to provide evidence that your view is the most reasonable one. Naturally your composition or speech will bear some resemblance to those of the other members of your group—you will have developed ideas as a team, so at least some of your ideas will be similar, even identical, to theirs. Don't be concerned about such similarities. Your composition or speech will be a unique effort if you (a) use supporting material from your own experience, observation, and research; (b) develop your own line of reasoning about that material; (c) employ your own ingenuity in designing an introduction and conclusion and in arranging the material in the body of your composition or speech; and (d) express your thoughts in your own words. For further guidance, consult the appropriate appendix—A for writing, B for speaking.

7

Express the Problem
or Issue

This stage in the creative process is the one most often neglected. The reason is not that people decide to be pigheaded and to proceed without having identified the best expression of the problem or issue. Rather, it is that they are convinced that the problem is self-evident and that it would be a waste of their valuable time to consider alternative ways of formulating it.

Such thinking is wrong. Like our first impressions of people, our initial perspectives on problems and issues are likely to be narrow or superficial. We see no more than what we have been conditioned to see, and stereotyped notions block clear vision and crowd out imagination. Most important, it happens without any alarms sounding, so we never realize it is occurring.

You can avoid this narrowness of perspective by developing the habit of expressing every problem or issue in as many different ways as you can. Before discussing the most effective forms of expression, we will note how to distinguish between problems and issues.

DISTINGUISHING PROBLEMS FROM ISSUES

As noted earlier, problems and issues differ in some respects. A problem is a situation that we regard as unacceptable; an issue is a matter about which intelligent, informed people to some extent disagree. Solving problems therefore means *deciding what action will change the situation for the best,* whereas resolving issues means *deciding what belief or viewpoint is the most reasonable.*

Whenever you are uncertain whether to treat a particular challenge as a problem or an issue, apply this test: Ask whether the matter involved tends to arouse partisan feelings and to divide informed, intelligent people. If it does not, treat it as a problem. If it does, treat it as an issue. Here are some sample problems: a student trying to study in a noisy dormitory, a child frightened at the prospect of being admitted to the hospital, a businesswoman dealing with subtle sexual harassment from her boss. And here are some sample issues: a public school teacher selecting a nondenominational prayer for the classroom, a college administrator increasing the work loads of faculty, an anthropologist stating that human beings are by nature violent.

Each of the situations in the first group is properly considered a problem because there is nothing about the situation itself that is likely to divide informed, intelligent people. Of course, someone, somewhere, might conceivably take an unusual view of a situation—for example, challenging the right of a student to a quiet dorm atmosphere—but that is likely to be a remote possibility. However, each of the situations in the second group is likely to provoke considerable disagreement because each involves *a matter that is itself controversial.*

EXPRESSING PROBLEMS

Both problems and issues are best expressed as questions, but the form of the question is different for each. The form most effective in expressing problems is the "How can . . . ?" form. Let's consider an actual case and see how this form applies. In the early 1980s almost 7000 public schools around the country closed their doors because of declining enrollments, budget cuts, and inflation.[1] Here are the various ways school officials might have expressed this problem:

- How can school enrollments be increased?
- What economies can be made to reduce school budgets?
- How can the impact of inflation on education be lessened?
- How can school buildings best be used after the schools are closed?
- How can the unused space in school buildings be used to generate income so the school will not have to be closed?
- How can school buildings be used in evenings and on weekends to generate income?
- How can the empty buildings be used after the schools are closed?
- How can the unemployed teachers be used after the schools are closed?

Let's consider another problem, the drug problem, arguably the greatest social challenge of our time. Here are just a few of the many ways this problem can be expressed:

- How can people be taught to shun drugs?
- How can people be discouraged from dealing in drugs?
- How can celebrities be persuaded to use their influence to combat drug use?
- How can the media assist in the antidrug effort?
- How can individual citizens support the federal government's antidrug program?

- How can law-enforcement agencies be made immune to corruption by drug lords?
- How can the support of drug-producing countries be enlisted?
- How can crops of drug-producing plants be spotted and destroyed before harvest?

There is room for disagreement about which expression of a problem is best. But there can be no disagreement that we are in a better position to make that decision, and to produce a creative solution, if we take the time to identify and consider all of the questions because *each question opens a different avenue of thought*. The kinds of solutions for teaching people to shun drugs are very different from those for destroying drug crops.

EXPRESSING ISSUES

The question form most effective in expressing issues is the "Is . . . ?" "Does . . . ?" or "Should . . . ?" form. Using such questions, in the sense we are considering here, does not mean asking for simple facts. Rather, it means probing the central elements of dispute. To determine these elements, just note the main points each side uses in its arguments and turn them into questions.

For example, in the abortion issue the prolife side argues that the fetus is a human being and therefore should be entitled to the protection of the law. The prochoice side argues that a woman's body is hers alone and therefore she alone should have the right to decide the fate of her fetus. Thus, your expression of the issue would be

Is the fetus a human being?

Does the fetus deserve the protection of the law?

Is a woman's body hers alone?

Should a woman have the right to decide the fate of her fetus?

In the issue of capital punishment, the pro side argues that when a person has been convicted of a capital crime, the government has the right to decide whether he or she should live or die. The anti side argues that capital punishment constitutes cruel and unusual treatment and is therefore a violation of a person's constitutional rights. Thus, your expression of this issue would be

Does the government have the right to decide whether someone convicted of a capital crime will live or die?

Is capital punishment cruel and unusual treatment?

Does capital punishment violate a person's constitutional rights?

The main points in an argument will either be directly expressed or at least clearly implied. They may, of course, be more numerous than those in the preceding examples.

The fact that "How can . . . ?" questions are the best kind for expressing problems and "Is . . . ?" "Does . . . ?" or "Should . . . ?" questions are best for expressing issues does not mean that other kinds of questions are without value. It means only that they have a different purpose than to focus a challenge. Questions that demand information—such as "Who?" "What?" "When?" and "Where?"—are useful in the investigating stage.° And questions that analyze—such as "Why?" and "How?"—are useful in the evaluation and refinement of ideas.

WHEN PROBLEMS BECOME ISSUES

It is possible to create a controversial issue where none existed. The way we express the problem (or at a later stage, the specific solution we choose) may provoke serious objection. Consider, for example, the last expression of the drug problem: "How can crops of drug-producing plants be spotted and destroyed before harvest?" Even people strongly committed to the war on drugs might respond as follows: "Most of the plants used for drugs could be used for other purposes. It is morally wrong to destroy such plants, especially if they are found in foreign countries on the lands of poor farmers."

Concerned about the high number of dropouts in West Virginia high schools (a problem in other states as well), officials devised an ingenious way to keep students in school—taking away the driver's licenses of students aged 16 to 18 who miss classes. The school notified the Department of Motor Vehicles, which sent a letter telling the offender to return to school or surrender his or her license.[2] This solution, however, was controversial. Some people argued that it violated the rights of students or that it transferred jurisdiction over minors from the parents to an agency of the government.

Good thinkers are sensitive to the implications of both their questions and their assertions. Whenever your questions or assertions create an issue, address it immediately. In the case of destroying drug plants, that would mean asking, "Are there any situations in which it would be morally wrong to destroy such plants?" and resolving the matter. (If you decided the most reasonable answer was affirmative, of course, you would either revise or delete the question "How can crops . . . be spotted and destroyed.") And in the case of the West Virginia school action, it would mean asking, "Does this action violate the rights of students? Does it transfer jurisdiction from parents? Is doing so defensible?"

°When the subject is noncontroversial, "Is . . . ?" and "Does . . . ?" are also in this category.

GUIDELINES FOR EXPRESSING PROBLEMS AND ISSUES

1. Examine the challenge. The moment you are aware that something you have experienced or read about is bothering you or that you are dissatisfied with some person, object, or situation (stage 1), examine the situation and raise your negative feeling to the conscious level. Ask yourself, "What exactly am I feeling? Sadness? Anger? Frustration? What is the source of this feeling?" Then decide whether what bothers you is best treated as a problem or as an issue.

2. Express the problem or issue. Using the appropriate form of questions—"How can ...?" for a problem, "Is ...?" "Does ...?" or "Should ...?" for an issue—express the problem or issue on paper rather than merely in your mind. There are two important reasons for writing your expressions. First, joining mental and physical effort and externalizing ideas often helps clarify them. Second, as any composition teacher will verify, *the very act of writing an idea has a way of triggering other ideas.* Press yourself to produce as many expressions of the problem or issue as you can.

3. Refine your expression. After you have expressed the problem or issue in as many ways as you can, refine the expressions. That is, replace vagueness with exactness and general words with specific ones. An expression is too vague or general whenever you can't be sure what kind of solution it points to. For example, "How can the school enrollment problem be solved?" and "How can the drug problem be eliminated?" point nowhere in particular and therefore should be revised.

BENEFITS OF CAREFUL EXPRESSION

It Helps You Move Beyond the Familiar and Habitual

The first perspective that occurs to you will usually be slanted heavily toward familiar, habitual ways of seeing and interpreting experiences. Thus, it is more likely than later perspectives to reflect bad thinking habits: mine-is-better, face saving, resistance to change, conformity, stereotyping, and self-deception. Creativity is not likely to arise out of these habits.

It Keeps Your Thinking Flexible

Once you adopt a perspective, even tentatively, it becomes difficult to entertain a different one. This is especially true with issues. Once you have reached a position on an issue, even casually, without any real analysis, you will be tempted to become inflexible about it. Thus, you will have difficulty considering it further, even in light of dramatic new evidence.

To appreciate the speed with which you can "lock into" a perspective and the difficulty of entertaining another perspective once you do so, look closely at each of these pictures for at least a minute. Then continue reading.

In the left-hand figure, you should be able to see both an old woman and a young girl; in the right-hand figure, both a vase and two faces. In each case, many people see one image quite readily but have difficulty seeing the other until it is pointed out to them. (If you still haven't seen both, turn to pages 242–243 for assistance.) Once you have seen both, however, you are able to move back and forth between them freely and quickly. It is much the same with perspectives on issues. If you force yourself to entertain a variety of perspectives, you are better able to maintain flexibility.

It Opens Many Lines of Thought

Once you have settled on a perspective, you close off all but one line of thought. Certain kinds of ideas will occur to you, but only those kinds and no others. Thus, if the handicapped man who invented the motorized cart had defined his problem as "How to occupy my time while lying in bed" rather than "How to get out of bed and move around the house," he would never have thought of his invention.

Have you ever looked closely at the wheels on a railroad train? They are flanged. That is, they have a lip on the inside to prevent them from sliding off the track. Originally, train wheels were not flanged; instead, the railroad *tracks* were. Because the problem of railroad safety had been expressed as "How can the tracks be made safer for trains to ride on?" hundreds of thousands of miles of railroad track were manufactured with an unnecessary steel lip. Only when someone thought to redefine the problem as "How can the wheels be made to grip the track more securely?" was the flanged wheel invented.[3]

The tendency to limit the lines of thought that are considered is one of the reasons that breakthrough ideas take years, even centuries, to develop. The development of modern periodontal surgery is a case in point. Before the idea of recording human history was invented, some toothless old person may have wondered, "How can I prepare food to make it edible without teeth?" Having asked the question, he or she may have hit upon the idea of pounding food with a rock to grind it into powder or paste. Later, history tells us, the ancient Etruscans asked, "How will we chew our food after our teeth have fallen out?" and proceeded to invent false teeth. But thousands of years passed before some dentist thought to ask, "How can we restore the gums to good health and make loose teeth more secure in the underlying bone?" and thereafter invented periodontal surgery. (Perhaps some creative person is at this very moment asking, "How can people's gums be permanently protected from disease?")

Keeping more than one line of thought open is especially urgent when dealing with issues. The human drive to make sense of things (a healthy drive, we should acknowledge) will often lead you to take sides too quickly in disputes. And once you have taken a side, ever afterward you are burdened with a powerful temptation to ignore all arguments and all evidence for the other side—indeed, to ignore the very questions that intellectual honesty requires you to ask.

For example, a strict creationist, who believes that the earth is only a few thousand years old, will tend to avoid pondering the question "Is it likely that scientific techniques for dating rocks and other materials are as inaccurate as my belief would suggest?" Similarly, a strict evolutionist, who attributes all that exists to strictly material causes, will tend to avoid pondering the question "Is it possible that a Supreme Being created the evolutionary process by which all things come into existence?" Surely both would be better thinkers for asking the questions they tend to ignore.

Keeping many lines of thought open when you address problems and issues can enable you to produce ideas that are ahead of your time and to avoid narrow-mindedness.

A SAMPLE PROBLEM

A situation that occurred recently in a college town illustrates the approach discussed here. Jean, a middle-aged woman, returned to college after many years to complete her degree. She was living off campus, in an apartment house. Directly below her apartment lived a young woman who played her stereo loud enough to reach Vladivostok with a favorable wind. At least it seemed that way to Jean. The sound and the woman's rudeness infuriated her. She pondered the problem and came up with these expressions of it:

How can I persuade her to turn it down?

How can I compel her to turn it down?

How can I frighten her into moving?

How can I escape the noise?

How can I bother her as much as she bothers me?

Deciding that the first expression of the problem was the best, Jean investigated how she might approach the woman. She tried to recall similarly difficult situations in the past that she had experienced or heard others tell about. Then she brainstormed the possible approaches she might take. After producing a generous number of ideas, she chose the best one, went to the woman, and tried it. It failed; the music continued to blare.

Disappointed, Jean looked at her list of expressions again and decided, probably because of her anger, that *compelling* might succeed where persuasion hadn't. She investigated again, produced ideas again, then selected and carried out not one, but two of them: reporting the matter to the apartment house's owner and registering a complaint with the police. The result was disheartening. The owner made a feeble appeal to the woman and the police gave her a halfhearted warning. After a day or two of quiet, the music blared again.

Now Jean decided her last expression of the problem was the best of the remaining ones. She gleefully listed dozens of hateful ideas for *bothering* the woman (including boring a hole in the floor and pouring water on the stereo). Then the insight came to her. An athletic woman, Jean loved to play tennis and jog. Why not use exercise as a weapon? So she did. She bought herself a jump rope and every morning, promptly at 4:00 A.M., she jumped rope in her bedroom—right over the sleeping woman's head. Wham, whump, thump. How sweet was revenge.

What happened next proved Jean's idea to be even more creative than she had realized. In a few days the woman knocked on Jean's door and explained sheepishly that Jean's jumping was keeping her awake. Jean seized the opportunity and said, "I'll tell you what—I'll stop jumping rope if you'll turn the stereo down." The woman agreed, and the problem was solved.

A SAMPLE ISSUE

The following situation illustrates how the expression of an issue would differ from that of a problem.° You read a newspaper story explaining that a national chain of convenience stores has decided no longer to sell magazines with a sexual emphasis. The chain's decision, the story says, reflects increasing public objection to all forms of pornography. You decide to address the challenge implicit in this subject.

Your first step is to decide whether the subject should be considered a problem or an issue. Because pornography divides informed, intelligent people—some regarding it as harmless and others as harmful—you decide it is an issue. Next you consider the essential elements of dispute found in the pro and con arguments concerning pornography. Those who believe pornography

---

°Because an adequate treatment of the issue illustrated here would demand greater space than is available, the discussion, unlike that of the sample problem, is limited to the expression of the issue.

is harmless often argue that (1) countries that take a liberal approach to the dissemination of pornography have no higher incidence of sex crimes than the United States, (2) looking at pornography provides a healthy release for sexual tension, and (3) the right of free speech applies to pornographers. On the other hand, those who believe pornography is harmful often argue that (4) it promotes a distorted view of sexuality and a negative view of women, and (5) it encourages irresponsible, immoral sexual behavior, including sadomasochism and sex between children and adults.

This consideration of the elements of dispute would lead you to the following expressions of the issue (the numbers correspond):

1. Is the incidence of sex crimes lower in countries that take a liberal approach to pornography?
2. Does looking at pornography provide a healthy release for sexual tension? In everyone? In certain people? Does the answer depend on the kind of pornography viewed?
3. Is the right of free speech applicable to pornographers?
4. Does pornography promote a distorted view of sexuality? A negative view of women? Does it do so for some people but not others? Is age a factor here?
5. Does all pornography encourage irresponsible, immoral sexual behavior, including sadomasochism and sex between children and adults? Does some pornography encourage these?

These questions would undoubtedly lead you to another, more comprehensive expression of the issue: Should the sale and distribution of pornography be in any way restricted?

WARM-UP EXERCISES

7.1. A hunter sees a squirrel on the trunk of a tall tree. The hunter approaches quietly, but the squirrel hears him and scampers to the other side of the tree. The hunter follows the squirrel around the tree, but the squirrel is very clever: It keeps moving at just the right pace to be on the side of the tree opposite the hunter. Around and around they move that way, on into the night. The question is: Does the hunter ever go around the squirrel? Explain your answer.

7.2. Is it possible for you to think of a city or a country that you have never been to? Explain your answer thoroughly.

7.3. Read the following dialogue carefully. Then state what you think Kenneth should say next to ensure that Karl will have no reasonable comeback.

> KENNETH: Every circle has an inside and an outside.
> KARL: I'll bet you can't prove that statement.
> KENNETH: Sure I can. . . .
> KARL: Remember, you said *every* circle. That's what you've got to prove.

APPLICATIONS

7.1. Select three entries from the lists you developed in response to Applications 6.1 and 6.3. Decide whether each of those entries represents a problem or an issue and express it, following the guidelines in this chapter.

Note: Do each of the following applications in this manner: First, express the problem or issue, using the guidelines explained in this chapter. Then investigate, as necessary, and produce as many ideas as you can to solve or resolve it. (Record all your thoughts as they occur to you, and be prepared to submit them to your instructor.) Finally, state which of your ideas you believe is best, and briefly explain why.

7.2. A Los Angeles woman and her husband were convicted of prostitution charges in an unusual case. The couple admitted accepting money from men for sexual favors, but they claimed that the sex acts were part of a religious ritual rather than prostitution. The husband testified he had a revelation from God to revive a 5000-year-old Egyptian religion. In his church, he explained, men's sins are absolved by having sex with the priestess, his wife.[4]

7.3. James Cook, president of the Thomas Alva Edison Foundation, noted that the number of patent applications in the United States had declined steadily in recent years and that a large number of the filed applications came from foreigners. He believed that the main reason for the apparent lack of interest in invention here was the poor image technology enjoyed, particularly among young people. He cited a UN study of the understanding level and appreciation of technology among the people of 19 industrialized countries. Japan scored first, the United States last.[5]

7.4. Ernest Digweed, a British recluse, died and left an unusual will. He bequeathed 30,000 pounds ($57,000 at that time) to Jesus Christ, provided Jesus return within 80 years. At the end of that time, his bequest, plus all accrued interest, would go to Digweed's closest relatives. The relatives, predictably, contested the will, and the matter was submitted to the London High Court.[6]

7.5. Hermione is a college student living in a dormitory room with two other women. Whenever she is trying to study, it seems, her roommates decide to have company, talk loudly, dance to the stereo, or do something else distracting. It's not that they *try* to bother Hermione, but the effect is the same.

7.6. The elementary school is located in a residential area of a small city. Lately there have been confirmed reports of strangers offering young children rides as they walk to and from school. Parents and school officials fear that the children may be in danger from one or more sexual deviates.

7.7. One apparent reason for the increase of violent crimes in recent years is that criminals' rights are as carefully protected as victims' rights. Criminals can break the law with greater boldness, knowing that even if they are caught, the slightest technicality—such as a police officer's failure to read them their rights or to permit them to call an attorney—will result in dismissal of their case.

7.8. As procedures for reporting and investigating child abuse grow more sophisticated, it becomes clear that the extent to which children are physically and emotionally victimized by their parents is much greater than most people realized.

7.9. In recent years there has been increasing concern about the competitiveness of U.S. industry in the world market. The quality of work and of employees' attitudes toward work has been researched and studied. American workers seem to feel less identification with their companies, less concern for increasing productivity, and less concern about the quality of their work than, for example, Japanese workers do. In one Japanese factory researchers found that the average worker submitted 10 suggestions for improving the company per year.[7]

7.10. Rocco is the manager of a movie theater. In recent years a number of competitors have cut into his business, and cable television and video rental stores have reduced the number of moviegoers still further. Rocco desperately needs to get more people to patronize his theater, particularly since he has begun to hear the owners talk of closing it and dismissing him if box office receipts don't improve.

7.11. Many authorities agree that one of the important reasons for the high divorce rate in this country is the naively romantic view of love many people have when they enter marriage.

7.12. Gail has always slept well. But lately she has been waking up at about 3:00 A.M. and having trouble getting back to sleep.

GROUP DISCUSSION EXERCISE

Discuss the following issue with two or three of your classmates. Observe the guidelines to group discussion presented in Appendix B. Consider all sides of the matter and try to reach consensus. Be prepared to report your group's deliberations to the class, describing how your analysis proceeded, what questions were asked, and what agreements were reached. If differences of viewpoint remain unresolved, be prepared to report them objectively.

The children of a deceased Mississippi smoker sued the company that made his brand of cigarettes and the company that distributed the product, charging that they were responsible because they knew the dangers of smoking before warning labels were placed on cigarette packs and therefore acted wrongly in withholding that information. In this case, as in most such cases, the jury absolved the companies of responsibility.[8] Consider the various arguments that could be made for and against tobacco companies' responsibility in such cases and decide under what circumstances, if any, the courts should return verdicts against them.

COMPOSITION OR SPEECH EXERCISE

Write a composition or, if your instructor specifies, a formal speech, presenting the view your group reached in the preceding group discussion exercise. (If you hold a dissenting view, present that instead.) Be sure to provide evidence that your view is the most reasonable one. Naturally your composition or speech will bear some resemblance to those of the other members of your group—you will have developed ideas as a team, so at least some of your ideas will be similar, even identical, to theirs. Don't be concerned about such similarities. Your composition or speech will be a unique effort if you (a) use supporting material from your own experience, observation, and research; (b) develop your own line of reasoning about that material; (c) employ your own ingenuity in designing an introduction and conclusion and in arranging the material in the body of your composition or speech; and (d) express your thoughts in your own words. For further guidance, consult the appropriate appendix—A for writing, B for speaking.

8

Investigate the Problem or Issue

It may seem strange to learn that investigation is a creative stage. You may think of it as a dull, plodding effort involving very little thinking of any kind, let alone creative thinking. In part, that is right. The way many people actually carry out their investigation involves little or no thinking—which is why their investigation is so often unproductive.

Investigation, as we define it, means more than routinely getting the same information as everyone else. It means getting information others overlook by searching in ways and places that never occur to the uncreative. It means using our resourcefulness and originality, being imaginative in our search.

Not every problem you encounter requires significant investigation. If, for instance, you decide to go beyond grumbling and kicking your gym locker when the string in your sweatpants slips out, you can apply the creative process without using the investigative stage at all. You can identify the problem in a number of ways—"How can I insert the string again easily?" "How can I avoid having it slip out again in the future?" "How can I eliminate the need for a string?"—and then go directly to the third stage of the creative process, producing as many solutions to the problem as you can.

In many other cases, however, the investigative stage is a crucial step in the process. The scientists who developed the creative surgical procedure in response to periodontal disease first had to investigate the nature of the disease; that is, its cause, its progress from initial infection to tooth loss, and the various technological methods, medical tools, and approaches available to be used. In the case of unwanted graffiti, the invention of Graffiti Gobbler depended on (1) a knowledge of what techniques had been unsuccessfully tried and (2) a basic understanding of chemistry. "Inspiration," wrote Louis Pasteur, "is the impact of a fact on a well-prepared mind." The investigation stage provides the mental preparation.

Investigation is especially important in complex or controversial issues. In such matters, unless you know all the relevant facts, including the various viewpoints involved and the different lines of reasoning people follow, you are not likely to make sound judgments and develop workable solutions. A. E. Mander makes the point vividly:

> The fewer the facts [one] possesses, the simpler the problem seems to him. If we know only a dozen facts, it is not difficult to find a theory to fit them. But suppose there are five hundred thousand other facts known—but not known to us! Of what value then is our poor little theory which has been designed to fit, and which perhaps fits, only about a dozen of the five hundred thousand known facts![1]

Sometimes a single fact can make a significant difference, as in a study of multiple personality disorders that revealed that 97 percent of the victims had been abused as children.[2]

The point is not that you should feel daunted by difficult problems and issues and give up. (That would certainly not help you to become a better thinker.) It is that you should appreciate the importance of being thorough in your investigations and refusing to rush in, like the proverbial fool, where angels fear to tread.

THREE SOURCES OF INFORMATION

Most people, if they bother to investigate problems and issues at all, do so unimaginatively. They have a very narrow mind-set about information. They know it is contained in libraries, but they aren't sure where else it may be found or how to go about getting it quickly and efficiently. That is unfortunate because knowing other sources can make handling problems and issues much easier and more enjoyable.

There are three sources of information: *yourself, the people around you,* and *authorities.* Let's look closely at each.

Yourself

The first source to consult in the investigation of any problem or issue is yourself; that is, your own experience and observation. You are literally a knowledge factory. You have been receiving sense impressions every moment of the day and night since birth. (Though sight and, to some extent, taste are dormant at night, hearing, touch, and smell remain active.) Calculated at the rate of one impression per second (a modest estimate), if you are now 18 years old, you have more than *56 million* perceptions stored in your mind. They include innumerable experiences of your own and experiences you witnessed or heard about from others. They include, too, all that you have read about or seen on television. In addition to all this information, you have all the ideas you have ever generated, consciously and unconsciously.

If you remind yourself from time to time that you have a wealth of information to draw on in solving problems, you'll be much more likely to make the effort to tap this priceless resource. And that effort is the first important step toward mastering the investigating stage of the creative process.

The next step is to be ready to receive insights from seemingly unlikely sources. Most of us grow up thinking that every subject, and often every aspect within a subject, is neatly and permanently separated from every other one. We would never dream of finding a scientific insight in a poem or a clue to an ethical problem in a math book. Yet many of the most creative insights come from just such unexpected places.

The forklift, for example, which makes it possible to move the heaviest objects effortlessly, was first conceived when the inventor was standing in a bakery. He noticed how the doughnuts were lifted out of the oven on steel "fingers" and thought, "Why shouldn't that same idea work in the warehouse?"[3] Similarly, the idea of the printing press first occurred to Johann Gutenberg while he was watching a winepress operating. He had long pondered how to achieve quicker book production; the current method was to carve words laboriously on blocks and then to rub paper against them. The winepress suggested the idea of transferring an image to paper by pressing an inked lead seal against it.[4]

What connection is there between a secretary's desk and an operating room? Or between the dolphins at Florida's Ocean World and the education of the retarded? "No connection at all," most people would say. And yet creative people have seen a very valuable connection. Surgeons are now using staples in place of sutures to save time and blood loss. And David Nathanson, a professor of psychology at Florida International University, has demonstrated that young people with Down's syndrome learn to speak more quickly and remember words longer when they are placed in pools with trained dolphins. He got the idea for the experiment when he noticed that retarded children who couldn't sit still and pay attention to a teacher would play with a puppy for a quarter of an hour. Speculating on how this interest in animals could best be used in teaching, he decided to use dolphins.[5]

In addition to searching for connections among ideas you encounter now, you can also search for connections you overlooked in past experiences and observations. You surely have thousands of experiences classified under only one heading that could be classified under several. For example, you may have gone swimming as a child, gotten a little too far from shore, struggled, panicked, and almost drowned, until a friend saved you. That experience and the circumstances surrounding it are probably etched in your mind as *narrow escape from drowning.* But think of the other possible classifications: *effects of fear on performance, importance of children's obedience to parents, role of personal sacrifice in friendship.* By seeing more connections between past experiences and observations, you multiply your store of useful information.

People Around You

The next source of information to consult in investigating a problem is other people. Like you, they are knowledge factories. If you were able to draw on all their perceptions, you would be rich indeed. By adding just nine other people's perceptions to your own, you would increase your total to half a billion.

Such total acquisition, of course, is out of the question. Nevertheless, you can learn a great deal from others if you approach them skillfully, with questions that stimulate their thinking and assist them in recalling relevant experiences.

Let's say your problem is how to overcome your fear of heights. You could ask a friend, "Have you ever been afraid of high places?" but that wouldn't be the best way to phrase the question. Any of his or her fears might give you helpful information, so your first question should be broader. And you should be ready with subsequent questions to direct your friend's recall in ways that seem helpful to you. Here's how you might proceed:

YOU: Have you ever had a nagging fear you wanted to overcome?

FRIEND: I don't know ... I guess so. Hmmm ... [trying to remember something specific].

YOU [STIMULATING RECALL]: I mean, like a fear of being closed in or dogs or high places.

FRIEND: Yeah, when I was about 12. I can remember being terrified of the dogs on my paper route.

YOU: Tell me about it. How did you feel?. . .

Later in the conversation you would ask how your friend thought the fear began and, more important, how he or she coped with and overcame it. You'd also ask whether he or she ever received any advice from others that proved helpful or knows any books and articles that speak to the question of overcoming fear. You might even share your fear with your friend and ask for comments.

Any time you try to draw on other people's experience in this way, keep two points in mind. First, some people are more helpful than others. You'll always do better asking a good thinker rather than a poor thinker or an open, talkative person rather than a shy, secretive one. Second, successful questioning depends not only on your ability to ask the right question at the right time but also on your willingness to listen at other times, to open yourself to the person's experience and not let other thoughts (even analytical ones) intrude.

It is also a good idea not to rely solely on your memory. Instead, get in the habit of taking notes. In most cases this is better done after the conversation rather than during it because many people will be distracted if you write while they speak.

Authorities

Although anyone who has had some experience with the problem you are addressing can be a source of helpful information, the best sources are usually authorities on the subject. Authorities are people who have expertise; that is, people who have mastered a subject well enough to know not only its principles and practices but also its areas of dispute. They are also familiar with the various theories and arguments advanced to extend the frontiers of knowledge in the subject.

Where do you find authorities? It's common for people to think, "There are no authorities around me. I don't live in New York or Los Angeles or Washington, D.C. And I don't know anyone in Harvard or Stanford. So I really have no access to authorities." That view is mistaken. Not all authorities live in big cities or work at prestigious universities. Many are nearer to you than you imagine. The biggest obstacle to recognizing them is the notion that if you know the person, he or she can't be an authority, that anyone possessing real expertise must live at least 100 miles away. (Familiarity, in this sense, unfortunately does breed contempt.)

If you are wrestling with a problem in psychology, why not consult a psychology professor on your campus? He or she is an authority in the subject and may even have published an article or book in the area of your concern. Similarly, if the question concerns the availability of jobs in a particular field, you can consult your college placement director. But what about questions in fields not represented at your college—for example, a question about architecture? With only a modest investment of imagination, you can turn to the yellow pages of your local telephone directory and look under "Architects."

And what if you find no such listing? In that case, you turn to your imagination once again and consider what related professions might be listed. *Building Contractor* is one example. Many contractors have had one or more courses in architecture. Even those who haven't may work closely with architects. Still other possibilities are state or county public works or highway departments, which usually employ architecturally trained people.

The advantage of this approach is that it offers a valuable bonus: If the people you contact can't answer your questions, they can usually offer suggestions on whom to consult or at least where to look. This is why so many professional writers use this method. If they are researching a story on a medical breakthrough, for example, they often begin by consulting their county or state medical association or a respected local physician.

MAINTAIN A QUESTIONING PERSPECTIVE

In the presence of an authority, particularly an eminent one, we are often tempted to yield to our sense of awe and surrender our judgment. To let that happen is a mistake. Being human, authorities are subject to making the same errors as anyone else. They can, for example, be blinded by personal preferences, cling stubbornly to outmoded views, and suffer lapses in reasoning.

Even when they manage to avoid such elementary errors, they may miss important new developments in their field or related fields, or they may misinterpret the significance of such developments. Research is constantly being done in every field, and the findings of such efforts often overturn previous conclusions. For example, for years expert medical opinion was in agreement that eating fats increases the risk of heart disease, that heavy salt consumption causes a rise in blood pressure, that the frequent consumption of eggs causes an increase in serum cholesterol, and that obesity in adulthood depends on childhood eating habits. Then new studies were published that challenged each of these conclusions and caused expert opinion to be modified.[6]

Complicating the matter further is the fact that new insights often take years to become general knowledge among the members of a profession. Psychologist Carol Tavris's excellent study *Anger: The Misunderstood Emotion,* which demolished the traditional assumption that venting hostility is beneficial for a person, was published in 1982. Yet articles are still being written endorsing the earlier idea, the authors apparently oblivious of Tavris's work, or irrationally committed to an erroneous view.

Accordingly, as important as it is to seek out authoritative opinion, it is equally important to maintain a questioning perspective. The best ways to do so are to consult several authorities of differing perspectives, to ask probing questions of each, and to compare their responses.

CONDUCTING AN INTERVIEW

Once you find your authorities, the next step is arranging interviews. Every interview should follow one basic rule: Be considerate of the interviewee. He or she is donating valuable time, so don't take your interviewee for granted. More specifically,

1. Call or write ahead for an appointment. Explain exactly what you wish to discuss and how long you'll take. (Keep the time as brief as you can, preferably under half an hour.) Make yourself available at a time that fits the interviewee's schedule best.
2. Before the interview, make an effort to learn the fundamentals of the subject you will be discussing. If the subject is controversial, know the issues in dispute and have at least a general notion of the competing arguments.
3. Prepare your questions carefully in advance. Make them clear and brief. Try to avoid those that can be answered yes or no; they won't be very helpful. For instance, instead of asking, "Do you agree with the governor's position?" ask, "What is your reaction to the governor's statement?" If you are sufficiently informed about a view that opposes the interviewee's views, ask, "Dr. _____ says such-and-such. How would you respond?" If you are insufficiently informed about opposing views, ask, "On what matters do those who oppose your view differ with you and how would you respond to their disagreement?"
4. Anticipate the responses to your initial questions, and prepare follow-up questions to probe those responses you feel don't go far enough or don't address the points you wish addressed.
5. Arrive on time. When you begin the interview, get right to the point. Keep your questions crisp and clear. Avoid thinking ahead to your next question. Instead, listen carefully to the reply. If any of your interviewee's comments open an aspect of the issue you did not consider but is

worth pursuing, be sure to pursue it. However, try not to overstay your welcome.

6. If at all possible, don't make the person wait while you take notes. If you can't take shorthand or write rapidly in longhand, consider the possibility of taping the interview. (Always obtain permission to tape an interview. Never merely assume it is acceptable to the other person.)

If the authority you wish to interview lives too far away for you to visit, consider a telephone interview. Such an interview is conducted as above, with two additional requirements. First, be sure to call or write in advance to determine when the interview will be most convenient. It is boorish to assume that because you are ready, your interviewee is, too. Second, remember that when conducting a telephone interview, it is especially important to speak clearly and to ask clear, concise questions.

USING THE LIBRARY

Fortunately, you needn't limit your investigation to those authorities available for interviewing. There is a way to consult those who live too far away to call, those who are too busy to receive your call, even those who are dead! It is to use the library. Perhaps you think of the library as a gathering place for dull, strange people, a place of little use to those who are lively and creative. That is a very shallow view. In fact, the library is best seen as *a formal meeting room for interviews with authorities not otherwise available.* That's precisely the way the very best thinkers regard it.

If your aversion to the library is based instead on the fear of lingering too long, you'll be pleased to learn that people who use the library most often—professional writers, speakers, and scholars—have even more reason than you to save time. They often have difficult deadlines to meet. Efficiency is not just a matter of preference with them—it's a dollars-and-cents concern. Yet they don't avoid the library; they simply use it more effectively.

The first step in using the library as professionals do is to determine all the headings and subheadings that might apply to your subject. Since the information sought may appear under different headings in the library's various sources, this is an important step. Start by giving free rein to your imagination and listing as many headings as you can. For example, for *crime* you may think of the subtopics *homicide, rape, shoplifting, kidnapping, vandalism,* and *burglary.* Next, expand your list of headings by consulting two sources available in most college libraries: the index volume of *Encyclopedia Americana* and the *Thesaurus of Psychological Index Terms,* a companion volume to *Psychological Abstracts.* You'll find such additional headings as *felonies, misdemeanors, antisocial behavior, behavior disorders, psychosexual behavior,* and *infanticide.*

Once you have determined the headings under which the information you are looking for is classified, get the information by using these simple and efficient approaches:

1. Consult a good encyclopedia for a broad overview of your subject. *Encyclopedia Britannica* and *Encyclopedia Americana* are generally considered to be the best. Note important facts. In addition, note special terms that might be useful in further research.
2. Consult an almanac, a collection of miscellaneous facts and statistical information about a wide variety of subjects. On the subject of crime, for example, you can find information under as many as two dozen specific listings. Most almanacs are published once a year. Thus, you can obtain comparative data—say, for 1970, 1980, and 1990—quickly and easily.
3. Consult the appropriate indexes. Indexes do not present the information you are looking for, but they tell you where to find it and so save you much time and energy. The following are among the most generally useful indexes. (Your librarian will be able to suggest others.)

   - For information in nontechnical periodicals—*The Readers' Guide to Periodical Literature.*
   - For information in specialized and technical publications—
       Applied Science and Technology Index
       Art Index
       Biography Index
       Biological and Agricultural Index
       Book Review Index
       Business Periodicals Index
       Education Index
       Engineering Index
       Essay and General Literature Index
       General Science Index
       Humanities Index
       Index to Legal Periodicals
       Magazine Index
       Music Index
       Philosopher's Index
       Psychological Abstracts
       Religion Index One: Periodicals.
       Social Science Index
   - For information in newspaper reports—the *New York Times Index.*
   - For information in government publications—the *Monthly Catalog of United States Government Publications* and the *Monthly Checklist of State Publications.*

4. Consult computer data bases and abstracting services. Data searches are easier than ever with modern information-retrieval technology. Your librarian can explain the data bases available to you. Ask, too, about abstracting services such as *Sociological Abstracts, America: History and Life,* and *Dissertation Abstracts International.*
5. Consult the *subject index* of the card catalog for books on your subject. Use broad subject headings as well as narrow ones; often a book that treats a larger subject will have a chapter or two on your subject.

6. Obtain and read the books and articles that are most relevant to your subject. Though the number of books and articles you read will depend on the scope of your project, the first five steps of the process should be followed for all but the very briefest of treatments.

These reference works are only the basic ones. For that reason it is important to remember that your most important resource in the library is the people who work there: the librarians and their assistants. They can suggest other research materials and help you expand your expertise.

KEEPING CREATIVITY ALIVE

As crucial as the investigation stage is in the solution of many problems, it can threaten creativity. The more information you accumulate, the greater the potential for confusion. To keep creativity alive, you will have to overcome that confusion. Here is how to do so.

Whenever you are confused by the amount or complexity of the information you have obtained and have difficulty sorting it out, pause for a moment, look back at your statement of the problem (stage 2), and use that statement to decide what is relevant and what is not. If you are dealing with an especially difficult problem, you may have to use this approach many times. Even the best and most creative thinkers lose their bearings from time to time, but they don't allow themselves to become discouraged. They just find their bearings again and continue.

A large amount of information can also have a daunting effect on your confidence. The more you probe a problem, the more you are likely to realize its complexity. In time you may find yourself thinking, "I didn't realize it would be this difficult. Maybe there is no solution. If other, more qualified people have been unable to find a solution, what business do I have trying?" When such thoughts occur, remind yourself that others may not have solved the problem precisely because they gave in to their feelings of apprehension—the ones that at this very moment threaten your creativity—or because, despite their expertise, they lacked the techniques for unlocking and applying their creativity. (After all, creativity is not a subject taught in most schools and colleges, so it is not surprising that otherwise educated people should be uninformed about it.) Remember, too, that whatever difficulties arise in thinking, there are effective methods for dealing with them, and your resources for producing creative responses to problems and issues are, as the next chapter will demonstrate, truly formidable.

WARM-UP EXERCISES

8.1. Read the following dialogue carefully. Then decide what you would say next if you were Veronica. Make your response so clear and effective that the matter would be settled.

PERRY: The only book a person ever needs to read is the Bible.

VERONICA: I don't agree. Other books surely have something to offer.

PERRY: Let me show you how wrong that is. If other books agree with the Bible, they are unnecessary. And if they disagree, they are irreligious and should be avoided.

8.2. Create as many new food recipes as you can. Include ingredients and preparation instructions.

8.3. Old toothbrushes are usually thrown in the trash. But are they really useless? Think of as many uses as you can for them.

APPLICATIONS

8.1. Each of the following cases was reported in the news. Most readers undoubtedly viewed them narrowly, believing each was entirely irrelevant to any but the most obvious subject. Yet to someone searching for more than surface connections, each case offers some interesting possibilities. For each of the following cases, list as many implied subjects or issues as you can. Be sure to specify what those implications are.

a. James Vance and Raymond Belknap, both of Nevada, each placed a shotgun under his chin and pulled the trigger. Vance died; Belknap survived but was horribly disfigured. Attorneys for the two sued CBS Records and rock group Judas Priest for millions of dollars, claiming that one of the group's albums, *Stained Class,* prompted the suicide attempt. Two experts examined the album and found the subliminal messages "do it" and "sign my evil spirit." The lyrics include such lines as "Keep the world with all its sin, it's not fit for living in."[7]

b. Some research findings suggest that personality differences among individuals are more a result of heredity than of environment. For example, University of Minnesota psychologists who studied 400 sets of adult twins found a strong genetic link for such qualities as anger, cautious behavior, and social-political-religious conservatism. And a Pennsylvania State University study of 700 sets of twins estimates that environment counts for only 10 percent of personality differences.[8]

c. A 9-year-old boy known as Robert M. pointed a toy gun at a New York City bank teller and robbed her of $118. He was placed on 2 years' probation after his attorney argued he was only playacting during the robbery. Then a year later, the same boy, with two accomplices, was arrested for stealing a sled from two boys at knifepoint.[9]

d. Three-year-old Chad Chancey was expected to be the youngest trial witness in Oklahoma's history. He was the only person with any knowledge of the events that took place the night his mother and sister were murdered. Chad reportedly heard a loud argument in the next room, women's screams, a sound he described as a loud handclap, then silence. He later identified the man who had been in the apartment that night from a police file photo. The defense attorney expressed concern that the child might be too young to separate fact from fantasy.[10]

e. In 1945 Charles Jamison was found badly wounded on a Boston dock. He carried papers identifying him as a first mate on the USS *Cutty Sark.* Yet no records could be found of the existence of such a ship, and all further investigations about the man revealed nothing. Interviews with him disclosed only that he had no family, had gone to sea at age 13, and believed his ship had been torpedoed. He remained in a Boston hospital until his death 30 years after his discovery on the dock.[11]

f. Dr. Martin Orne, a psychiatrist and expert on memory and hypnosis, and Dr. Elizabeth Loftus, a psychologist and memory expert, presented information to the American Association for the Advancement of Science that suggested that using hypnotism to get witnesses to recall details of past events may be ill advised. Their research showed that memory may be unintentionally altered by the form of the hypnotist's questions. "If the hypnotist has certain beliefs," said Dr. Orne, "he will create memories in the subject's mind."[12]

g. After 60 years of business the American Seed Company closed its doors. In 1981, its fifth straight year of losses, the company lost $600,000. One of the principal reasons for the company's demise was the refusal of the children who sold the seeds to pay the company its share of the money they earned. (The arrangement was fair: The company was to receive 40 cents and the child 20 cents for each packet of seeds sold.) According to the *Wall Street Journal,* when the company appealed to the children's parents, it got little or no cooperation. "Far from lending a helping hand," the *Journal* wrote, "the parents often sided with their outlaw offspring" by saying essentially, "You're a big company; you don't need the money and you're only trying to cheat my child."[13]

h. A director of the National Credential Verification Service, a company that checks job applicants' academic backgrounds for employers, reports that one-third of its investigations uncover false credentials. College officials corroborate the estimate. Such misrepresentation is not limited to young applicants. Many middle managers also practice deception.[14]

i. Some studies have suggested that the hormone secretion and levels of certain chemicals in a mother's blood may affect an unborn child in more far-reaching ways than ever realized. Not only physical effects, but also behavioral effects, are demonstrable. For example, children exposed to progestins before birth turn out to be more independent and self-assured, whereas those exposed to estrogens are more disposed to group dependency. There is even speculation that transsexuality may be linked to a decrease in testosterone during the fetal period.[15]

j. A human fetus survived to full term after it was extracted from its mother's womb for surgery and then returned to the womb following surgery. The surgery, which took place in the twenty-fourth week of pregnancy, corrected a life-threatening urinary tract obstruction.[16]

8.2. Woebegone College is having a problem with grade inflation. The average grade submitted by many professors is a B+, despite the fact that the average entrance examination score of Woebegone's students has declined steadily over the past decade. It appears that work that would have received a C 10 or 15 years ago is now being given a B or B+. One effect has been that 60 percent of the student body is on the dean's list. Find the best expression of this problem. Then investigate it, as necessary, using the approaches explained in the chapter, and produce as many solutions as you can. (Record all your thoughts as they occur to you, and be prepared to submit them to your instructor.) Finally, state which of your solutions you believe is best and briefly explain why.

8.3. Every so often someone writes an article about the poor state of composition teaching, usually with a title such as "Why Dick and Jane Can't Write" or "The Scandal in the English Classroom." The public then gets excited and calls for a study of the problem, and the media explore methods of developing students' language skills. But no lasting creative solution to the problem ever seems to be found. Identify and solve this problem, following the directions in Application 8.2.

8.4. Economic recessions can cause a bad employment situation to grow much worse. Some people grew pessimistic about this country ever being able to guarantee a job for everyone who wants work, no matter how desirable that goal might be. Identify and solve this problem, following the directions in Application 8.2.

8.5. Alcohol and drug abuse are associated with crime in the streets, health problems, the breakdown of the family, and poor job performance. Identify and solve this problem, following the directions in Application 8.2.

8.6. Women and racial and ethnic minorities have faced job discrimination for many years in this country. Then in the 1970s and 1980s the government instituted affirmative action programs that attempted not only to ensure present fairness but also to compensate for past grievances. The idea was to give some job preference to those who had been discriminated against in the past. Yet these programs drew criticism for creating *reverse discrimination*—in other words, for being as unfair as the system they were designed to correct. Identify and solve this problem, following the directions in Application 8.2.

8.7. In many Third World countries, the United States seems to be faced with a difficult choice: either to support the existing governments and risk alienating the masses of people who are victimized by them, or to support rebel groups and create political instability. Identify and solve this problem, following the directions in Application 8.2.

8.8. In many states the schools are financed primarily by property taxes. This system, of course, tends to favor wealthy areas over poor areas and often results in inequality of educational opportunity. Identify and solve this problem, following the directions in Application 8.2.

8.9. On the one hand, the federal government forbids cigarette advertising on radio and television and requires health warnings to be printed on every pack of cigarettes sold. On the other hand, the same government heavily subsidizes tobacco farming. Address this challenge, following the directions in Application 8.2.

8.10. The state of Montana prohibits discrimination by sex or marital status in insurance premiums or policy benefits. Various women's groups applaud this legislative initiative, but insurance companies have lobbied vigorously against it.[17] Address this challenge, following the directions in Application 8.2.

8.11. For roughly the first half of the 1980s many Americans were convinced that a positive mental attitude could help prevent and cure various diseases, including cancer. A number of books and articles, notably Norman Cousins's *Anatomy of an Illness* (1979), lent credibility to this idea. Then in 1985 the *New England Journal of Medicine* published a study that cast doubt on the popular view.[18] Address this challenge, following the directions in Application 8.2.

8.12. Some members of Congress, noting the impressive revenues raised by state lotteries, once proposed having a *national* lottery. The idea evoked both positive and negative responses.[19] Address this challenge, following the directions in Application 8.2.

8.13. The U.S. Patent and Trademark Office announced in 1987 that it "considers nonnaturally occurring nonhuman multicellular living organisms, including animals, to be patentable subject matter." Some people consider this development a logical extension of earlier rulings that allowed patenting of plants and of genetically engineered microorganisms. But others see it as a dangerous precedent.[20] Address this challenge, following the directions in Application 8.2.

8.14. Getting a company's products displayed in a movie is not a new advertising idea, but it has been getting wider use lately. Ford Motor Company, for example, gave free cars for *License to Kill* in exchange for having James Bond drive a Lincoln Continental. And director John Badham displayed Alaska Airlines, Apple computers, Bounty paper towels, and Ore-Ida frozen french fries in his film *Short Circuit*. Badham probably speaks for many advertisers and filmmakers when he says, "If we can help each other, and it doesn't intrude on the movie, it's fine."[21] But not everyone would agree. Address this challenge, following the directions in Application 8.2.

GROUP DISCUSSION EXERCISE

Discuss the following issue with two or three of your classmates. Observe the guidelines to group discussion presented in Appendix B. Consider all sides of the matter and try to reach consensus. Be prepared to report your group's deliberations to the class, describing how your analysis proceeded, what questions were asked, and what agreements were reached. If differences of viewpoint remain unresolved, be prepared to report them objectively.

In many urban areas, one cannot walk on major streets without meeting panhandlers asking for (or demanding) a handout and people sleeping on the sidewalk or wandering aimlessly, mumbling to themselves or shouting to no one in particular. The experience is unpleasant at best and often carries with it the threat of robbery or physical assault. In recent years public tolerance has turned to resentment, even outrage. What can be done to solve this problem?

COMPOSITION OR SPEECH EXERCISE

Write a composition or, if your instructor specifies, a formal speech, presenting the view your group reached in the preceding group discussion exercise. (If you hold a dissenting view, present that instead.) Be sure to provide evidence that your view is the most reasonable one. Naturally your composition or speech will bear some resemblance to those of the other members of your group—you will have developed ideas as a team, so at least some of your ideas will be similar, even identical, to theirs. Don't be concerned about such similarities. Your composition or speech will be a unique effort if you (a) use supporting material from your own experience, observation, and research; (b) develop you own line of reasoning about that material; (c) employ your own ingenuity in designing an introduction and conclusion and in arranging the material in the body of your composition or speech; and (d) express your thoughts in your own words. For further guidance, consult the appropriate appendix—A for writing, B for speaking.

Produce Ideas

Imagine a pearl diver on an island in the South Seas. He pushes his canoe off from shore, paddles out into the lagoon, dives deep into the water, picks an oyster off the bottom, surfaces, climbs into his boat, paddles to shore, and opens the shell. Finding nothing but an oyster inside, he pushes his canoe off again, and begins paddling into the lagoon. "Wait a minute," you're probably thinking; "he's wasting an awful lot of time. The right way to do it is not to paddle back to shore with one oyster but to dive again and again, to fill the canoe with oysters, and then return to shore."

You're right. Pearls are rare; a diver must open many oysters before finding one. Only a very foolish diver would waste time and energy making a separate trip for each oyster.[1] *And it's exactly the same with producing ideas.* Foolish people think of a single solution to a problem and then proceed as if that solution *had* to be creative. But creative ideas, like pearls, occur infrequently. So sensible people produce many ideas before expecting to find a creative one.

Researchers have found a clear relationship between the number of ideas produced and the quality of the ideas. The more ideas produced, the better the chances of having one or more good ones.[2] There are two reasons for this. The first is a matter of simple probability. Creative ideas are statistically uncommon. As Alfred North Whitehead explains, "The probability is that nine hundred and ninety-nine of [our ideas] will come to nothing, either because they are worthless in themselves or because we shall not know how to elicit their value; but we had better entertain them all, however skeptically, for the *thousandth* idea may be the one that will change the world."[3]

The second reason is that initial ideas are usually poorer in quality than later ideas. Just as water must run from a faucet for a while to be clear and free of particles, so thought must flow before it becomes creative. "Early ideas," Herbert Spencer warned, "are not usually true ideas."[4] Exactly why this is so is not known, but one very plausible hypothesis is that familiar and safe responses lie closest to the surface of our consciousness and therefore are naturally thought of first.[5] In any case, success in creative thinking depends on continuing the flow of ideas long enough to purge the common, habitual ones and produce the unusual and imaginative.

In dealing with problems, the ideas you should seek to produce are answers to the "How can . . . ?" questions you asked in expressing the problem. In dealing with issues, your ideas should be broader, including not only direct answers to your "Is (Are) . . . ?" and "Should . . . ?" questions but also all other ideas that can help you answer those questions. Not infrequently, the idea that provides a key to resolving an issue will seem, at first consideration, irrelevant.

STIMULATING YOUR IMAGINATION

Producing a large quantity of ideas is the first way to produce creative solutions, but it is not the only way. Another important way is to stimulate your imagination. Studies confirm that most people behave unimaginatively not because they lack imagination but because they fear the reaction their ideas will receive. In time they grow used to suppressing ideas that differ from the norm, ideas that might raise eyebrows. They do themselves a great disservice because creativity depends on imagination. "No great discovery is ever made without a bold guess," observed Sir Isaac Newton.[6] And Albert Einstein added, "I believe in imagination. . . . Imagination is more important than knowledge."[7]

It takes more than determination to stimulate your thoughts, of course, particularly if you have gotten into the habit of suppressing them. You'll need some strategies for activating your creative imagination. Following are seven effective strategies. Some will fit problems better than issues; others, the reverse.

1. Force uncommon responses.
2. Use free association.
3. Use analogy.
4. Look for unusual combinations.
5. Visualize the solution.
6. Construct pro and con arguments.
7. Construct relevant scenarios.

Force Uncommon Responses

We noted that common, familiar ideas tend to come first. Nothing can be done to avoid this pattern. Therefore, your best approach is to expect them, even encourage them, to free your mind for more original ideas. Begin by asking yourself what responses most people would think of. Write them all down. When you have produced a number of these, and you can't think of any others, ask yourself what responses others would probably *not* think of. Press yourself for as many as you can produce.

One predictable outcome of this effort is the listing of some outrageous or silly ideas. Chances are you will feel a little uncomfortable with such ideas. "How can they be helpful?" you'll think. "Problems and issues are serious matters—no room for foolishness here." *Resist that feeling.* Playfulness, as we saw, is one important characteristic of creative people; it contributes to their dynamism. There's nothing wrong with writing even the most outrageous ideas on paper. Listing them is not the same as endorsing them; you can always cross them out later. But don't screen them out now; you might inadvertently discard an original insight in the process.

Don't misunderstand this advice. It doesn't mean you should try to be outrageous or ridiculous. It means you should tolerate being so when it occurs as a natural consequence of striving for uncommon ideas.

Use Free Association

Free association means letting one idea suggest another. It differs from forced response in that you are not directing your mind at all but giving it free rein, relaxing your control over it momentarily and observing what ideas, what associations, result. Some of them may be quite unexpected and point out interesting and profitable directions. As with forced responses, you should not screen any associations as they occur to you. Rather, write them all for later examination. Often what seems totally irrelevant when it occurs to you may later prove valuable.

A word of warning is in order. The purpose of this strategy is to help you retrieve relevant information you originally classified too restrictively. Because this strategy involves relaxing mental control and allowing your thoughts to drift, it can slip into aimless daydreaming. You should therefore use it as a variation on other strategies and not as a substitute for them.

Use Analogy

An analogy is a reference to one or more similarities between two otherwise very different things. An analogy might be made, for example, between a football halfback's broken field running and the movements of a jaguar or cheetah.

The history of creative achievements documents the value of analogical thinking. Creative breakthroughs often occur when a person makes a connection between something outside his or her field. (This fact suggests the value of a broad education. Narrowness of training all too often breeds a narrowness of perspective that hinders creativity.) When Gutenberg observed a winepress in operation and conceived of the printing press and when the inventor of the forklift got his insight from the doughnut machine, they were using analogical thinking.

To use analogy in your thinking, simply ask what the problem or issue is like, what it reminds you of. Where appropriate, you may also ask more specific questions, such as "What does this *look* like (or sound, taste, smell, or feel like)?" or "What does this *function* like?"

Look for Unusual Combinations

Sometimes the best solution to a problem will be to combine things not usually combined. The miner's cap (combining a flashlight and a protective hat), the wheelchair, and the clock radio are examples of how combinations result in invention. Perhaps the most common example of this kind of invention is the recipe. Every time a cook blends different ingredients to make a dish differently, he or she is inventing by combination. The first person to put a slice of mozzarella cheese on a veal cutlet invented veal parmigiana, and the ingenious person who couldn't afford veal and substituted a slice of meatloaf invented meatloaf parmigiana.

This same strategy works well in other kinds of creativity as well—finding solutions to social problems, for example. One problem of growing concern today is the increasing cost of our prison system. Someone wrestling with that problem might well consider combining prisons with factories—that is, have convicts work for private industry behind bars, be paid for their efforts, and reimburse the taxpayers for the cost of the imprisonment. (The idea might even come through analogy, by noting that prisons sometimes resemble large factory complexes.)

Visualize the Solution

This strategy consists of imagining the problem solved and visualizing what it would look like then. For example, before the problem of automobile travel on snow- and ice-covered roads was solved, a man forced to drive in such conditions would have pictured in his mind not the reality of tires mired in snow or spinning on ice but the condition he *wished for:* wheels turning smoothly, tires biting into the snow and grasping the ice firmly. His imagination thus stimulated, he'd have asked himself, "What would those tires look like if they were able to perform the way I wish?" And he might just have visualized pieces of metal wrapped around the tire (chains) or spikes protruding from the tire to grip the road (studs).

Construct Pro and Con Arguments

This strategy, an essential one in dealing with issues, consists of listing all conceivable arguments that might be advanced on either side of the issue. To use it, simply address your expression(s) of the issue—"Is . . . ?" "Does . . . ?" or "Should . . . ?"—and list as many "yes" responses as you can, together with the reasoning that supports them, and as many "no" responses as you can, together with the reasoning for them. If, for example, the issue you examined were whether technology has had a positive or negative effect on human society, you would include these points, among others. (For the sake of brevity, supporting arguments are omitted.)

POSITIVE EFFECT ARGUMENTS	NEGATIVE EFFECT ARGUMENTS
Has shortened the workweek, creating more leisure time for workers.	Has made many jobs very routine, increasing workers' boredom.

Has increased the variety of goods and services available.	Has decreased the quality of goods and services in many cases.
Has created many new skilled occupations.	Has eliminated many unskilled jobs.
Has increased the monetary reward to both employers and employees.	Has caused many workers to hate what they do for a living.
Has created the need for new kinds of education—vocational and technical.	Has undermined the role of the liberal arts in education.

An important warning—expect yourself to be biased, and expect your bias to affect your efforts to construct arguments. Unless you are perfectly neutral about the issue, an unlikely circumstance, at the very outset of this strategy you will believe one side of the issue to be right, and that belief will incline you to construct your list accordingly. In other words, consciously or unconsciously you will present more and better arguments for the side of the issue you prefer. The only safeguard against such bias is to *go out of your way to think of arguments that might be advanced on the other side of the issue.* (If your investigation of the issue gave a fair hearing to both sides, this safeguard should not be too difficult to accomplish.)

Construct Relevant Scenarios

We often tend to think of ideas exclusively as *assertions,* claims about what is or should be, such as "Respect for the rights of others is decreasing in our society" and "Ethics instruction belongs in the nation's schools." Those are ideas, to be sure, but so are *scenarios,* which are imaginatively conceived examples of situations and events that are relevant to the issue under consideration. Well-constructed scenarios have a special value that assertions lack: They represent reality itself and not just conclusions about reality.

Let's say that the issue you are analyzing concerns whether a woman must have offered "earnest resistance" to a man's sexual advances for a rape charge to be filed in the courts. (This was still a legal requirement in some states as recently as 1982.) Here are three scenarios you might construct:

- A woman has just returned from a date with a young man whom she has known for some time, has dated previously, and has had sexual intercourse with on several occasions. She invites him into her apartment and proceeds to engage in sexual foreplay. When he proposes that they have intercourse, she says no several times but does not stop him from performing the act.
- A woman is lying in a hospital bed, heavily sedated after experiencing a nervous breakdown. A male nurse realizes she is unable to resist his advances and so assaults her sexually.

- Walking from the campus library to her dormitory one evening, a college student passes through a dimly lighted wooded area. Suddenly, two men jump out at her, one brandishing a knife and warning that if she resists sexual intercourse with them, he will kill her. Fearing for her life, she submits.

A close reading of these scenarios will reveal the importance of constructing more than a single scenario and of taking care that those constructed cover the broad range of possibilities. All of these are believable—an indispensable qualification that every scenario must meet. However, they do not shed equal light on the issue of whether "earnest resistance" is a reasonable legal requirement. Taken alone, the first scenario might be considered to support an affirmative answer. Yet as the other two make clear, such an answer would be shallow. Under the very plausible circumstances they present, the requirement of "earnest resistance" is quite unreasonable.

These seven strategies will give you significant help in activating your imagination. But don't expect to be able to use them smoothly right away. Give them time to become familiar. If you are inclined to give up after a few tries, remind yourself how awkward you felt the first time you dribbled a basketball or drove a car. That, too, seemed impossible to learn, but you mastered it. Whenever your turning from one strategy to another confuses you, simply look back at your statement of the problem, regain your bearings, and continue producing ideas.

AIMING FOR ORIGINALITY

In the popular view, originality is a kind of genetic endowment. Either you have it or you don't, and if you don't have it, you have no hope of learning it. Research has demolished this idea. Like every other creative skill, *originality can be learned.* If you don't produce original thoughts, it is only because you have acquired the habit of being unoriginal. One study revealed that originality can be stimulated simply by letting a person know it is expected.[8]

To achieve originality in your thinking, demand it of yourself. Remind yourself that there is nothing mysterious about originality; it lies just a step or two beyond the commonplace. Don't restrict your ideas to those you have heard or thought of before. Every time you address a problem and try to find solutions, stretch your mind a little, reach for thoughts a little more daring than you have entertained before.

There is one additional method that can help you be more original: *Watch your fringe thoughts.* The term *fringe thoughts* was coined by Graham Wallas.[9] It means thoughts occurring on the edge or fringe of consciousness, much the same way objects appear on the periphery of our vision. When walking down the street or driving a car, we focus our gaze in one direction but continue to see objects outside that focus. When something unusual or unexpected appears there, we are able to turn our attention to it. Since original ideas often appear first on the fringe of consciousness, the more alert you are to what is happening there, the more original ideas you will discover.

WITHHOLDING JUDGMENT

Judgment is an essential part of thinking. Without it, we wouldn't be able to distinguish between good and bad solutions or select the best and most workable one. But the timing of our judgment can make all the difference. Most people don't time their judgment well: They are impulsive, evaluating ideas as soon as they are produced, sometimes even screening out certain ideas before they are fully conceptualized. At the first inkling of an idea, they say, "No, that's no good" or "This is silly" or "That can't be a solution."

Yet often the most creative ideas are the ones that seem silliest at first. Rushing to judgment, therefore, causes some of the best ideas to be discarded—and the least creative ones to be approved mindlessly. Ironically, it ensures that people will be uncreative just when they want most to be creative.

Research has documented that thinkers who resist judging ideas during the idea-producing stage and who extend their effort to produce ideas beyond the point where they are tempted to stop are rewarded with a greater proportion of good ideas.[10] As you do the applications for this and subsequent chapters, and whenever you look for solutions to problems outside this course, don't allow yourself to judge any idea until after you have produced as many ideas as you can. Don't set artificial limits on the number of your ideas. When you find yourself thinking, "I've got 10 (or 20 or 30) ideas now—that's enough," remember that the best solution to the problem very likely lies 10 or 20 ideas beyond that point. It can only be reached by pressing on. Moreover, just to be sure you are not unconsciously setting limits on your thinking, look back occasionally at previous efforts—the applications you did in the last few chapters, for example—and decide whether you stopped producing ideas too soon.

OVERCOMING OBSTACLES

The three most common obstacles to the effective production of a large and varied number of ideas are thinker's block, vagueness and confusion, and inflexibility. Learning how to recognize each, and mastering a few simple responses, can prevent your problem-solving efforts from being frustrated.

Thinker's Block

Like writer's block, which prevents an author from putting words on the page, thinker's block prevents us from producing ideas. It makes us sit idle and grow increasingly nervous, waiting for ideas that do not come. Poor thinkers are not the only ones afflicted with thinker's block. Everyone experiences it from time to time. But good thinkers have learned that they needn't be victimized by it, that there are effective methods for dealing with it.

The best way is to minimize the chance of its occurring by doing something we have already discussed: *developing the habit of withholding judgment while you are producing ideas.* Every time you stop the flow of ideas to make a judgment, even if you stop for only a second or two, you run the risk of not being able to start again. On the other hand, the more you resist the temptation to stop and instead sustain your idea production, the less trouble thinker's block causes you.

When it occurs despite your best efforts to avoid it, try one or more of the following approaches, in the order they are presented:

1. Look back at the ideas you have written. Read them carefully, concentrating on each as you read it. Usually one of those ideas will suggest another that you have not written. As soon as it does, write it. Now that the ideas are flowing again, don't stop until you have to. It doesn't matter if the first few ideas are off target. You can gently direct the flow back to the problem or issue.
2. Run through the strategies for stimulating your imagination again. That is, force uncommon responses (however outrageous), use free association and analogy, look for unusual combinations, and so on through the list of strategies. You'll seldom get beyond the first or second strategy before the ideas are flowing again.
3. Copy your list of ideas over again and again, concentrating on each idea as you are writing it. Be alert to the appearance of a new idea on the fringe of your consciousness. This approach keeps you active and prevents frustration and apprehension.
4. Walk away from the problem for a time (an hour, a day, a week). Return to it only when you can take a fresh look at it, unburdened of anxiety.
5. If all else fails, go back to the second stage of the process and consider other expressions of the problem or issue.

Vagueness and Confusion

Even the greatest thinkers experience this obstacle to problem solving. Einstein, for example, began considering the problem that led to his relativity theory when he was 16 years old. He struggled with it for 7 years before reaching a solution. During that time he experienced vagueness, confusion, and puzzlement to the point of depression and despair.[11]

Whether this obstacle appears during the investigating stage or the idea-producing stage, it is most often caused by losing sight of the problem. The best way to overcome it is the way noted in Chapter 8: *Look back at your statement of the problem or issue and get your bearings.* In the beginning you may have to stop the flow of ideas to take this backward look, but with a little practice you will be able to do it without stopping the flow. You will merely slow it down a little. It's much like steering a car. A beginning driver often has to come to a complete stop to straighten the car's direction, but very soon he or she learns to make slight corrections with the steering wheel while maintaining speed.

You will find this kind of mental steering easier to master if you write your expression of the problem on a card or sheet of paper and keep it handy while working on the problem.

Inflexibility

This obstacle is characterized by too many ideas of one type, with little or no variation. It is caused by unconsciously directing your thinking along one narrow line of thought. Whenever you find this obstacle in your work (a simple glance back over your ideas will reveal whether it is present), make a special effort to stimulate your imagination. Any of the seven strategies we discussed may be used, but the first two and the last—forcing uncommon responses, using free association, and constructing relevant scenarios—are especially helpful.

HOW INSIGHT OCCURS

The most dramatic experience of the idea-producing stage—indeed, of the entire creative process—is the arrival of an insight. The moment of insight has been described in many ways. One is the *Aha!* reaction, such as Archimedes experienced when he sat down in a tub of water, noticed the displacement of the water by the mass of his body, and instantly conceptualized the principle of specific gravity. "Eureka! I have found it," he is said to have shouted, as he ran naked through the streets. (Apparently the law against indecent exposure was not well enforced then, or else he ran very fast. In any case, he seems to have escaped arrest.) Another way of describing the moment of insight is an intense feeling of satisfaction, such as we get when we find a missing puzzle part. But perhaps the most common experience is sudden illumination, like the light bulb glowing above the head of a cartoon character.

For some reason many insights come during moments of rest. One of the building blocks of modern science, an idea called "the most brilliant piece of prediction to be found in the whole range of organic chemistry," occurred at such a time. Friedrich August von Kekulé lay dozing by the fire one day in 1865 and suddenly realized that the molecules of certain organic compounds were not open structures but ring-shaped. Here's how he described the experience:

> I turned my chair to the fire and dozed. . . . Again the atoms were gambolling before my eyes. This time the smaller groups kept modestly in the background. My mental eye, rendered more acute by repeated visions of this kind, could now distinguish larger structures, of manifold conformation; long rows, sometimes more closely fitted together; all twining and twisting in snakelike motion. But look! What was that? One of the snakes had seized hold of its own tail, and the form whirled mockingly before my eyes. As if by a flash of lightning I awoke.[12]

The fact that many imaginative leaps have come during periods of leisure or rest has led to the misconception that insight comes without effort. Authorities on the creative process are in agreement that insight is not associated with idleness. (If it were, the village loafer would hold the record for creative achievement.) Nor does it arrive during any type of leisure. Rather, it arrives during the leisure that follows periods of intense activity, in which the thinker grapples with the problem or issue, is momentarily defeated by it, and turns away in frustration. Authorities theorize that the conscious mind then turns the problem over to the unconscious, which continues working. Insight comes from that effort.[13]

Sudden insights, like all dramatic experiences, tend to be more widely publicized and more memorable than everyday occurrences. However, the fact is that many, sometimes the vast majority, of creative solutions come about more quietly. They are the result of alertness to details and careful analysis of ideas. Such solutions, though they arrive with no fanfare, are no less valuable for that. And they have one great advantage over sudden insights. We can, to a significant extent, make them happen.

A SAMPLE PROBLEM

You are a bill collector for a magazine. You have wasted countless hours in waiting rooms hoping to see the magazine's debtors. But most secretaries have been instructed to let you wait until you get tired and leave. You examine the problem from all sides and consider a number of expressions. Finally you decide that the best expression is "How can I get to see debtors despite their secretaries' refusal to let me do so?" Here is how your production of ideas might proceed.

You begin listing all your ideas. The first ones are outrageous, but that doesn't bother you. You know you shouldn't stop to evaluate them.

- Carry a shotgun and threaten the secretary.
- Threaten to kidnap the debtor's wife and kids.
- Bring an attack dog to the office.
- Scale the building and climb in the debtor's window.
- Tell the secretary you are the boss's brother or sister.
- Tie up the secretary and barge into the office.

You encounter thinker's block, so you apply one or more of the strategies recommended in the chapter for overcoming this obstacle. The ideas begin to flow again.

- Sweet-talk the secretary.
- Call and make an appointment first.
- Send a letter requesting payment.
- Fax the debtor repeatedly.
- Change jobs.
- Take a course in quick thinking.

- Cancel the debtor's subscription.
- Take legal action.
- Sit and wait until the office closes.
- Take an attorney with you.
- Send someone else to wait in your place.

At this point you become confused; you believe you've lost sight of the problem. A glance back at the ideas you've just produced confirms this. They do not address the problem as you expressed it. You reread your expression and begin producing again.

- Bother the secretary.
- Give him or her a box of candy.
- Take him or her to lunch.
- Try bribery.
- Beg to see the debtor.
- Wait for the secretary to go to lunch and then barge in.

You run dry again, so you start once more with the first strategy, looking back over the ideas you have produced. Starting with the most recent, you read, "Wait for the secretary to go to lunch . . . beg to see the debtor, bribery. . . ." Suddenly you realize your inflexibility: You have slipped into producing ideas of the same type, with little or no variation. You try to stimulate your imagination, first by forcing uncommon responses. The ideas begin again.

- Pretend to be someone else.
- Catch the debtor outside the office.
- Bother the other people in the waiting room.
- Cause a disturbance.
- Be obnoxious.

The ideas stop once more, so you stimulate your imagination. When you fail to force uncommon responses, you turn to free association. Several of your ideas suggest a number of associations. Specifically, "Pretend to be someone else" suggests

- A telephone repairer
- A janitor
- A job applicant
- A police officer
- An office-supplies salesperson
- A priest or nun
- An electrician
- A newspaper reporter
- A magazine contest representative (to award a prize)
- A window washer

"Bother the secretary" suggests

- Ask to be announced every few minutes.
- Sit on the secretary's desk.
- Talk to him or her incessantly.

"Bother the other people in the waiting room" suggests

- Talk loudly about your recently contracted contagious disease.
- Tell everyone loudly that the debtor has been named in a paternity suit.
- Tell them the truth about the debtor's bill.

"Cause a disturbance" suggests

- Fall down and feign a seizure.
- Practice the tuba.
- Yell, "Fire!"
- Jump up and down on a whoopee cushion.
- Sing off-key.
- Pitch a tent (literally).
- Make howling noises.
- Put up signs saying, "This guy doesn't pay his bills."

"Be obnoxious" suggests

- Put on a horrible mask and fake blood.
- Rub your clothing with garlic and onion.
- Soak your clothes in skunk spray.

At this point you'd have produced enough good ideas, including a number of creative ones, to stop producing and select your best one. Which would that be? A real bill collector, Andy Smulion of London, uses the very last one with great success. He soaks his clothes in skunk spray, walks quietly into the debtor's office, and hands the secretary a note saying, "I'll leave when you pay." Needless to say, he doesn't have to wait long.

A SAMPLE ISSUE

You read in the newspaper that the Television Information Office, an organization financed by the television industry, has issued a six-page research paper arguing that television is not the cause of declining reading scores in the nation's schools. The research paper claims that children's reading scores have more to do with "socioeconomic factors" than with the amount of television they watch and that heavy viewing doesn't cause reading problems but is the result of those problems. It states, "Children having difficulty with classroom study and with homework will turn to television . . . precisely because of their reading difficulties."[14]

You realize that this is a matter that informed people disagree about, so you approach it as an issue and decide that the best expression of it is "Is television viewing in any way a causative factor in declining reading scores?" After reading several scholarly articles in the library and interviewing an education professor and a reading skills instructor (both of them on your campus), you develop ideas as follows.*

The television industry financed the study, so it could be biased.

The conclusion says television doesn't cause reading deficiencies. That makes me more suspicious, though it proves nothing.

[*A move to interpretation*] The claim that reading scores have more to do with "socioeconomic factors" suggests that the disadvantaged are the only ones with reading problems. Yet that's not the case.

Middle- and upper-class students' reading deficiencies must be caused by something else.

What about reading problems causing heavy television viewing? Sounds odd, but the authorities I consulted agreed that it can happen that way.

How exactly would this happen? Let's see. . . .

[*Now constructing a scenario*] Kids have trouble reading in school, grow frustrated, and so are motivated not to pick up a book but to escape. They come home, switch on the television set, and watch the evening away.

It makes sense. In cases like this, reading deficiencies probably do cause excessive television viewing.

[*Now playing devil's advocate*] But how are those kids any different from the average kid? Don't many good readers watch television just as much? If reading problems don't cause them to be enslaved by the boob tube, maybe they don't always cause poor readers to do so. Is it possible that the study is in error, that television viewing does cause reading problems, after all?

What would have to happen in order for television viewing to be the cause? It would have to *precede* reading deficiencies. Kids would first have to be hooked on television. Let me get a clearer picture of the sequence.

[*Now another scenario*] First, the TV viewing. When, exactly? In early childhood. How? The kids plays while a parent is busy. The parent leaves the television set on as a kind of baby-sitter. The kid watches it, hour after hour, day after day, from age 1 to age 5. By the time the child begins learning to read, at age 6 or so, he or she has already watched thousands of hours of TV. . . .

---

*The form and content of this sample do not reflect what you would typically do. You would undoubtedly list your ideas in fragmentary fashion so as not to interrupt the flow of thought; yet for the sake of clarity, ideas are presented here in complete sentences. Moreover, your analysis would involve actually conducting investigations and then reflecting on each to generate more ideas, whereas here, because of space limitations, the investigations are only suggested. The emphasis here is not on research completeness but on the process by which one strategy leads to another and produces ideas.

That's not only plausible—it's what actually happens in many cases. TV does exert influence in a child's life much earlier than formal education.

[*Now an attempt to interpret*] What exactly is the influence of television? What happens on television that could affect reading?

[*Now yet another scenario, this one of a typical television hour, during a soap opera*] The hour begins with a cluster of commercials, then for ten minutes or so moves back and forth among two or three story lines. Then there's another cluster of three or four commercials and perhaps a newsbreak before returning to the several story lines. . . .

What does all of that translate to? Frequent shifts from scene to scene, frequent commercial breaks, frequent shifts of viewer's attention, no demands on the mind, no difficulties or challenges. No wonder reading seems impossibly difficult by comparison.

WARM-UP EXERCISES

9.1. Many actors and actresses drop their given names and take stage names that are easy to remember and that project a particular image. Thus, the silent screen had Theda Bara (her last name was derived by reversing *Arab*), and later films have had Tyrone Power, Victor Mature, Rip Torn, and so on. Think of as many creative stage names as you can. The image you aim to project may be macho male, female sex symbol, charming child, or any other you wish.

9.2. Think of as many creative names as you can for a restaurant. Consider all types of establishments from the fancy high-priced variety to the lowly coffee shop, and all types of cuisines.

9.3. Most of us complain that we don't have enough closets. Yet we seldom use very efficiently the closet space we already have. Redesign your closet at home (or if you prefer, the one at college) to achieve maximum use of its space. Do "before" and "after" sketches of the closet.

APPLICATIONS

For each of the following applications, find the best expression of the problem or issue, investigate it as necessary, and then produce as many ideas as you can, applying what you learned in this chapter. (Record all your thoughts as they occur to you, and be prepared to submit them to your instructor.) Finally, state which of your ideas you believe is best, and briefly explain why.

9.1. You've entered a snow sculpture contest. The most important judging criterion, according to the organizers of the contest, will be creativity. There is no special theme, nor are there any restrictions on size or form.

9.2. Some creative person got the idea of making a calendar serve an educational purpose and produced the 365-New-Words-a-Year Calendar. Think of as many other educational purposes a calendar might serve; then select your best idea and prepare a formal presentation to the class, including an explanation of how you would implement your plan.

9.3. In Chapter 8 we noted that the problem of having the string slip out of your sweatpants can be expressed in a number of ways, but we did not discuss that problem's solution.

9.4. Marian's roommate has developed the habit of borrowing Marian's clothes without permission. On top of that, she is careless with them, more often than not returning them soiled or even torn. Marian has tried speaking to her, but it hasn't seemed to help.

9.5. Newton's friends are a partying crowd. Almost every night they are either having a party themselves, attending a party in someone's dorm room or apartment, or making the rounds of the local bars. Newton wants to do his best academically and would prefer to drink only on weekends—and even then only moderately. He'd like to explain this to his friends, but he's sure they wouldn't understand; they'd either try to pressure him into conforming or feel he was rejecting them.

9.6. Many corporations have initiated drug testing for all job applicants. Policymakers reason that they are within their rights in rejecting drug users from hiring consideration.

9.7. You are the editor of the college newspaper. Your staff consists of two other people, who limit their work to a few hours a week. To get the paper out each week, you've had to spend many more hours than your course load permits. On several occasions you've stayed up all night and slept through the next morning's classes. You've tried putting ads in the paper to get more staff members, but no one answers them.

9.8. In some cultures, the elderly are greatly respected and made to feel important. Their views are considered especially valuable because they are formed out of a lifetime of experience. In our culture it is quite different. Those over 60 are regarded as having nothing to offer society.

9.9. Many people, notably students, believe that extracurricular activities in high school complement the curriculum and provide valuable opportunities for personal growth and achievement. Yet many communities are finding the cost of financing today's schools an intolerable burden and are looking for ways to reduce that cost. Some are deciding, reluctantly, that they must cut extracurricular activities (including varsity sports) from the school budget.

9.10. The welfare program is a financial drain on the country. Many argue for abolishing it. Yet others object that such a move would abandon the poor, the disabled, innocent children, and the elderly to starvation.

9.11. More U.S. citizens have been lost on the nation's highways than on the battlefields of war. Drunk driving is one major cause. The illegality of driving under the influence of alcohol (or drugs) seems not to make much difference.

9.12. The American Lung Association is looking for ways to warn teenagers about the dangers of cigarette smoking. Assist the association.

9.13. Many parents place intense pressure on children to win in competitive sports. These parents can be seen screaming at, and even hitting, Little Leaguers when they make a mistake or have a bad day. And when the children get older and compete at a higher level, the parents are always hovering about, grim-faced, missing no opportunity to cajole, nag, and intimidate them to succeed. Authorities agree that such pressure is harmful to children.

9.14. Going to the hospital for the first time can be a frightening experience, particularly for small children. Think of as many ways as you can to make the children's ward of a hospital a nonthreatening, cheery place.

9.15. At least 15 states still consider adultery a crime and can legally impose monetary fines or prison sentences on anyone convicted of it.

9.16. The AIDS epidemic has led many people to argue for mandatory testing of individuals in high-risk groups, such as active homosexuals and drug users.

GROUP DISCUSSION EXERCISE

Discuss the following issue with two or three of your classmates. Observe the guidelines to group discussion presented in Appendix B. Consider all sides of the matter and try to reach consensus. Be prepared to report your group's deliberations to the class, describing how your analysis proceeded, what questions were asked, and what agreements were reached. If differences of viewpoint remain unresolved, be prepared to report them objectively.

> The growing concern over juvenile crime has prompted some to entertain new ideas for solving the problem. One controversial proposal is that parents be held responsible for their children's crimes. Test the idea by considering the variety of situations that might arise. Decide whether any such law could be so devised as to be fair and reasonable. If you decide that it could be, explain the provisions that would make it so.

COMPOSITION OR SPEECH EXERCISE

Write a composition or, if your instructor specifies, a formal speech, presenting the view your group reached in the preceding group discussion exercise. (If you hold a dissenting view, present that instead.) Be sure to provide evidence that your view is the most reasonable one. Naturally your composition or speech will bear some resemblance to those of the other members of your group—you will have developed ideas as a team, so at least some of your ideas will be similar, even identical, to theirs. Don't be concerned about such similarities. Your composition or speech will be a unique effort if you (a) use supporting material from your own experience, observation, and research; (b) develop your own line of reasoning about that material; (c) employ your own ingenuity in designing an introduction and conclusion and in arranging the material in the body of your composition or speech; and (d) express your thoughts in your own words. For further guidance, consult the appropriate appendix—A for writing, B for speaking.

PART 3

Be
Critical

The Role of Criticism

Gilbert Keith Chesterton once described a poet as a person with his head in the clouds and his feet on the ground. That description also fits good thinkers. They are able to entertain the boldest ideas, the undreamt-of solutions to problems—yet they are also able to fit their ideas to the exacting demands of reality. They are not only imaginative but practical as well. We have examined the former, creative phase of thinking. Now we will examine the latter, critical phase.

Critical thinking, as we define it here, means reviewing the ideas we have produced, making a tentative decision about what action will best solve the problem or what belief about the issue is most reasonable, and then evaluating and refining that solution or belief.

WHY CRITICISM IS NECESSARY

The role of criticism in problem solving is important for two reasons. First, no solution is ever perfect. However creative it may be, there is always room for improvement. Moreover, even the best ideas seldom occur in refined form. Like fine gems, they must be cleaned and polished before their potential worth is realized. Second, in many cases solutions cannot just be put into effect; they must first be approved by others. Ideas for the improvement of the office or factory, for example, may require the approval of an employer or supervisor. Ideas about overcoming difficulties in family relationships may depend on the cooperation of other family members. And creative solutions to social problems often require the support of government leaders or the endorsement of the voters. In such cases, the best idea in the world is of little value until others are persuaded of its worth.

Criticism is equally important in resolving issues. A viewpoint may seem eminently reasonable, the ideal ground for compromise between opposing views, yet contain subtle flaws. Sometimes these become evident only when the idea is translated into a course of action.

In the early 1970s, for example, in response to the issue of fairness in divorce settlements, the idea of "no-fault" divorce became law in California, and in subsequent years, in most other states. It was considered at the time an ingenious way to permit a marriage to be dissolved easily and fairly, without squabbling and bitter accusations. Now many critics believe they have found an effect of no-fault divorce that no one anticipated when it was instituted: the impoverishment of divorced women and their children.[1]

Although there can never be a guarantee that even the most thorough criticism will reveal every flaw in an idea, your responses to issues are more likely to be reasonable if you subject your ideas to rigorous evaluation before reaching a judgment. Critical thinking reduces your chance of error.

FOCUS ON *YOUR* IDEAS

The focus of this and the following chapters is not on criticism of other people's solutions. It is rather on a much more difficult, even painful criticism: that of *your own* solutions. Like everyone else, you are vulnerable to a variety of errors. You may receive inaccurate reports from others, including the media. In addition, you may misunderstand accurate reports, fall prey to rumor and hearsay, let emotion color your judgment, and suffer lapses in logic. For these reasons the ideas you produce need criticism.

Ironically, though you are undoubtedly ready to criticize others' ideas freely, like most people you are probably blind to the need for criticism of your own thinking. There are several reasons for this. First, your ego is inclined against it. Once you have settled on an idea, you feel a proprietary interest in it. "It is mine," you tell yourself, "so it must be good." And once in that frame of mind, you are ready to defend the idea against all attack, even the attack that your own good judgment might mount against it. The situation is something like that of a dog with a bone. The dog will cling to it tenaciously and growl and snarl when anyone approaches, not because the bone is worth anything (it may long since have been chewed out), but simply because it is the dog's possession.

Another reason you will be reluctant to evaluate your own ideas is that their familiarity makes it difficult to see flaws in them. The longer you work on a problem or issue, the more accustomed you become to its details. And once your effort yields a solution, you have usually gotten so close to the problem that it is difficult to distance yourself from it, to step back mentally from your solution and see it objectively.

OVERCOMING OBSTACLES TO CRITICAL THINKING

This blindness toward imperfections in your ideas will make it tempting to approach criticism of your ideas with, at best, mock analysis followed by a vigorous nod of approval. There are two ways you can safeguard against this mistake. The first is to say to yourself, before you begin to take a critical look at any idea, "I know this idea is going to look good to me and that I am going to feel it's pointless to look for flaws. That's natural. I thought of it, so I want it to be perfect. *But I'm going to disregard this reaction and force myself to examine it critically.*"

The second safeguard is to turn your ego to advantage. Whenever you find yourself ready to stop evaluating your idea before you really should, reflect for a moment on how it would feel to have a serious flaw pointed out by someone else, particularly by someone you don't much care for. Visualize the situation; imagine yourself squirming with embarrassment and awkwardly offering face-saving excuses. Such a mental picture ought to motivate you to continue evaluating your idea.

APPLYING CURIOSITY

We have seen how curiosity increases awareness of problems and issues, enabling you to feel dissatisfactions and annoyances more consciously and to regard them more productively, as challenges and opportunities. We have seen, too, that curiosity keeps your mind dynamic and contributes to the playfulness Einstein regarded as "the essential feature of productive thought." That same curiosity is also a valuable aid to critical thinking.

Perhaps you've had the experience of adding up a column of figures and getting the same answer—the *wrong* answer—again and again. Psychologists have long recognized that when we travel a particular mental route a second or third time, we often follow our earlier footsteps without realizing that we are doing so. That's what happened when you added up those figures. You had the impression that each new total was fresh and independent. In reality, though, you were trapped by your initial miscalculation.

That same kind of mistake can occur when you examine your ideas critically. You can look at an idea again and again and still not see its flaws. For this reason, merely spending a lot of time criticizing is not necessarily effective. You need to examine the idea from different perspectives in order to break out of your first view. That's where curiosity comes in. By approaching criticism inquisitively, asking, "How will my idea work when it is applied?" and "How will others react to it?" you will increase your chances of finding the imperfections and complications that need to be addressed.

AVOIDING ASSUMPTIONS

To assume is to take something for granted, to expect that things will be a certain way because they have been that way in the past, or because you want them to be that way. It's natural to make assumptions. Everyone makes them continually. You assume, for example, that your professor will be in class when class is scheduled, that the cafeteria will not serve lunch two hours early, that the college will not rent your room to someone else and change the lock on the door, that the bank that has always cashed your checks will continue to do so, and that the elevator is really going up when the indicator says it is. Making such assumptions is reasonable, even if on occasion they later prove to be incorrect.

However, while refining your ideas, it is wise to make no assumptions at all. The reason for this is not only that unexpected outcomes can cause you embarrassment but also, and more important, that *what you take for granted you do not examine critically*. Assumptions obstruct the refining process.

It would be impossible to list all the assumptions you will be tempted to make while refining your ideas. However, the following assumptions occur often enough, and interfere with critical thinking seriously enough, to warrant special mention:

1. *The assumption that others familiar with the problem or issue will share your enthusiasm for your ideas.* Although this might seem to be a reasonable expectation, it seldom is. The more familiar people are with a problem or issue, the more likely they are to have their own ideas.
2. *The assumption that small imperfections in your idea will not affect people's acceptance of it.* When people have their own ideas, which differ from yours, they are likely to magnify small imperfections without even realizing it because, subconsciously, they are looking for an excuse to reject yours. Small imperfections may provide that excuse.
3. *The assumption that if your idea is clear to you, it will be clear to others.* If you've ever sat in a classroom and heard a teacher offer an explanation that didn't make the slightest sense to you, you should appreciate this assumption. *Your* understanding of what you are expressing does not constitute clarity. If you want the solution and its presentation to be clear, you must *construct* it to be so and not just assume that it is.
4. *The assumption that the people who stand to benefit most from your idea will accept it automatically without any persuasion on your part.* This assumption has caused creative people incalculable grief. For example, when Elias Howe invented the sewing machine, he knew it would be a boon to the garment industry. It would revolutionize garment construction and make the clothing business much more profitable. He may very well have assumed that the mere unveiling of his invention would be sufficient to have the leaders of that industry praising it and him. But reality didn't match that assumption. Howe couldn't get a single American firm interested enough to buy the machine. He was forced to go to England to find a favorable reception. To save yourself considerable disappointment, never assume that the value of your ideas will be universally recognized. Expect to have to persuade everyone.

REFINING YOUR SOLUTIONS TO PROBLEMS

Refining your solutions means making your best ideas even better—that is, making the results of your creative thinking even more effective, more workable, more attractive. Although much of what you will be doing in this stage is finding flaws and complications, the emphasis is not negative but positive. Your aim is to *improve* your ideas.

Not every idea, of course, requires refinement. With the problem of the string that slips out of your sweatpants, for example, there is little or no need for refinement and no need to present the solution for others' approval. Once you have decided on a solution, you can just implement it. Most of the important problems and issues you will encounter, however, are more demanding.

Later chapters will develop the refinement and presentation of ideas more fully. The basic approach that follows will enable you to begin using these steps and developing skill in applying them even while you are studying each in greater depth. The approach consists of asking and answering these four questions:

1. How exactly will your solution be applied? (List all steps and all important details.)
2. What difficulties could arise in application and how would these best be overcome?
3. What reasons might others find for opposing this solution? What modifications could you make to overcome their opposition?
4. Who, specifically, will have to be persuaded of the merit of your solution? What kind of presentation would be most likely to persuade them?

A SAMPLE PROBLEM

The following problem was included in Chapter 9's applications.

> You are the editor of the college newspaper. Your staff consists of two other people, who limit their work to a few hours a week. To get the paper out each week, you've had to spend many more hours than your course load permits. On several occasions you've stayed up all night and slept through the next morning's classes. You've tried putting ads in the paper to get more staff members, but no one answers them.

Let's say you identified the problem as "How to reward students for joining the staff." (This is one good expression of the problem, though not, of course, the only one.) Let's say further that after investigating the problem and producing a number of possible solutions, you chose *giving college credit to those who work on the paper* as the best one. Here is how to apply the critical approach.

1. How exactly will your solution be applied?

Here you'd have to decide and list the requirements for obtaining credit for the work. You'd also have to decide which department would grant credit, how much credit would be granted, and whether it would be elective credit or would fulfill some course requirement.

2. What difficulties could arise in the application and how would these best be overcome?

The most obvious difficulty would involve course requirements and evaluation of student performance. Who would teach the course? Where? (In a classroom? In the newspaper office?) How could one, two, or three time periods per week satisfy the demands of producing the paper? How would the instructor evaluate performance? Would the editor have to meet a different standard than a reporter or layout person? If so, how would the registrar clarify on each student's transcript what standard was met? These and other questions would have to be raised and answered satisfactorily.

3. Why might others resist this solution? What modifications could you make to overcome this resistance?

Here you'd consider such reasons as the inappropriateness of the new course to any curriculum on campus (assuming the campus did not offer a journalism major), the lack of journalistic expertise among campus faculty, and the possible course overload the solution would represent for faculty.

4. Whom would you have to persuade of the solution's value? What kind of presentation would be most likely to persuade them?

You'd surely have to persuade the college administration and the faculty, particularly the faculty of the department you would have teach the course.

REFINING YOUR POSITIONS ON ISSUES

We noted earlier that though the terms *problem* and *issue* both refer to disagreeable situations that challenge our ingenuity, an issue also tends to divide people into opposing camps, each sure that it is right and the opposition wrong. We noted, too, that whereas the aim of problem solving is to find the best course of action, the aim of issue resolving is to find the most reasonable belief, and so we express problems and issues differently and produce different kinds of ideas for each.

Now we will consider another difference. Your approach to refining your positions on issues is to decide not whether the idea works but whether it meets the tests of logic. Thus you must take the following steps:

1. State your argument. That is, state the belief you have decided to be most reasonable concerning the issue and give your reasons for so deciding.
2. Examine your evidence for relevance, comprehensiveness, and reliability.
3. Examine your argument for flaws in reasoning; for example, errors of narrow perspective, confusion, or carelessness.

In cases where your aim is solely to form a reasonable belief and not to take any action about it, this approach will constitute refinement of the issue. However, in cases in which you wish to recommend or take action and resolve the issue, you will next answer questions quite similar to those used for refining solutions to problems, questions designed to plan a course of action and then to evaluate it critically. Here are those questions:

What action do you recommend be taken and how exactly will it be taken? List all steps and important details.

What difficulties could arise in taking this action and how would they best be overcome?

To see how this approach works, let's consider a sample issue.

A SAMPLE ISSUE

Let's say that you are addressing the matter of the United States giving monetary aid to foreign governments that victimize their citizens and deny them their human rights and that you have expressed the main issue as "Is it morally right for the U.S. government to provide such aid?" Let's also say that your argument is as follows:

> It is morally wrong for the U.S. government to provide monetary aid to foreign governments that victimize their citizens and deny them their human rights because the United States is a democracy and holds that government exists for the good of the people and that the people are "endowed with certain unalienable rights." To support tyranny in this way, while preaching human rights, is hypocritical.

Next you examine your argument for reasonableness and find only one serious flaw, the unwarranted assumption that giving monetary aid to such countries is *necessarily* supporting tyranny and therefore is hypocritical. On reflection, you decide that if the people would be worse off without the aid, giving it would represent the lesser of two evils and therefore a moral course of action. You modify your argument, replacing the last sentence with this one: "Giving monetary aid in such circumstances is justifiable only if the people would be worse off without it and no other effective way to help them can be found."

Taking Action on the Issue

Recognizing that your argument is a challenge to find a better approach than giving money to corrupt governments, you proceed with your critical thinking as follows:

> What action do you recommend be taken and how exactly will it be taken?

Let's say that the action you choose is to give aid in the form of technological education and employment opportunities, with the stipulation that the governments end all victimization of the people. You would then detail the kinds of technological education and employment opportunities you have in mind. You would also decide whether the teachers and employers will be sponsored by our government, by private enterprise, or by a combination of the two. Finally, you'd detail any special employment conditions, including wages and benefits.

> What difficulties would arise in taking this action and how would they best be overcome?

The most obvious difficulty would be policing the country's government—deciding how to ensure that it ended human rights violations. (This problem could be overcome by having a UN task force monitor the situation.) Another difficulty would be preventing the corrupt officials from using your plan in a manner you do not intend, taking advantage of the new cheap labor for their own financial gain. (This difficulty could be overcome by establishing profit-sharing plans and cooperatives so that the people would enjoy the fruits of their labor.)

One final suggestion: If you ever become discouraged about imperfections and complications in your work—if you are inclined to say, "How can I ever be expected to work out all the flaws I discover? It's an impossible task!"—try this approach: Treat each significant imperfection or complication as a miniature problem, first finding the best expression, investigating it if necessary, and finally generating as many possible solutions as you can. Not every issue warrants such meticulous attention. But the more important ones will. And by using a familiar process to address them, you bolster your confidence, overcome discouragement, and stimulate your imagination.

WARM-UP EXERCISES

10.1. Old dishwashing liquid containers (the plastic ones that Dawn, Joy, and Ivory liquid come in) are usually discarded when empty. But perhaps they could be put to some use. Think of as many uses for them as you can.

10.2. A law student hired a tutor to help him with his law studies. He promised to pay for the tutor's services as soon as he passed his bar exam, set up practice, and won his first case. He subsequently passed the exam and set up practice, but a year passed and he still had not won a case. The tutor grew tired of waiting and sued him for payment. The young lawyer then wrote the tutor a letter and said, "If your suit against me goes to court and I win it, I won't have to pay you. And if I lose it, I still won't have to pay you, because the terms of our agreement (my winning my first case) will not have been met."[2] Do you agree with the young lawyer's reasoning? Explain thoroughly.

10.3. In the following dialogue, Lily admits she is confused. Perhaps Daisy is, too. Clear up the confusion for them.

DAISY: What is the meaning of life?
LILY: There is no one meaning.
DAISY: There's got to be—otherwise everyone makes his or her own, and that would create chaos.
LILY: No, everyone *decides* his or her own. Whatever a person says, that's it.
DAISY: Do you mean if I say the meaning of life is "eat, drink, and be merry, for tomorrow we die," that *is* the meaning of life?
LILY: Yes, for *you* it is, though maybe not for me.
DAISY: That would mean that no one can be wrong in his or her view. And if that's the case, why is everyone so concerned about finding the meaning of life?
LILY: I don't know. That's always puzzled me.

APPLICATIONS

10.1. In Application 7.9 you applied your creativity to a question concerning the quality of American workers' performance and their attitudes toward work (see pages 109–110). Refine your best solution to that application, using the approach explained in this chapter.

10.2. In Application 9.11 you applied your creativity to a question concerning drunk driving (see page 139). Refine your best solution, using the approach explained in this chapter.

10.3. Since you graduated from high school, you've been wondering what single improvement could be made in your school system between kindergarten and twelfth grade that would have the best and most lasting impact on students. Now you've come up with the answer: Have the students be taught *how to think*, directly and systematically. Now take that idea and refine it.

10.4. You are a Hollywood film producer. You have just been tried in federal court for agreeing to buy 5 ounces of cocaine. The judge deferred final judgment of your case for a year but put you on probation and offered you this challenge: "If you put your talents to work fighting drug abuse by children, I will wipe your record clean." You feel remorse for your own drug use and resolve to meet the challenge. Identify and solve this problem; then refine your best solution.

10.5. Tens of thousands of shoplifting arrests are made across the country every year. In many cases the shoplifters have a checkbook, a credit card, or enough cash to pay for what they steal. To jail these offenders costs the taxpayers money. Yet to treat them leniently encourages shoplifting and adds to the cost of consumer goods. Identify and solve this problem; then refine your best solution.

10.6. Your older sister shares this personal problem with you: Her daughter is only a toddler, but before long your sister will have to explain the best advice about being honest in daily life. Yet she herself is confused. Here's how she explains her dilemma to you: "Mom and Dad always told us that 'honesty is the best policy' in every case. Yet every other day, it seems, I read about workers who report corruption in their company or in government and then lose their jobs for their honesty. I want to give my daughter the best advice, and yet I'm not sure what the best advice is." Identify and solve your sister's problem; then refine your best solution.

10.7. There's probably not a home in the land that has managed to avoid wrangling over whether the parents' generation or the children's generation had a more difficult time growing up. Apply your creative and critical thinking to this issue as you did in previous applications.

10.8. Michael is very excited. He has just gotten his first job, delivering newspapers in a residential neighborhood. The only problem is that he has to pass several large dogs on his route and he has been afraid of dogs for as long as he can remember. Identify and solve Michael's problem; then refine your best solution.

10.9. For as long as anyone in your town can remember, there has been a manger scene on the village square at Christmastime. But this year a group of civil libertarians challenged the placing of such scenes on public property, claiming a violation of the constitutional prohibition of the "establishment of religion." There is strong feeling on both sides of the question. Apply your creative and critical thinking to this issue.

10.10. Millions of American adults are functionally illiterate. These people cannot decipher a bus, train, or airline schedule; write a letter; or fill out a job application. Such illiteracy is estimated to cost the United States billions of dollars annually in welfare and unemployment payments. With the federal government decreasing its aid to education, that cost is likely to increase. Apply your creative and critical thinking to this problem as you did in previous applications.

10.11. Zeb and Jeb are engaged in a spirited discussion. Read it carefully, identify and resolve the issue, and refine your best solution.

> ZEB: There's one thing I don't think belongs in our Constitution.
> JEB: What's that?
> ZEB: The freedom-of-religion clause.
> JEB: But that's one of the basic freedoms we all enjoy.
> ZEB: As I see it, it's a dangerous business allowing people to practice any religion they want with no restrictions. What if people want to worship the devil? Do you think that's right?
> JEB: No, I don't personally, but I wouldn't deny others the right to do so.
> ZEB: You're just repeating empty formulas you were taught. What if a group made sexual orgies their main ritual? Would you approve that?
> JEB: Hey, man, where do I sign up for that religion?
> ZEB: Be serious. There were lots of religions in the past that practiced some pretty weird and disgusting things. Like the sacrifice of young girls to ensure a good harvest and the murdering of servants so some king or queen could be properly attended in the afterlife. Do you approve of that kind of stuff?
> JEB: No, I guess not, but. . . .
> ZEB: Right. The more you think about the issue, the more you've got to agree my fears make good sense. We should change the Constitution.

10.12. Follow the directions for Application 10.11.

> BABETTE: Sebastian, do you approve of euthanasia?
> SEBASTIAN: Do you mean "mercy killing"?
> BABETTE: Yes.
> SEBASTIAN: No, I don't. It leaves a person's life at the mercy of people who may have other interests than his or her well-being: for example, the doctor who has received an urgent request for a heart, liver, or kidney and wishes to hasten the person's death to meet that request; or the relatives of a terminally ill patient who are lusting after his or her estate.
> BABETTE: I approve of it. It not only spares terminally ill patients pain and suffering but also saves their families the staggering medical expense of long-term intensive care and protracted grief.
> SEBASTIAN: A person's life is a sacred and precious thing—too much so to be ended by other people, no matter how well-intentioned or merciful they are. As a matter of fact, I believe it is too precious for the person himself or herself to assign others the right to pull the plug.

GROUP DISCUSSION EXERCISE

Discuss the following issue with two or three of your classmates. Observe the guidelines to group discussion presented in Appendix B. Consider all sides of the matter and try to reach consensus. Be prepared to report your group's deliberations to the class, describing how your analysis proceeded, what questions were asked, and what agreements were reached. If differences of viewpoint remain unresolved, be prepared to report them objectively.

> Damian Williams, who was captured on videotape assaulting truck driver Reginald Denny and performing a victory dance during the Los Angeles riots, offered these reasons for his actions: (a) ignorance in that he didn't think about what he was doing at the time; (b) the fact that he was raised entirely by his mother and never knew his father; and (c) his mother's explanation to him that "the devil" was responsible.[3] Are these reasons credible? How else might Williams's behavior, and that of other assailants, looters, and rioters, be explained?

COMPOSITION OR SPEECH EXERCISE

Write a composition or, if your instructor specifies, a formal speech, presenting the view your group reached in the preceding group discussion exercise. (If you hold a dissenting view, present that instead.) Be sure to provide evidence that your view is the most reasonable one. Naturally your composition or speech will bear some resemblance to those of the other members of your group—you will have developed ideas as a team, so at least some of your ideas will be similar, even identical, to theirs. Don't be concerned about such similarities. Your composition or speech will be a unique effort if you (a) use supporting material from your own experience, observation, and research; (b) develop your own line of reasoning about that material; (c) employ your own ingenuity in designing an introduction and conclusion and in arranging the material in the body of your composition or speech; and (d) express your thoughts in your own words. For further guidance, consult the appropriate appendix—A for writing, B for speaking.

Refine Your Solution to the Problem

How might the human voice be carried over distances beyond the normal range of hearing? That was the problem facing Alexander Graham Bell. The solution, as we all know, was the telephone. But how did Bell actually invent it? Most of us probably have the vague notion that once he got his creative idea, he merely retired to his workshop, built a model of the machine, sold it, and became rich and famous. In fact, it wasn't that simple. Although Bell was an expert in sound, he knew virtually nothing about electricity. Before he was able to make his idea a reality, he had to learn all about electricity and then put his knowledge to work and solve the technical problems.

The refinement of solutions to problems does not always demand learning an entirely new field, but it is seldom the easy matter many people assume. As Eliot Hutchinson explains,

> There is nothing trifling, incidental or dilettantish about this business of [refining solutions]. It is work, days and nights of it, months and years of it, the perspiration that is nine-tenths genius. And it tires, discourages, exhausts. . . . The history both of art and of science is largely the history of man's personal endurance, his acceptance of labor as the price of success. To be sure, some men dash off a brilliant piece of work, spread themselves for a time. But 90 percent of reputable authors, no matter how sure their technique, and well-nigh all reputable scientists revamp their work until what was given in insight is so overlaid with secondary material that it is hardly to be recognized. Elaboration is for the mature only; it is for the rigorous, the exacting, the profound.[1]

THREE STEPS IN REFINING

Because refinement can spell the difference between success and failure, you should approach it very seriously. Yet there is no reason to be frightened by the task. It usually requires no special gift or talent. Rather, it is achievable by

153

anyone who is willing to work hard and patiently. Three steps are involved: working out the details of the solution, finding imperfections and complications, and making improvements.

Step 1: Working Out the Details

The first step means determining exactly how your solution will be applied. It's easy to overlook this step or to ignore its significance. After all, most of the things we use every day and take for granted—the concepts, the processes and systems, the products and services—appear to us in refined form. We seldom have occasion even to imagine how they appeared in rough form or to appreciate the difficult challenges their refinement posed for their creators.

Consider the ballpoint pen. It was first conceived of in the United States in 1888 by John Loud. He even obtained a patent for his idea of using a rotating ball to deliver the ink to the paper. Yet he never was able to refine the pen enough to make it write cleanly. In 1919 Laszlo Biro of Hungary reinvented this pen, but he was unable to complete his design and market his idea until 1943—and even then the ink came out in splotches. Finally, Franz Seech of Austria worked out the basic difficulties in 1949 (the key to his pen's performance was fast-drying ink) and marketed his pen successfully. Thus, *61 years* elapsed from conception to refinement.[2]

When William Addis, a prisoner in a British jail, got the idea for the first toothbrush in 1870, he faced a number of challenges to his ingenuity. (In case you didn't know, before 1870 people cleaned their teeth by rubbing them with a rag.) What would be the right size for the invention? What shape would be best? What should it be made of? What kind of bristles would work best? How should they be held together? What could be used to contain the bristles? Addis saved a bone from his supper; bored tiny holes in it; obtained some bristles from his prison guard; cut, tied, and glued them together; and inserted them into the bone. When he was released from prison, he marketed his invention and became a business success.[3]

The refinement of the typewriter posed even greater challenges. How to place the keys, how to arrange the keyboard, how to make the keys strike, how to hold the paper, how to make it move so that the keys wouldn't strike the same place over and over, how to move from line to line without turning the carriage by hand, how to ink the keys—these were just some of the details that had to be worked out. In light of the numerous and complex problems, it is perhaps not surprising that before Christopher Sholes and Samuel Soulé completed their first working model in 1867, *51 other inventors* had tried and failed.[4]

We could cite many other examples of the refinement difficulties facing the originators of most new ideas. The point is that even the most creative idea does not become useful until the details of its application are worked out. The following approach will help you work out the details of your solutions more effectively:

If your solution involves *doing* something (as, for example, in a new process), answer these questions:

- How exactly is it to be done, step by step?
- By whom is it to be done?
- When is it to be done? (According to what timetable?)
- Where is it to be done?
- Who will finance it?
- What tools or materials, if any, are to be used?
- From what source will they be obtained?
- How and by whom will they be transported?
- Where will they be stored?
- What special conditions, if any, will be required for the solution to be carried out?

If your solution involves *making* something (as in a new product), answer these questions:

- How will it work? Be specific.
- What will it look like? Be specific as to size, shape, color, texture, and any other relevant descriptive details.
- What material will it be made of?
- What will the product cost to make?
- Who will pay for it?
- How exactly will it be used?
- Who will use it? When? Where?
- How will it be packaged?
- How will it be delivered?
- How will it be stored?

Step 2: Finding Imperfections and Complications

After you have worked out the details of your solution, your next step is to examine those details for imperfections. Remember that despite the normal tendency to regard your solution as perfect and to view this step as unnecessary, it is almost certain that your solution, like any other, contains at least minor flaws. Remember, too, that your success in persuading others of your solution's value will depend in no small part on your willingness to improve your idea in any way you can.

Until you are experienced in examining solutions critically, the biggest difficulty you are likely to encounter is knowing what kinds of imperfections and complications to look for and how to go about looking for them. The following four approaches will prove helpful both in overcoming that initial difficulty and in assuring that your analysis will be comprehensive.

1. *Check for common kinds of imperfections.* The following areas are the ones in which imperfections most commonly occur. (Not every one, of

course, will apply to every type of solution.) Although the list is not exhaustive, and therefore you should not limit yourself to it, it is an excellent starting point for examining most solutions.

- Clarity: Is the solution difficult to understand?
- Safety: Does the solution create any danger for those who use it or those for whom it is used?
- Convenience: Is the solution awkward to use or implement?
- Efficiency: Does using the solution involve significant delays?
- Economy: Is the solution too costly to build or implement?
- Simplicity: Is the solution unnecessarily complex in design or format?
- Comfort: Is the solution uncomfortable to use?
- Durability: Is the solution likely to break or malfunction?
- Beauty: Will most people find the solution ugly or unappealing?
- Compatibility: Does the solution clash with any other product or process it should harmonize with?

2. *Compare the solution with competing ones.* Examine the existing product or process your solution is designed to replace, or study another proposed solution competitive with yours. Determine how the existing product, process, or competing solution has the advantage over yours. (Although your solution should be superior in most major respects, there will often be one or two inferior respects. Any such area should be considered an imperfection.)
3. *Consider what changes your solution will cause.* Ask yourself what will occur if your solution is implemented. Don't overlook even minor changes. Decide which of them, if any, will cause complications.
4. *Consider the effects your solution will have on people.* Look among the physical, moral, emotional, intellectual, and financial areas of life to see how any would be affected. Be sure to consider even the remote effects that might occur to any person or group. Most of the changes you list will undoubtedly be beneficial. But those that are in any way undesirable will often signal imperfections or complications in your solution.

Step 3: Making Improvements

The third and final step in refining your solutions is to make improvements that will eliminate imperfections. Here, classified according to the types of solutions they are usually associated with, are the kinds of improvements you will find applicable in most situations.

For a new or revised *concept:*

- Change the terminology—make it simpler, easier to remember, more eye-catching.
- Change the way it is explained—use different illustrations, analogies, and so on.
- Change the application—use it in other situations or in different ways.

For a new or revised *process, system,* or *service:*

- Change the way it is done, the step-by-step approach.
- Change who does it.
- Change the place where it is done.
- Change the tools or materials used.
- Change the source from which the tools or materials are obtained.
- Change the place the tools or materials will be stored.
- Change the conditions required.

For a new or modified *product:*

- Change its size, shape, color, texture, and so on.
- Change its composition (the material it is made of).
- Change the way it is used.
- Change who will use it or when or where it will be used.
- Change the way it is packaged or delivered.
- Change the way it is stored.

Whenever you address an imperfection and are trying to think of ways to improve your solution, be sure to consider using the approaches for producing ideas explained in Chapter 9. Specifically, you should consider *forcing uncommon responses, using free association and analogy, looking for unusual combinations,* and *visualizing the possibilities.* Each imperfection and complication is, after all, a miniproblem in itself and will therefore respond to the creative process much as the larger problem did.

Most important, be sure not to settle for the first improvement that occurs to you. Instead, extend your effort to produce ideas, and withhold judgment of any one idea until you have produced a generous number of possibilities.

Occasionally you will encounter an imperfection that requires you to return to the second stage of the creative process and investigate the matter more deeply—much as Alexander Graham Bell did when he took time out to master the principles of electricity. In extreme cases you may even find that your solution is too badly flawed to be workable. At such times you will feel as if all your efforts were wasted. But they will not really have been wasted. *To find out what does not work is an important step toward determining what does.*

TWO SAMPLE PROBLEMS

The First Problem

Now let's apply this approach to some cases and note how it works. The first case concerns Rocco, the manager of the movie theater. His problem was discussed in Application 7.10: "In recent years, a number of competitors have cut into his business, and cable television and video rental stores have reduced the number of moviegoers still further. Rocco desperately needs to get more people to patronize his theater, particularly since he has begun to hear the owners talk of closing it and dismissing him if box office receipts don't improve."

Let's say that after considering several expressions of this problem, you decide that the best is "how to attract moviegoers away from other theaters to Rocco's, and how to attract people that ordinarily don't go to movie theaters." Let's say, further, that after investigating the problem and producing a number of possible solutions, you decide that three ideas, in combination, are the best solution: to present interesting displays, to provide entertainment, and to offer discounts to groups. Here is how you would refine this solution. (Only one or two ideas are provided for each point. You would, of course, consider many more in your analysis.)

Step 1: Working Out the Details

To present interesting displays:

- What displays? Arts and crafts, for example.
- Which artists and craftspeople? There would be no restrictions.
- How would Rocco find people to display their work? He could check with area arts and crafts councils.
- Where would the displays be set up? In the lobby.
- What supplies would be needed and how would they be provided? Tables, chairs, and display shelves. Each displayer would provide his or her own.

To provide entertainment:

- What entertainment? Amateur or professional musicians, performing individually or in small groups.
- How would Rocco find them? He could advertise on posters in the lobby or check with area high school music teachers or the local musicians' union.
- How would he pay them? He could let them pass the hat for donations from theater patrons, or let them put up a sign listing their phone number, so they could get jobs by word of mouth among theater patrons.

To offer discounts to groups:

- Which groups? Senior citizens' organizations, employees of particular businesses in the area, members of a union (any union).
- How would he let people know of this discount? He could highlight the fact in his usual newspaper advertisements.

Steps 2 and 3: Finding and Overcoming Imperfections and Complications

To present interesting displays in the lobby:

- Complication: Such displays might block the flow of traffic in and out of the theater and thus create problems of inconvenience and even a violation of the safety code.

- Improvement: Limit the number of displays provided and put them in an out-of-the-way corner. Change them each week.

To provide entertainment:

- Complication: The musicians' union might object to members working for no pay.
- Improvement: Limit the entertainment to young amateurs (high school students, for example).
- Complication: Amateurs might not want to hire out for other jobs, so advertising their skills might not be an incentive.
- Improvement: Pay them in free admissions, one week free for every night of playing.

To offer discounts to groups:

- Imperfection: Senior citizens might not want to attend at night because they fear street crime.
- Improvement: Offer them discounts for matinees.

The Second Problem

We first encountered the second problem in Application 9.14. It was phrased this way: "Going to the hospital for the first time can be a frightening experience, particularly for small children. Think of as many ways as you can to make the children's ward of a hospital a nonthreatening, cheery place."

Let's say your best solution to this problem was a combination of these ideas: to have the hospital staff dress in colorful outfits, to have children's music playing, and to decorate the lounge appealingly. Here is how you would refine this solution. (As in the previous case, only one or two ideas are provided for each point. You would consider many more in your analysis.)

Step 1: Working Out the Details

To have the staff dress in colorful outfits:

- What would the colors be? Would the uniforms have a design on them? They'd be pastel colors and have pictures of animals, clowns, and nursery rhyme characters.
- Who would wear them? Doctors, nurses, aides, secretaries—anyone who worked on the children's ward.
- What kinds of outfits would they be? Lab coats for the doctors, smocks or aprons for the secretaries, nurses, and aides.

To have children's music playing:

- What kind of music? Nursery songs, songs from children's movies, and so on.
- Where would the music be playing? Throughout the children's ward—rooms, halls, and in the lounge.

To decorate the lounge appealingly:

- What decorating ideas would you use? I'd have special furniture made and use wallpaper on the walls.
- What furniture specifically, and what would be special about it? Child-size heavy plastic furniture—chairs, bookcases, a table for games, perhaps a small seesaw. Each piece would be in a bright color and be shaped like an animal. For example, a chair could be shaped like a kangaroo, with the seat where the pouch would be.
- What pattern would you have for the wallpaper? Scenes from Mother Goose.

Steps 2 and 3: Finding and Overcoming Imperfections and Complications

To have colorful outfits:

- Complication: Doctors would be unlikely to want to dress in, say, a Pluto coat. People on other wards might think them strange when they made their hospital rounds. Nurses and others would undoubtedly object to such an unprofessional outfit, too, even though they'd be sympathetic to the idea of making the ward cheery.
- Improvement: Let the *children* have colorful gowns and even colorful sheets instead.

To have children's music playing:

- Imperfection: Children's music at the nurses' station might upset the work being done there. And it wouldn't be appropriate in some rooms, either—for example, the rooms with very ill children or those who have just returned from surgery.
- Improvement: Have the music piped into the rooms of those who want it. Also, have it playing quietly in the lounge.

To decorate the lounge appealingly:

- Complication: The cost of such extensive redecorating and refurnishing might be prohibitive.
- Improvement: Appeal to a local service organization (Lions, Kiwanis, Rotary, for example) to donate funds.

All the improvements presented overcome the imperfections and complications they address without creating new difficulties. Naturally, not all the improvements you think of will do this. Many will create greater imperfections and complications than the ones they correct. For this reason, you should exercise care in selecting your improvements.

WARM-UP EXERCISES

11.1. The chain letter is usually associated with dishonesty, superstition, and even illegality. (The mailing of money is illegal in many places.) But it could be used constructively and beneficially. Think of as many such ways as you can to use the chain letter, modifying it in whatever ways you wish.

11.2. Suppose that you are looking at a star, say Sirius, on a dark night. Astronomers tell us that light waves started to travel from Sirius many years ago. After all that time they reach Earth, strike your retinas, and cause you to say you are seeing Sirius. But the star about which they convey information to you, the star that existed at the time the rays began their journey, may no longer exist. To say that you see what may no longer exist is absurd. Therefore, whatever you see, it is not Sirius.[5] Is this reasoning sound? Explain your thinking thoroughly.

11.3. Oscar and Felix are having a discussion.

> OSCAR: I'll prove to you there's no such thing as a pile of sand.
> FELIX: That's ridiculous. You can't do it.
> OSCAR: Oh yeah? Listen carefully. A single grain of sand is not a pile, right?
> FELIX: Right, so what?
> OSCAR: If we add another grain of sand, that's still not a pile, right?
> FELIX: OK, OK. Get on with it.
> OSCAR: If we add another grain, and another, up to 10 million and beyond, we'd never reach a point where *no pile of sand* is converted to *pile of sand*. So there's no such thing as a pile of sand.

What should Felix say next to prove Oscar wrong?

APPLICATIONS

11.1. Cigarette smoking is now known to be a causative factor in a number of serious diseases and a contributing factor in health care cost increases and lost productivity in business. Yet smoking continues to be attractive to many people, including many teenagers. Identify and solve this problem; then refine your best solution as explained in the chapter.

11.2. Hundreds of thousands of homeless people live on the streets of America's cities, finding temporary shelter in abandoned buildings, in parks, under bridges, and in alleys. Their numbers include alcoholics, drug addicts, derelicts, and the mentally deficient who were released from institutions but have nowhere else to go. Lacking proper nutrition, they often have health problems. They are vulnerable to victimization by thugs, and in some cases they victimize others. Identify and solve this problem; then refine your best solution as explained in the chapter.

11.3. Most experts seem to agree that children from one-parent homes have more problems (including health problems) than children from two-parent homes.[6] Yet one-parent families are on the increase not only because of the high divorce rate but also because it has become fashionable among some unmarried middle-class women to have a child and raise it alone. Identify and solve this problem; then refine your best solution as explained in the chapter.

11.4. Several years ago you bought a house for $90,000, about twice the amount you could comfortably afford at the time. Because your business prospects seemed favorable, you expected to be in much better financial shape in a year or two. Unfortunately those prospects did not materialize. Now you'd like to sell the house (you can't afford the mortgage payments much longer), but the interest rates are so high you haven't been able to find a buyer. Identify your problem and solve it; then refine your best solution as explained in the chapter.

11.5. College athletes are supposed to be amateurs. That is, they are not allowed to receive money for performing their sport. The National Collegiate Athletic Association publishes a 322-page manual governing the way colleges recruit athletes, the academic requirements athletes must meet to remain eligible for play, and the limitations on financial and other assistance they may receive. But college athletics is big business; national rankings bring lucrative television payments to colleges and help finance costly educational programs. So colleges are tempted to ignore the NCAA rules. A decade ago Notre Dame's basketball coach publicly stated that at least seven colleges, and probably more, pay their star basketball players $10,000 a year under the table.[7] Identify and solve this problem; then refine your best solution as explained in the chapter.

11.6. You are the parent of two children, an 8-year-old daughter and a 6-year-old son. They love to watch television, but you believe that most programs are either a waste of time or promote harmful attitudes and values. Identify and solve this problem; then refine your best solution as explained in the chapter.

11.7. The Federal Communications Act of 1927 established in law that the airways belong to the public. Radio and television station licenses are supposedly granted only if the station's programming practices serve the public interest. Yet the practice of interrupting programs every 10 minutes with commercials that all too often assault the senses and insult the minds of viewers is, in the judgment of most people, decidedly not a service to the public. Identify and solve this problem; then refine your best solution as explained in the chapter.

11.8. Professor Danielle Murphy teaches literature at a small liberal arts college. She begins every term hoping to do little lecturing and to devote the larger part of each class period to class discussion. Yet she is invariably disappointed with the students' response. No matter what the assigned work of literature, only one or two students will volunteer their comments, and discussion quickly fizzles out. The rest of the class sit and stare at their desks or cast nervous glances at the clock. Identify and solve Professor Murphy's problem; then refine your best solution as explained in the chapter.

GROUP DISCUSSION EXERCISE

Discuss the following issue with two or three of your classmates. Observe the guidelines to group discussion presented in Appendix B. Consider all sides of the matter and try to reach consensus. Be prepared to report your group's deliberations to the class, describing how your analysis proceeded, what questions were asked, and what agreements were reached. If differences of viewpoint remain unresolved, be prepared to report them objectively.

Mike Diana draws cartoons about child molestation, rape, necrophilia, cannibalism, mutilation, and murder and publishes them in his homemade magazine, *Boiled Angel*. He is just one of a substantial group of individuals who publish magazines that most people would find revolting.[8] What restrictions, if any, should there be on the publication and/or distribution of such magazines?

COMPOSITION OR SPEECH EXERCISE

Write a composition or, if your instructor specifies, a formal speech, presenting the view your group reached in the preceding group discussion exercise. (If you hold a dissenting view, present that instead.) Be sure to provide evidence that your view is the most reasonable one. Naturally your composition or speech will bear some resemblance to those of the other members of your group—you will have developed ideas as a team, so at least some of your ideas will be similar, even identical, to theirs. Don't be concerned about such similarities. Your composition or speech will be a unique effort if you (a) use supporting material from your own experience, observation, and research; (b) develop your own line of reasoning about that material; (c) employ your own ingenuity in designing an introduction and conclusion and in arranging the material in the body of your composition or speech; and (d) express your thoughts in your own words. For further guidance, consult the appropriate appendix—A for writing, B for speaking.

12

Evaluate Your
Argument on the Issue

Because your main objective in addressing an issue is not to find the most effective action but to determine the most reasonable *belief,* your main task in refining an issue is to evaluate your argument to be sure that it is free from error. There are two broad kinds of error to consider. The first affects the *validity* of the argument, the quality of the reasoning by which the conclusion is reached. The second affects the *truth* of the statements in the argument. A sound argument is not only valid but also true.

ERRORS AFFECTING VALIDITY

To determine an argument's validity, we must examine the entire argument. It is the relationship between the premises and the conclusion that make an argument valid or invalid. The logical principles governing the validity of arguments are the substance of *formal logic,* the area of logic concerned with the various forms of argument. Since a detailed treatment of formal logic is beyond the scope of this book,* we will focus on an essential error that commonly occurs in controversial issues: the *illegitimate conclusion.*

An illegitimate conclusion is one that does not follow logically from the premises preceding it. Before examining an illegitimate conclusion, let's first look at a legitimate one:

> Anything that shortens people's attention span harms their concentration. Television commercials shorten people's attention span. Therefore, television commercials harm people's concentration.

---

*For a brief introduction to the basic principles of formal logic, see Appendix C, "The Fundamentals of Logic."

This conclusion is legitimate because if anything that shortens people's attention span harms concentration, and if television commercials do shorten that span, they therefore must harm people's concentration. Commercials, after all, are a thing, so they fit in the *anything* specified in the first premise. When we are checking for the validity of the reasoning, remember, we are not checking for the truth of the premises or conclusion. That concern is a separate matter. Thus, even a ludicrous argument could be technically valid. Here is an example:

> Anything that gives people indigestion harms their concentration. Television commercials give people indigestion. Therefore, television commercials harm people's concentration.

Let's now look at some illegitimate conclusions and see what makes them so.

> All people who take courses significantly above their level of competency will surely fail. Samantha is taking a course well within her level of competency. Therefore, Samantha will surely pass.

Even if it were true that all people who take courses well above their competency level necessarily fail, this would not eliminate the possibility of other reasons for failure, reasons that apply to the competent as well as the incompetent. In other words, the first premise does not imply that *only* the incompetent will fail. Samantha may be extraordinarily proficient and still fail because she cuts classes and does not submit the required work.

Here is another example of an illegitimate conclusion:

> People who care about the environment will support the clean air bill now before Congress. Senator Boychik supports the clean air bill. Therefore, Senator Boychik cares about the environment.

The first premise of this argument says that people—all people*—who care about the environment will support the bill. However, it does not say that no one else will support the bill. Thus, it leaves open the possibility that some who do not care will support it, perhaps for political reasons. Which group Boychik belongs to is unclear. Therefore, the conclusion is illegitimate.

Illegitimate conclusions can also occur in hypothetical (if-then) reasoning. Of course, not all hypothetical reasoning is faulty. Here is an example of a valid hypothetical argument:

> *If* a person uses a gun in the commission of a crime, *then* he should be given an additional penalty. Simon used a gun in the commission of a crime. *Therefore,* Simon should be given an additional penalty.

---

*Though the premise says *people*, not *all people*, the sense of *all* is clearly conveyed. Usually, when no qualifying word or phrase—such as *some, many, the citizens of Peoria*—is present, we presume the universal *all* is intended.

The first premise sets forth the conditions under which the additional penalty should be applied. The second presents a case that fits those conditions. The conclusion that the penalty should apply in that case is legitimate. Here, in contrast, is an illegitimate conclusion:

> *If* a person uses a gun in the commission of a crime, *then* he should be given an additional penalty. Simon was given an additional penalty for his crime. *Therefore,* Simon used a gun in the commission of the crime.

Here the first premise sets forth one condition for an additional penalty. It does not *exclude* the possibility of other conditions carrying additional penalties. For this reason, we have no way of knowing whether Simon's additional penalty was for using a gun or for some other reason.

The following is another example of an illegitimate conclusion:

> If a person has great wealth, he can get elected. Governor Mindless got elected. Therefore, Governor Mindless has great wealth.

The first premise of this argument specifies one way of getting elected. There may be others. Did Governor Mindless get elected in this or in some other way? We can't be sure from the information given, so the conclusion is illegitimate.

Occasionally an illegitimate conclusion in hypothetical arguments takes a slightly different form: the reversal of conditions. The following argument illustrates this:

> If the death penalty is reinstated, the crime rate will drop. Therefore, if the rate of crime is reduced, the death penalty will be reinstated.

The error here is reversing what is not necessarily reversible. The clear implication in the first premise is that there is a cause-and-effect relationship between the reinstatement of the death penalty and a drop in the crime rate. To reverse that relationship makes the effect the cause, and vice versa. Such a reversal does not logically follow.

A SPECIAL PROBLEM: THE HIDDEN PREMISE

An argument's expression in ordinary discussion or writing is not always as precise as our examples. The sentence order may vary; the conclusion, for example, may come first. In place of the word *therefore,* a variety of signal words may be used. *So* and *it follows that* are two common substitutes. Sometimes no signal word is used. These variations make the evaluation of an argument a little more time consuming, but they pose no real difficulty. There is, however, a variation that can cause real difficulty: the *hidden premise.* A hidden premise, known in formal logic as an *enthymeme,* is a premise implied but not stated. Here is an example of an argument with a hidden premise:

ARGUMENT WITH PREMISE HIDDEN	SAME ARGUMENT, PREMISE EXPRESSED
Liberty means responsibility. That is why most men dread it.	Liberty means responsibility. Most men dread responsibility. Therefore, most men dread liberty.

There is nothing necessarily wrong with having a hidden premise. It is not an error. In the preceding case, the hidden-premise argument is from the writing of George Bernard Shaw. In either of the forms shown, the argument is perfectly valid. The only problem with hidden premises is that they obscure the reasoning behind the argument and make evaluation difficult. Accordingly, whenever a premise is hidden, it should be identified and expressed before the argument is evaluated.

Here are several more examples of hidden-premise arguments. Note how much easier it is to grasp the reasoning when the hidden premise is expressed.

PREMISE HIDDEN	PREMISE EXPRESSED
Prostitution is immoral, so it should be illegal.	Everything immoral should be illegal. Prostitution is immoral. Therefore, it should be illegal.
Newspapers are a threat to democracy because they have too much power.	All agencies that have too much power are a threat to democracy. Newspapers have too much power. Therefore, newspapers are a threat to democracy.
If Brewster Bland is a good family man, he'll make a good senator.	If a person is a good family man, he'll make a good senator. Brewster Bland is a good family man. Therefore, Brewster Bland will make a good senator.
AIDS is a costly and at this time terminal disease. Therefore, health insurance companies should be able to suspend coverage when people contract AIDS.	Insurance companies should not have to provide coverage for costly, terminal diseases. AIDS is a costly and at this time terminal disease. Therefore, health insurance companies should be able to suspend coverage when people contract AIDS.
Many celebrities believe that a 35,000-year-old spirit entity known	If many celebrities believe something, it is by that fact worthy

as Ramtha speaks through channeler J. Z. Knight. Therefore, this belief is worthy of respect.

of respect. Many celebrities believe that a 35,000-year-old spirit entity known as Ramtha speaks through channeler J. Z. Knight. Therefore, this belief is worthy of respect.

EVALUATING COMPLEX ARGUMENTS

Not all arguments can be expressed in two premises and one conclusion. Many are complex, involving a network of premises and conclusions. Moreover, some of these may be unexpressed, like the hidden premises we have discussed. Consider, for example, this argument:

> People who lack control over their sexual urges are a threat to society, so homosexuals should be banned from the teaching profession.

At first glance, only one premise may seem to be missing from this argument. Actually it is a complex argument and much more is missing. Here is how it would be expressed if nothing were omitted:

> People who lack control over their sexual urges are a threat to society. Homosexuals lack control over their sexual urges. Therefore, homosexuals are a threat to society. Furthermore, people who are a threat to society should be banned from the teaching profession. Homosexuals are a threat to society. Therefore, homosexuals should be banned from the teaching profession.

Here are two more examples of complex arguments. In each case, the argument is first expressed in the abbreviated form often used in everyday conversation and then in its complete logical form.

1. *Abbreviated:* The government wastes billions of tax dollars, so I'm not obligated to report all my income.
   Complete: The government wastes billions of tax dollars. Wasting tax dollars increases every individual's tax burden unnecessarily. I am a taxpayer, so the government is increasing my tax burden unnecessarily. Furthermore, when the government increases the taxpayers' tax burden unnecessarily, the taxpayers are not obligated to report all their income. Therefore, I'm not obligated to report all my income.

2. *Abbreviated:* The communications and entertainment media have more influence on young people than parents and teachers, so the media are more responsible for teenage pregancy, drug and alcohol abuse, violence, and academic deficiency.
   Complete: The agency that has the greatest influence on young people's attitudes and values bears the greatest responsibility for the behavior caused by those attitudes and values. Although parents and teachers used to have the greatest influence on young people's attitudes and values, the media now have a greater influence. In addition, the messages

disseminated by the media generally oppose the lessons of home and school. Typical media messages—that each person creates his or her own reality and morality, that self is more important than others, that restraint of one's urges is harmful, and that feelings are a more reliable guide than thought—tend to lead to impulsiveness and the demand for instant gratification and create or aggravate such problems as teenage pregnancy, drug and alcohol abuse, violence, and academic deficiency. Therefore, the communications and entertainment media bear the greatest responsibility for these problems.

In a world of complex realities, a world of controversial issues with no simple solutions, complex arguments are often unavoidable. Yet such arguments are frequently flawed precisely because of their complexity. For this reason, we must exercise special care in identifying all the premises and conclusions our arguments contain.

ERRORS AFFECTING TRUTH

Unlike validity errors, errors affecting truth are not necessarily found in the relationship between premises and conclusion. In fact, in many cases these errors are confined to a single premise. That fact, however, does not make them less harmful to an argument. (Remember that for an argument to be sound, it must not only be valid but true as well.) It merely means that they are usually found by testing the accuracy of the premises and the conclusion *as individual statements*, rather than by examining the reasoning that links them.

There are numerous errors affecting truth. The first and most obvious error of this kind is simple factual inaccuracy. If we have investigated the issue properly and have taken care to verify our evidence wherever possible, such errors should not be present. We will therefore limit our consideration to the more subtle and most common errors:

- Either/or thinking
- Avoiding the issue
- Overgeneralizing
- Oversimplifying
- Double standard
- Shifting the burden of proof
- Irrational appeal

Either/Or Thinking

This error consists of believing that only two choices are possible in situations in which there are more than two choices. A common example of either/or thinking occurs in the creationism-versus-evolution debate. Both sides are often guilty of the error. "The biblical story of creation and scientific evolution cannot both be right," they say. "It must be either one or the other." They are mistaken. There is a third possibility: that there is a God who created everything but did so through evolution. Whether this position is the best one may, of course, be disputed. But it is an error to ignore its existence.

Either/or thinking undoubtedly occurs because in controversy the spotlight is usually on the most obvious positions, those most clearly in conflict. Any other position, particularly a subtle one, is ignored. Such thinking is best overcome by conscientiously searching out all possible views before choosing one. If you find either/or thinking in your position on an issue, ask yourself, "Why must it be one view or the other? Why not both or neither?"

Avoiding the Issue

The attorney was just beginning to try the case in court when her associate learned that their key witness had changed his mind about testifying. The associate handed the attorney this note: "Have no case—abuse the other side." That is the form avoiding the issue often takes: deliberately attacking the person in the hope that the issue will be forgotten. It happens with lamentable frequency in politics. The issue being debated may be, for example, a particular proposal for tax reform. One candidate will say, "The reason my opponent supports this proposal is clear—it is a popular position to take. His record is filled with examples of jumping on the bandwagon to gain voter approval. . . ." And so on. Of course, what the candidate says may be true of the opponent, and if it is, then it would surely be relevant to the issue of whether the opponent deserves to be elected. But it is not relevant to the issue at hand, the tax-reform proposal.

Avoiding the issue may not necessarily be motivated by deceit, as the preceding errors are. It may occur because of unintentional misunderstanding or because of an unconscious slip to something irrelevant. But it is still error, regardless of its innocence. To check your reasoning, look closely at each issue and ask whether your solution really responds to it. If it doesn't, make it do so.

Overgeneralizing

Overgeneralizing means taking a valid idea and extending it beyond the limits of reasonableness. Here are some examples:

- Women who have abortions are poor and unmarried.
- Convicted criminals must be imprisoned or the public safety will be threatened.
- Women are athletically inferior to men and more emotional than rational.
- Men are coarse and insensitive, inept at cooking and cleaning, and unable to give affection freely.

Each of these statements could be true at times. That is, we could find examples of poor, unmarried women who have had abortions, convicted criminals whose release would endanger the public, and so on. Yet in each case we could also find examples that do not fit the assertion. That is what makes these statements overgeneralizations. (The fact that your overgeneralizations do not take the most extreme form, stereotypes, which we discussed in Chapter 3, should not make you complacent about correcting them. They still mar your arguments, usually significantly.)

To find overgeneralizations in your arguments, be alert to any idea in which *all* or *none* is stated or *implied*. (That is the case in each of the preceding four examples.) Occasionally you will find a situation in which *all* or *none* is justified, but in the great majority of cases critical evaluation will reveal it is not valid. To correct overgeneralizations, decide what level of generalization is appropriate and modify your statement accordingly. For example, in the four cases discussed, you would consider these possibilities:

Some Many Most All A specific number	. . . of women who have abortions are poor and unmarried.
Some Many Most All Certain types	. . . of convicted criminals must be imprisoned or the public safety will be threatened.
Some Many Most All In certain cultural conditions	. . . women are athletically inferior to men and more emotional than rational.
Some Many Most All In certain cultural conditions	. . . men are coarse and insensitive, inept at cooking and cleaning, and unable to give affection freely.

Oversimplifying

There is nothing wrong with simplifying a complex reality to understand it better or to communicate it more clearly to others. Teachers simplify all the time, especially in grade school. Simplification is only a problem when it goes too far—when it goes beyond making complex matters clear and begins to distort them. At that point it ceases to represent reality and *mis*represents it. Such oversimplification is often found in reasoning about causes and effects. Here are three examples of this error:

- The cause of the economic recession in the early 1980s was excessive welfare spending.
- The American Nazi party has a beneficial effect on the intellectual life of the country. It reminds people of the constitutional rights of free speech and assembly.
- A return to public executions, shown on prime-time television, would make crime less glamorous and thus in time make us a less brutal, more civilized society.

These statements contain an element of truth (many authorities would say a very small element). Yet they do not fairly or accurately represent the reality described. They focus on one cause or effect as if it were the only one. In fact there are others, some of them significant.

To find oversimplifications in your arguments, ask what important aspects of the issue your statements ignore. To correct oversimplifications, decide what expression of the matter best reflects the reality without distorting it.

Double Standard

Applying a double standard means judging the same action or point of view differently depending on who does or holds it. It can often be recognized by the use of sharply contrasting terms of description or classification. Thus, we may attack a government assistance program as a welfare handout if the money goes to people we don't know or don't identify with but defend it as a necessary subsidy if it goes to our friends. Similarly, if one country crosses another's border with a military force we may approve the action as a "securing of borders" or condemn it as "naked aggression," depending on our feelings toward the countries involved.

Be careful not to confuse the double standard with the legitimate judgment of cases according to their circumstances. It is never an error to acknowledge real differences. Accordingly, if you find you have judged a particular case differently from other cases of the same kind, look closely at the circumstances. If they warrant different judgments, you have not been guilty of applying a double standard. However, if they do not warrant it—if your reasoning shows partiality toward one side—you have committed the error and should revise your judgment to make it fair.

Shifting the Burden of Proof

This error consists of making an assertion and then demanding that the opposition prove it false. This is an unreasonable demand. The person making the assertion has the burden of supporting it. Though the opposing side may accept the challenge of disproving it, it has no obligation to do so. Suppose, for example, you said to a friend, "Mermaids must exist," your friend disputed you, and you responded, "Unless you can disprove their existence, I am justified in believing in them." You have shifted the burden of proof. Having made the assertion about mermaids, you have the obligation to support it. To overcome this error in your arguments, identify all the assertions you have made but not supported and provide adequate support for them. (If you find you cannot support an assertion, withdraw it.)

Irrational Appeal

This error bases your position on an appeal that is unreasonable. The most common forms of irrational appeal are the appeal to *common practice* ("Everyone does it"), the appeal to *tradition* ("We mustn't change what is long established"), the appeal to *fear* ("Awful things could happen"), the appeal to *moderation* ("Let's not offend anyone"), and the appeal to *authority* ("We have no business questioning the experts"). Of course, there is nothing necessarily wrong with defending common practice or tradition, warning about dangers, urging moderation, or supporting the views of experts. It is only when these appeals are used as a substitue for careful reasoning—when they aim for an audience's emotions rather than their minds—that they are misused. To correct irrational appeals, refocus your argument on the specific merits of your ideas.

STEPS IN EVALUATING AN ARGUMENT

The following four steps are an efficient way to apply what you learned in this chapter—in other words, to evaluate your argument and overcome any errors in validity or truth that it may contain.

1. State your argument fully, as clearly as you can. Be sure to identify any hidden premises and, if the argument is complex, to express all parts of it.
2. Examine your argument for validity errors; consider the reasoning that occurs from premises to conclusion. Determine whether your conclusion is legitimate or illegitimate.
3. Examine each part of your argument for errors affecting truth. (To be sure this examination is not perfunctory, play devil's advocate and *challenge* the argument, asking pointed questions about it, taking nothing for granted.) Note any instances of either/or thinking, avoiding the issue, overgeneralizing, oversimplifying, double standard, shifting the burden of proof, or irrational appeal. In addition, check to be sure that the argument reflects the pro and con arguments and is relevant to the scenarios you produced earlier. (See Chapter 9.)
4. Revise your argument to eliminate any errors you find. The changes you will have to make in your argument will depend on the kinds of errors you find. Sometimes only minor revision is called for—the adding of a simple qualification, for example, or the substitution of a rational appeal for an irrational one. Occasionally, however, the change required is more dramatic. You may, for example, find your argument so

flawed that the only appropriate action is to abandon it altogether and embrace a different argument. On those occasions, you may be tempted to pretend your argument is sound and hope no one will notice the errors. Resist that hope. It is foolish and dishonest to invest time in refining a view that you know is unsound.

To illustrate how you would follow these steps, we will now examine two issues.

THE CASE OF PARENTS VERSUS BROADCASTERS

You have read a number of articles lately about protests over television commercials and programming. The protesters are mostly parents of school-age children. They have spoken out either individually or through organizations they belong to, expressing concern that the values taught by school and home are being undermined by television. Specific complaints include the emphasis on sex and violence in television programming, the appeal to self-indulgence and instant gratification in commercials, and the promotion of "if it feels good, do it" in both programming and commercials. The protestors are urging concerned citizens to write to the companies that sponsor programs and threaten to boycott their products unless these offenses are eliminated.

Let's say you identify the main issue here as "Are parents justified in making such demands on companies?" After considering the matter and producing a number of ideas, you decide that the best answer is "No, they are not justified" and state your argument as follows:

> Only those who pay for television programming and advertisements are entitled to have a say about them. The companies alone pay. Therefore, the companies alone are entitled to have a say.

You examine your argument for validity errors and find that it contains none. Then you examine it for errors of truth or relevance. Playing devil's advocate, you ask, "*Do* the companies alone pay?" "How exactly is payment handled?" Not being sure, you ask a professor of business and learn that the sponsorship of television programs and other advertising are part of the overall product budget. You also learn that these costs, along with other costs of raw materials, manufacturing and packaging, warehousing and delivery, are reflected in the price of the product.

"Wait a minute," you reason. "If programming and other advertising costs are reflected in the price of the product, that means consumers are paying for every television show and every commercial. And if that's the case, parents (and other consumers) *are* entitled to have a say, make demands, and threaten boycotts." And so you revise your argument accordingly.

> Those who pay for television programming and commercials are entitled to have a say about them. Consumers pay. Therefore, consumers are entitled to have a say.°

THE CASE OF THE RETARDED GIRLS

This case is one we encountered earlier, in Application 2.7h. The parents of three severely retarded girls, you may remember, brought court action seeking the legal right to make the decision to sterilize the girls. The larger issue here continues to be controversial. Let's say you express it as follows: "Should anyone have the right to make such a significant decision for another person?" After investigating the issue and producing a number of ideas, including the major pro and con arguments and several relevant scenarios, you state your argument thus:

> Those who have the child's interest at heart can be expected to judge wisely if they are properly informed. Most parents or guardians have the child's interest at heart. Therefore, most parents or guardians can be expected to judge wisely if they are properly informed. Furthermore, knowing whether the child will ever be able to meet the responsibilities of parenthood constitutes being properly informed. A qualified doctor can tell parents or guardians whether the child will ever be able to meet the responsibilities of parenthood. Therefore, a qualified doctor can properly inform parents.

You examine your argument (a complex one that cannot be expressed adequately in two premises and a conclusion) and decide that it is valid and true.

WARM-UP EXERCISES

12.1. Willy Joe and Joe Willy are having a conversation of sorts:

> WILLY JOE: There's no such thing as reality, man.
> JOE WILLY: No way . . . like, I mean . . . it makes no sense that way. . . . No, there's no way.
> WILLY JOE: OK, man, you say there's a reality. So describe it to me.
> JOE WILLY: Um . . . ah . . . uh. . . .
> WILLY JOE: You can't describe it, so it can't exist. Case closed.

°Such a formal, logical ($a + b = c$) statement of your argument is essential when you are evaluating your reasoning. However, it is seldom appropriate for a central-idea statement in a piece of writing. In this case, your central-idea statement might be "Because consumers pay for television programming and commercials, they are entitled to make demands and threaten boycotts."

How would you answer Willy Joe? Explain your thinking carefully.

12.2. One thing, at least, is indisputable about rock music: It produces groups with very creative names. But perhaps you can do even better. Think of as many creative names as you can for a rock group, names you've never heard before.

12.3. In Strangeville it was decided that the local barber should shave all those, and only those, who did not shave themselves. Did the barber shave himself? Explain your thinking thoroughly.

APPLICATIONS

2.1. Check each of the following arguments to be sure that it contains no hidden premises and, if it is a complex argument, that all parts are expressed. Revise each, as necessary, to make the expression complete. Then evaluate the argument and decide whether it is sound. Explain your judgment.

   a. Having great wealth is a worthy goal because it is difficult to attain and many famous people have pursued it.
   b. Low grades on a college transcript are a handicap in the job market, so teachers who grade harshly are doing students a disservice.
   c. The Bible can't be relevant to today's problems—it was written many centuries ago and is filled with archaic phrasing.
   d. It is dishonest to pretend to have knowledge one does not have, so plagiarism is more virtue than vice.
   e. The credit card habit promotes careless spending, particularly among young people. Therefore, credit card companies should not be permitted to issue credit cards to anyone under age 21.
   f. No one who ever attended this college achieved distinction after graduation. Marvin attends this college. Therefore, Marvin will not achieve distinction after graduation.
   g. Drug dealing should not be a crime because it does not directly harm others or force them to harm themselves.
   h. A mature person is self-directing, so parents who make all their children's decisions for them are doing their offspring a disservice.
   i. There's no point in attending Professor Drone's class; all he does is lecture in a boring monotone.
   j. Power must be evil because it can corrupt people.
   k. If the theory of evolution is true, as scientific evidence overwhelmingly suggests, a human being is nothing more than an ape.
   l. Rock musicians are contributing to the decline of language by singing in a slurred, mumbling manner.
   m. If emphasis on error paralyzes effort, this college is paying my English professor to make it impossible for me to learn English.
   n. Nuclear power is a threat to world peace. Nuclear energy stations generate nuclear power. So nuclear energy stations are a threat to world peace.
   o. Lew Fairman is the best candidate for governor because he is in favor of the death penalty.
   p. All religious authorities are concerned about the dangers of nuclear war. All politicians are concerned about the dangers of nuclear war. Therefore, all politicians are religious authorities.

q. The government should undertake a comprehensive censorship program because censorship eliminates undesirable books and films from the market.

r. If the Social Security system is further weakened, the elderly will have to fear poverty. Therefore, if the Social Security system is not further weakened, the elderly will not have to fear poverty.

s. Challenging other people's opinions is a sign of intolerance, so debating courses have no place on a college campus.

t. It's ridiculous to think that there will be fewer deaths if we ban handguns. Handguns don't kill people; *people* kill people.

u. The antiabortionists say that the fetus is human, but they have not proved it. Therefore, they have no reasonable basis for opposing abortion.

v. We must either defeat communism or be defeated by it. To be defeated by communism is unthinkable. Therefore, we must defeat communism.

w. There is no way that anyone can ever deserve to live better than his neighbors, so capitalism is an immoral economic system.

x. If an expectant mother drinks, smokes, takes drugs, or fails to get proper rest, she may damage her unborn child. Therefore, if an expectant mother does these things and her child is born with a defect or ailment that can be traced to them, the mother should face criminal charges.

y. Custom is a form of folk wisdom. In some parts of the world it is customary for "bride buyers" to buy (or sometimes kidnap) young women from their parents and sell them to men looking for wives. Even though we might find this practice distasteful, it would be morally wrong for us to object to others practicing it.

12.2. Identify, investigate (as necessary), and resolve each of the following issues. Be sure you do not just accept your reasoning uncritically. Evaluate it by using the approach explained on pages 173–174. Then modify your argument as necessary and decide how you could most effectively demonstrate its soundness.

a. Radar detectors give speeders a warning so that they can slow down in time to avoid getting a ticket. Some people believe they should be banned because they help people break the law. Others disagree, arguing that they should be able to protect themselves from the sneaky practices of highway patrols.

b. One proposal for combating the drug problem is government seizure of the property (cars, homes, etc.) of convicted drug dealers. One objection to this proposal is that such seizure could violate the rights of innocent parties, such as spouses and children.

c. Since smoking is not permitted at one's desk in many companies, significant time is presumably lost in unauthorized smoking breaks in restrooms or outside of buildings. A company could save itself that time, and the money it represents, by establishing a policy of hiring only nonsmokers. Predictably, of course, some people would consider such a policy discriminatory.

d. London test-tube baby pioneer Dr. Robert Edwards and a colleague announced that they planned to freeze spare embryos and donate them to infertile women. They explained that their test-tube technique involved the removal of eggs from a woman's ovary, fertilization with the husband's sperm, and reimplantation of one of the many embryos that result. Instead of destroying the unused embryos, they proposed to offer them (with the mother's permission) to infertile women at a later time. Freezing the embryos would have permitted implantation at the best moment in the woman's menstrual cycle. A controversy arose over the legal and moral implications of the plan.[1]

e. A number of states and many foreign countries have programs forcing alcoholics to receive treatment. A person arrested for drunken driving, for example, is required to receive treatment as a stipulation of probation. Or a welfare recipient will be threatened with loss of benefits if he or she does not comply. The programs range from individual therapy to group therapy to the taking of such drugs as Antabuse (which can make a person violently ill if he or she drinks within three days after ingesting it). There is sharp disagreement over such programs. Many feel they are a violation of civil rights.[2]

f. In recent decades tens of thousands of aliens, including many illegal aliens, have come to the United States. The numbers from Mexico, Cuba, and Latin America have been especially great. The traditional attitude in this country has been to accept anyone who wishes to flee poverty or oppression abroad and build a new life here. Many still feel that way. Yet others believe that stricter limits should be imposed, particularly because today's immigrants often come from an entirely different culture and tend to resist assimilation.

g. Video games are not welcome everywhere. At least one college administration banned them from campus out of fear that students would take too much time from their studies to play them. Many people, of course, regard that decision as unreasonable.

GROUP DISCUSSION EXERCISE

Discuss the following issue with two or three of your classmates. Observe the guidelines to group discussion presented in Appendix B. Consider all sides of the matter and try to reach consensus. Be prepared to report your group's deliberations to the class, describing how your analysis proceeded, what questions were asked, and what agreements were reached. If differences of viewpoint remain unresolved, be prepared to report them objectively.

A woman in Hastings, Nebraska, was charged with felony child abuse for drinking so heavily during her pregnancy that her daughter was born two months prematurely. (The daughter survived and was placed with foster parents.) However, a district judge dismissed the charge because the state's child abuse laws don't apply to a fetus.[3] Should it be a crime for a woman to drink heavily during a pregnancy? To smoke heavily? If so, what exactly should the crime be? Examine this issue thoroughly, being sure to consider the implications of the various answers that might be given.

COMPOSITION OR SPEECH EXERCISE

Write a composition or, if your instructor specifies, a formal speech, presenting the view your group reached in the preceding group discussion exercise. (If you hold a dissenting view, present that instead.) Be sure to provide evidence that your view is the most reasonable one. Naturally your composition or speech will bear some resemblance to those of the other members of your group—you will have developed ideas as a team, so at least some of your ideas will be similar, even identical, to theirs. Don't be concerned about such similarities. Your composition or speech will be a unique effort if you (a) use supporting material from your own experience, observation, and research; (b) develop your own line of reasoning about that material; (c) employ your own ingenuity in designing an introduction and conclusion and in arranging the material in the body of your composition or speech; and (d) express your thoughts in your own words. For further guidance, consult the appropriate appendix—A for writing, B for speaking.

13

Refine Your Resolution of the Issue

Not all issues require the treatment described in this chapter. In many cases, your analysis of an issue will be complete when you evaluate your argument on the issue and, if necessary, revise it to overcome deficiencies. For example, the issue may concern whether General Dwight Eisenhower, as supreme commander of allied forces in Europe, made a tactical error in waiting for the Soviet army before advancing into Berlin. Once you have found the answer that is most reasonable in light of the evidence, nothing more need be done.

On the other hand, in many other cases you will not be content with deciding what belief is most reasonable; you will wish to consider what action should be taken on that belief. If you were to decide, for example, that television programming and commercials have a seriously negative effect on young people's intellectual development, you would probably consider what should be done to eliminate or counteract that effect. And if you came to believe that handgun control would significantly reduce the number of lives lost in accidents, you might devise a plan to get handgun legislation passed in Congress.

This chapter concerns the latter kinds of cases, those in which your positions on the issues prompt you to recommend further action. In such cases, you must decide what exactly should be done, what difficulties might arise in doing it, and how those difficulties could best be overcome, in much the same manner as you would proceed in refining your solutions to problems. To appreciate the importance of these decisions, you need only reflect on the fact that an ill-considered plan of implementation can make even the most reasonable belief appear deficient.

STEP 1: DECIDING WHAT ACTION SHOULD BE TAKEN

This step consists of asking and answering appropriate questions. Though not all of the following questions will apply in every case, most of them will apply in the majority of cases.

- What exactly is to be done?

- How is it to be done? (If, for example, it is to be done in stages, specify the stages. If a special procedure is needed, detail that procedure.)
- By whom is it to be done?
- Will those doing it volunteer for the job or be enlisted? If enlisted, how will this be accomplished?
- Will these individuals need to be trained? If so, what will the training consist of ? How, when, and by whom will the training be given?
- When is the action to take place? (According to what timetable?)
- How will this action be financed? Publicized?

STEP 2: RECOGNIZING AND OVERCOMING DIFFICULTIES

At first consideration, you may be tempted to regard your plan of action as foolproof. That view is unwise because no matter how carefully a plan has been conceived, it is likely to encounter difficulties. By acknowledging this fact and making an effort to identify those difficulties in advance, you increase the chances for successful implementation. Following are four approaches to identifying potential difficulties.

1. Check for common kinds of imperfections, such as these:

   Safety: Does your plan create any danger for those who use it or those for whom it is used?

   Convenience: Will the plan be awkward to implement?

   Efficiency: Will the plan involve significant delays?

   Economy: Is the plan too expensive to implement?

   Simplicity: Is the plan unnecessarily complicated?

   Compatibility: Will the plan clash with any other procedure it should harmonize with?

   Legality: Does the plan conform to the law or at least include provision for changing a law with which it conflicts?

   Morality: Does any aspect of the plan violate one or more ethical principles? (See Chapter 2.)

2. Compare your plan of action with competing ones. If there is a competing plan, compare it with yours. Determine whether the competing plan has any worthwhile features yours lacks.

3. Consider what changes your plan will cause in the existing situation. List all the changes that would occur if your plan were implemented, taking care not to overlook any significant ones. Note any undesirable changes.

4. Consider the effects your plan will have on people, including not only physical effects but also moral, emotional, intellectual, and financial effects. Be sure to consider remote effects as well as proximate ones, and subtle as well as obvious ones.

After you have used these four approaches and identified the difficulties that might arise in implementing your plan, consider how the difficulties might most effectively be overcome. As with all idea production, defer judgment and extend your effort to produce a variety of ideas for overcoming each difficulty. Then select the best ideas and modify your plan accordingly.

To see how these steps would be applied in actual cases, let's examine two issues. The first is the case of the retarded girls, discussed in Chapter 12.

THE CASE OF THE RETARDED GIRLS

You might work out your plan as follows: Parents of a severely retarded child should be permitted to have the child sterilized only if a qualified physician certifies that the child will never be able to meet the responsibilities of parenthood.

In considering the possible negative effects of your plan, you would imagine a variety of situations that might arise if the plan were implemented. Among those situations would be the following:

1. The parents have strange notions about sexuality and are obsessed with the fear that their child will bring shame on them. They pressure the doctor to certify that their child will never be able to fulfill parental responsibilities even though that is not really the case. The doctor is qualified but unscrupulous—as long as the fee is paid, the doctor is willing to certify anything.
2. The parents are responsible and the doctor is not only qualified but above reproach morally. The decision is made to sterilize the child at age 4. Several years later medical science finds a way to overcome the child's retardation. The child becomes normal, but the sterilization cannot be reversed.

To prevent the first situation from occurring, you would revise your plan to specify that certification be made by a board of physicians, rather than a single physician. You might also decide the composition of the board. (All surgeons? One or more psychologists? An authority on mental retardation?) The second situation, unfortunately, is not entirely preventable; nevertheless, the chance of its occurring can be minimized by stipulating that no sterilization will be permitted before the onset of puberty.

SHOULD CHILDREN PLEDGE ALLEGIANCE?

From time to time the issue of pledging allegiance to the flag is revived and debate rages around the United States. One highly publicized occasion was during the 1988 presidential campaign. The issue was expressed as this:

"Should public school students be required to recite the pledge of allegiance in unison at the start of each day?" Let's assume that after careful analysis, and some revision of your initial view, you reasoned as follows:

> A system of government built on respect for the essential dignity and the corresponding rights of every human being deserves the allegiance of its citizens. Whatever its lapses of application may be, the United States is built on respect for the essential dignity and the corresponding rights of every human being. Therefore, the United States deserves the allegiance of its citizens. Furthermore, any effort to develop in citizens the understanding and appreciation that underlie such allegiance is acceptable as long as it does not violate the dignity of the individual or cause him or her to compromise personal beliefs. Unfortunately, requiring public school students to recite the pledge of allegiance in school does in some cases cause them to compromise their personal beliefs or be subjected to abuse.° Therefore this requirement is not acceptable.

Because your argument does not merely reject the required pledge but also affirms the value of allegiance and the cultivation of the understanding and appreciation that underlie allegiance, you would probably feel it was appropriate to recommend action on the issue. Accordingly, you might decide that school districts should mandate that teachers begin each day with a period of silence for students to reflect on what they owe their country and their fellow citizens for the blessing of living in this country. Further details of your idea could include the provision of statewide guidelines for the conduct of this period of reflection and a dissemination of these guidelines to the public to avoid any misunderstanding.

In examining this plan for imperfections and other difficulties, you might decide that though it would be noncontroversial, it would not accomplish its purpose. Students might use the time to think about their social life, personal problems, and so on. And even if they used it as intended, there would be no way to ensure that their reflection helped them grow in understanding and appreciation.

In this case, your examination might well lead you to change your recommendation to one that holds greater promise. For example, you might recommend that one period a week (a homeroom period, perhaps) be set aside for a class discussion of the rights and responsibilities of living in a democracy. You might further specify that the focus of the discussion be on important historical incidents that dramatize those rights and responsibilities, or timely problems and issues.

°In the 1930s hundreds of Jehovah's Witnesses were given the choice of reciting the pledge or being expelled from school. Because their religion holds that it is a form of blasphemy to recite the pledge, they chose expulsion. As a result, most suffered verbal abuse; some also suffered physical abuse. In Richwood, West Virginia, police forced nine Witnesses to swallow large amounts of castor oil after they refused to recite the pledge. Elsewhere Witnesses were attacked, tarred and feathered, and in one instance castrated. In Kennebunk, Maine, an angry mob of 2500 pillaged and set fire to the local Kingdom Hall. At first the Supreme Court upheld the rights of municipalities to require the pledge; then in 1943 it reversed itself.

A final note about refining your resolution of issues: Critical examination of a plan you are enthusiastic about requires real self-discipline. But that self-discipline is one of the qualities that distinguishes outstanding thinkers. Moreover, it is one of the principal reasons for their effectiveness in persuading others to endorse their views.

WARM-UP EXERCISES

13.1. Decide whether the following argument is sound. Explain your judgment thoroughly.

Unicorns must exist because no one has ever been able to prove that they don't.

13.2. Decide whether the following argument is sound. Explain your judgment thoroughly.

It is wrong to blame people for being born with a disease. Criminality is a disease some people are born with. Therefore, it is wrong to blame people for committing crimes.

13.3. A logician died and left this will: "I leave $1000 to be divided among my four daughters. Some of the money is to go to Annabel or Beatrice. I know that Beatrice and Clarissa are under Deirdre's thumb, so if any of the money goes to either of them, she is to have none. I want Beatrice and Clarissa treated alike—in fact, all four, or as many as possible, are to receive equal treatment." Who was the logician's favorite daughter, and what was the size of her legacy?[1] Explain your reasoning fully.

APPLICATIONS

Directions: Apply your creative and critical thinking to the following issues. After resolving each issue, decide whether it would be appropriate to take action on your belief. (In most cases, it would be appropriate.) Where action is called for, apply the two steps explained in this chapter.

13.1. Gambling is still illegal in most states. Yet by running lotteries, many state governments are themselves involved in gambling. These facts lead some people to conclude that all legal restrictions concerning gambling should be lifted. Others, of course, believe such legalization would be an error with serious consequences.

13.2. For decades Nobel laureate Linus Pauling and others have argued that vitamin C can limit the severity of, and taken in time even prevent, colds. This view has its supporters and its opponents. What is the truth about vitamin C? Does it perform as Pauling believes?

13.3. Carelessly used, fireworks can cause severe burns or blindness. That's why many states have outlawed their purchase by the general public. (In those states, fireworks displays on holidays are put on by professionals.) Some people believe that it is not a proper function of government to protect people from their own negligence nor to forbid anyone from buying what a relative few will misuse.

13.4. The concept of statutory rape is somewhat controversial. Essentially the concept means that below a certain age (18 in many states) a person, usually a girl, is not legally able to consent to sexual intercourse. Any adult who engages in sexual intercourse with a person below that age is technically guilty of rape and may be so charged. Some people believe the concept ridiculous, others that it is very sensible, and still others have no quarrel with the concept but disagree over the age.

13.5. Woodrow Collums stood at the foot of his brother's nursing home bed, raised his .38 caliber pistol, and pumped five bullets into his brother's chest and abdomen. The act was a mercy killing. Collums loved his brother and couldn't bear to see him lying helpless, unable to speak, his brain cells degenerating from Alzheimer's disease, slowly sliding toward death.[1] The case was widely publicized and excited anew the controversy over mercy killing.

13.6. Steven Michael White pleaded guilty to first-degree manslaughter in the strangulation death of Mary Collins. (Both were patients at a psychiatric center when the slaying occurred.) Then the Appellate Division of the New York Supreme Court overturned White's conviction on the grounds that when he confessed to the crime, he had not understood his right to remain silent.[2] There is much disagreement over whether this right is a reasonable one and, if so, how much weight it should be given in cases involving serious crimes.

13.7. Environmentalists in many cases believe the government has an obligation to protect plants and animals threatened with extinction. Others believe that if individuals want to take up that cause, that is their right but that it is not the government's business.

13.8. Some people believe that religious proselytizing (attempting to convert people to one's religion) is not only morally justifiable but a moral obligation. Others believe it is morally wrong.

13.9. For years a controversy has raged over pornography. Some people believe it affronts human decency and should be outlawed. Others regard it as quite harmless. Still others claim it is beneficial, that it helps people overcome their inhibitions and provides a means to ventilate strong sexual urges.

13.10. Controversy extends even to such a basic question as the nature of humankind. Are human beings essentially good and noble creatures who are corrupted by society in the course of their development? Or are they inherently violent and savage, their darker tendencies kept in check only by the threat of punishment? (There have been intelligent and educated supporters of each view.)

13.11. "Not guilty by reason of insanity." That decision would be heard no more if a majority of Americans had their way. A nationwide poll revealed that 87 percent of those surveyed believe too many people accused of murder are using the insanity plea to escape prison. Sixty-nine percent favor abolishing the insanity defense in murder cases.[3] Yet many knowledgeable people argue that the insanity defense is absolutely necessary. "How can a person be held guilty for an act he or she wasn't aware of committing, an act he or she had no control over?" they ask.

13.12. The idea of sex education classes in the upper grades and high school is not as explosive an issue as it was 10 or 15 years ago. But feelings still run high on both sides, some people believing that the teaching of sex belongs in the home, and others believing that many parents simply cannot do the job properly because of ignorance or embarrassment. They believe the school has an obligation to help students understand this vital aspect of life.

13.13. In 1981 Albert Goldman published a biography of Elvis Presley entitled *Elvis*. Many people objected to Goldman's negative descriptions of Presley's looks near the time of his death, home, manner of dress, relationship with his mother, and sexual habits. They felt Goldman had grievously wronged a man's good name and that the offense was compounded by the fact that Presley could no longer defend himself. Yet the law is on Goldman's side. It is impossible under the law as it stands to libel a deceased person. Only the living are afforded that legal protection.

13.14. After years of educating the children of illegal aliens without charge, the state of Texas passed a law cutting off the state's share of the cost of educating these children. Some localities announced that all children of illegal aliens would have to pay a tuition fee if they wished to enroll in the public schools. A group of parents asked the federal courts to intervene, and the U.S. Supreme Court decided, 5 to 4, that the Texas law was unconstitutional. In other words, the Court declared that Texas must provide free education for the children of people living there illegally.[4]

GROUP DISCUSSION EXERCISE

Discuss the following issue with two or three of your classmates. Observe the guidelines to group discussion presented in Appendix B. Consider all sides of the matter and try to reach consensus. Be prepared to report your group's deliberations to the class, describing how your analysis proceeded, what questions were asked, and what agreements were reached. If differences of viewpoint remain unresolved, be prepared to report them objectively.

> Violence has become epidemic in America. It can be found not only in the inner city, but in suburbia and rural areas as well. It has even invaded the schoolhouse. This was not the situation 50 years ago. What is responsible for this tragic change? And what can be done to make America safe again? (In deliberating these questions, make a special effort to consider responses other than those found in popular writing.)

COMPOSITION OR SPEECH EXERCISE

Write a composition or, if your instructor specifies, a formal speech, presenting the view your group reached in the preceding group discussion exercise. (If you hold a dissenting view, present that instead.) Be sure to provide evidence that your view is the most reasonable one. Naturally your composition or speech will bear some resemblance to those of the other members of your group—you will have developed ideas as a team, so at least some of your ideas will be similar, even identical, to theirs. Don't be concerned about such similarities. Your composition or speech will be a unique effort if you (a) use supporting material from your own experience, observation, and research; (b) develop your own line of reasoning about that material; (c) employ your own ingenuity in designing an introduction and conclusion and in arranging the material in the body of your composition or speech; and (d) express your thoughts in your own words. For further guidance, consult the appropriate appendix—A for writing, B for speaking.

PART 4

Communicate Your Ideas

14

Anticipate Negative Reactions

Boris Noodnik is just finishing his presentation to the Parent-Teachers' Association meeting: "To summarize my proposal, ladies and gentlemen, every teacher in our school system should make students write a composition of from one to three paragraphs every day of the school year and make helpful suggestions for improvement on each paper submitted. This is the only sensible way to have our students become proficient in their use of the written word." He pauses while the audience applauds his presentation and then asks, "Are there any questions?"

A woman in the back of the room raises her hand, Boris acknowledges her, and she stands to speak. "Mr. Noodnik," she begins, "I have done some rough calculating while you were making your presentation. Each teacher in our system has, on the average, 27 students in class. Figuring an average of 7 minutes to correct a composition (a conservative estimate), it will take each teacher an additional 15 hours a week to correct those papers. Teachers already do most of their planning for class in the evenings and on weekends. Just when do you expect them to get the time to correct all those papers?"

Boris's face reddens. "Uh-h-h, well, u-h-h-h, ma'am," he stammers, "ah, let me see . . . I'll have to check out those figures. I really don't know right this minute." Poor Boris. However viable his idea seemed to him, and perhaps to many in the audience, it is very likely dead now. And it's not really the woman in the audience who's responsible for its demise. Boris is. If he really wanted the audience to accept his proposal, he should have taken the trouble to anticipate any negative reactions and been prepared to answer them.

Although readers' reactions are less dramatic and less potentially embarrassing than the reaction of a live audience, they are no less real or critical. Readers may not be able to stand up and ask the hard questions in person, but they can still think them. Any audience, whether to the spoken or the written word, has a right to expect that those offering a solution to a problem or issue be prepared to answer objections that might be raised. If that expectation is not met, the audience quickly loses confidence in the speaker or author.

"Forewarned is forearmed," as the saying goes. This chapter will teach you how to determine in advance the reactions your solutions are likely to receive, so that you can plan a presentation incorporating your answers to those reactions.

HOW COMMON ARE NEGATIVE REACTIONS?

It is tempting to think that when you unveil your creative responses to problems and issues, people will shout, "Bravo! Magnifique!" and schedule ticker-tape parades for you. Unfortunately that is not the case for anyone, even the geniuses whom later generations honor.

When Nicolaus Copernicus presented his original idea that the sun, rather than the earth, is the center of the solar system, he was not applauded but scoffed at. Martin Luther responded to the idea by saying, "This fool wishes to reverse the entire scheme of astronomy." And John Calvin said mockingly, "Who will venture to place the authority of Copernicus above that of the Holy Spirit?" Thirty-one years later, Copernicus had the deathbed reward of seeing his ideas published—but even then they were not accepted.

When Galileo took up Copernicus's cause, he fared no better. He was thought to be a madman and would have been executed as a heretic had not good friends in high places interceded for him. The price he had to pay for his life was public renunciation of the idea he knew to be true.

Women scientists of Galileo's time—particularly midwives and physicians—faced another peril: being tortured or executed as witches. An estimated 40,000 women were executed for witchcraft during the seventeenth century alone, and the practice continued well into the nineteenth century. For this reason, only the most brilliant women could succeed in the sciences. One example is Maria Gaetana Agnesi, the gifted eighteenth-century linguist, mathematician, and philanthropist whose writings were essential to the foundations for integral calculus. Although she was called the "witch of Agnesi" for her mathematical genius, she was fortunate enough not to be persecuted as a witch. However, her most famous mathematical formula is called the witch of Agnesi to this day.

The history of ideas is filled with examples of new ideas being laughed at, then accepted. When Charles Newbold invented the cast-iron plow, farmers rejected it because they believed it would pollute the soil. When Horace Wells first used gas as an anesthetic to pull teeth, his peers ridiculed him. Joseph Lister's pioneering of antiseptic surgery was dismissed as needless housekeeping. William Harvey's discovery of the blood's circulation was rejected for 20 years and earned him derision, abuse, and the loss of much of his medical practice. Secretary of State William H. Seward's purchase of Alaska from Russia for 2 cents an acre was considered a mistake and dubbed "Seward's Folly." Ignaz Semmelweis was rewarded for his discovery of the cause of puerperal fever by being fired from two university medical centers and hounded into a lunatic asylum. Before Chester Carlson finally found a company that took an interest in his copying machine, known today as the Xerox copier, 5 years had elapsed and more than 20 companies had rejected his idea. The lesson in all these cases, and thousands of others like them, is that negative reactions to creative ideas are not only common—they are also predictable. Knowing that, wise thinkers do their best to anticipate negative responses and prepare to meet them before they occur.

WHY PEOPLE REACT NEGATIVELY

It is easier to deal successfully with negative reactions if we understand why people react that way. Sometimes it seems that meanness or resentment or simple jealousy is the reason. To be sure, one or another of these is often involved, at least to some extent. But these emotions do not explain the numerous cases in which the rejected ideas are beneficial to the very people who spurn them. As we will see, the causes usually are less personal and petty.

One cause of negative reactions to solutions is *lack of understanding* about what the solutions are and how they will work. Most people don't listen or read attentively. One study showed that the average person listens with between 25 percent and 50 percent accuracy.[1] The level of reading attentiveness is often not much better. And even when readers do make a conscious effort to grasp the ideas presented, they may grow apprehensive and confused if the subject or treatment seems difficult.

A second cause is *bad thinking habits.* If you recall the habits hindering effective thinking that were discussed in Chapter 3 and consider the difficulty you had overcoming those that you'd acquired, you'll appreciate how seriously those habits can affect the thinking of people who don't realize they have them. Mine-is-better thinking, face saving, conformity, stereotyping, self-deception, and particularly resistance to change can effectively block acceptance of your new solutions. And the more insecurity, laziness, or blind acceptance of tradition that underlies the resistance, the greater the obstacle. *Thobbing* (*th*inking out the *o*pinion that pleases them and *b*elieving it) will pose a formidable threat to your solutions.

Still another cause of negative reactions is *ignorance of creativity.* It's important to remember that the creative process is not widely known. Few textbooks treat it at all; few colleges offer courses that introduce it, even to future teachers. Most people are more likely to be familiar with popular misconceptions about creativity than with the facts. They themselves probably approach problems and issues vaguely and without any conscious strategy, therefore producing only the most common and unimaginative responses. So the independence and originality of your thinking, and your confidence in it, may frighten them away. Your most creative ideas may seem bizarre to them, and you may appear to be a "radical."

All this is especially true of your resolutions of issues. Many people are so used to seeing controversial matters in either/or, right/wrong fashion that they will not understand your efforts to bridge controversies. And because they find it extremely difficult to achieve a balanced perspective on issues, they will be suspicious of your perspective. On occasion you may find that your very effort to bridge a controversy not only fails to win the approval of both sides but actually alienates both sides.

There is yet another cause of negative reactions to solutions. It is markedly different from the other three, which represent failures on the part of the audience. This final cause is *a real or apparent flaw in your solution.* It therefore represents not the audience's failure, but yours. It is difficult to anticipate negative reactions caused by flaws in your solution, but it is crucial that you do so. There is nothing quite so disheartening as to have a solution rejected by others because of legitimate negative reactions you could have anticipated and headed off. The time to make the effort, to scrutinize your work carefully, is at this stage, not later. Later is often too late.

COMMON NEGATIVE REACTIONS

Exactly what kinds of reactions can you expect your solutions to receive? It is impossible to predict all of them because they can vary with the particulars of your solutions. Nevertheless, certain broad reactions tend to occur again and again. The following are the most common kinds of negative reactions:

- The idea is *impractical.*
- The idea is *too expensive.*
- The idea is *illegal.*
- The idea is *immoral.*
- The idea is *inefficient.*
- The idea is *unworkable.*
- The idea will be *disruptive of existing procedures.*
- The idea is *unaesthetic* (that is, ugly or lacking in taste).
- The idea is *too radical.*
- The idea will be *unappealing to others* (for example, to the public).
- The idea is *unfair* (that is, it favors one side of the dispute at the expense of the other).

ANTICIPATING SPECIFIC REACTIONS

Your aim in anticipating others' reactions is twofold. First, you want to identify the valid objections others might raise to your idea so that you can modify the idea and eliminate the objections. Second, you want to identify invalid objections that others might raise because of their misunderstanding and confusion, bad thinking habits, or suspicion of new ideas, so that you can prepare responses to them.

To stimulate your speculation about negative reactions, two techniques are especially useful: brainstorming and imaginary dialogue.

The Brainstorming Technique

This technique is an adaptation of the third stage of the creative process, the production of ideas. The aim here is to think of as many possible objections to your solution as you can, however outlandish they seem. Here's how to use this technique. Look back at the common negative reactions and use them as a checklist to guide your brainstorming. In other words, first ask whether anyone might find your solution impractical, and then list as many possibilities as you can think of; next ask in what ways people might find your solution too expensive, and list the possible ways; and so on, proceeding through all the common reactions.

Caution is in order here. Whenever you use the brainstorming technique, be sure to withhold all judgment so that the flow of ideas isn't interrupted. Keep in mind that extended effort will always reward you: Some of the most helpful reactions will not occur to you until you have purged your mind of obvious and familiar ideas. When you've completed brainstorming all 11 common reactions, then you can decide which possibilities are most likely to occur.

The Imaginary Dialogue Technique

This technique, as the name implies, consists of imagining yourself discussing your solution with someone who objects to it. For best results, think of a specific person, preferably someone you know quite well and are sure would disagree with you. Be sure to put aside any feelings of awkwardness or embarrassment while using this technique. If you find yourself thinking, "What would people think of my talking to myself this way?" tell yourself that no one need know and that you are not doing it out of compulsion but as a deliberate strategy to aid your thinking.

Here is an example of how the imaginary dialogue technique works. You will recall that in Chapter 2 (pages 30–31) we discussed the case of Ralph, the father who befriended the coaches and used that friendship to gain a special advantage for his son Mark over the other players. We decided that Ralph behaved immorally—that though his actions achieved some good (the development of his son's skills), they caused more harm. They deprived other players of the opportunity to develop their basketball skills, probably caused those players to become bitter, and undoubtedly caused Mark to believe that it is acceptable to disregard other people's rights and needs to achieve his own goals.

If you were addressing the larger issue this case raises, the issue of at what point a father's helping his son or daughter athletically slips from morally acceptable into morally unacceptable behavior, and attempting to resolve the issue by offering guidelines for parents to follow, you would want to anticipate negative reactions. And if you wanted to use the imaginary dialogue technique to help stimulate your speculation, what better person would there be to talk with than Ralph himself? Surely he would not look upon your disposition of his case favorably.

Just how would you conduct the dialogue in your imagination? First, you'd make an assertion expressing your view. Then you'd put yourself in his position, enter his frame of mind, and answer for him. Next you'd express a second view, construct the answer he'd probably give to it, proceed to a third view, and so on. The resulting dialogue might go like this:

YOU: Your actions were immoral, Ralph.

YOU-AS-RALPH: That's ridiculous. All I did was help my boy.

YOU: But you developed those friendships with the coaches so that you could use them later. That's dishonest.

YOU-AS-RALPH: You mean I have no right to choose my friends, that I have to avoid friendships with coaches if my boy is an athlete?

YOU: Not at all. There's a difference between developing a friendship because you like someone and developing it to use the person for your son's advantage.

YOU-AS-RALPH: It's a rough world out there. A boy needs an advantage to get ahead.

YOU: But you gained that advantage at other people's expense. Look at what you did to the other boys on the team.

YOU-AS-RALPH: I can't be concerned with them as much as I am concerned about my own son. That's unrealistic.

YOU: That's true enough. But we're not talking about your being concerned or not concerned. We're talking about specific actions you took, deliberately, that hurt them.

YOU-AS-RALPH: But they didn't have the interest or the talent my Mark had.

YOU: That was not for you to judge. It was the coaches' decision to make. Besides, if you were so sure of your son's talent, there would have been no need for you to gain an unfair advantage for him. His talent would have given him all the advantage he needed.

YOU-AS-RALPH: I did it because I love my son. Is it immoral to help your own flesh and blood?

YOU: Is it an act of love to teach your son that the rules of decency and fairness don't apply where his desires are involved, that he can do whatever he wants because he's special?

The dialogue shows the benefit of this approach to your thinking. Used properly, it not only reveals the negative reactions you are likely to get from others but also helps you develop better responses to shallow or uninformed reactions. In actual practice, however, it is not necessary for you to detail your own responses while you are conducting the dialogue. It is sufficient to contribute just enough to move the dialogue along, to prod the "other person" to respond. The most important part of the dialogue, after all, is not your views but the other person's thoughts and feelings about them. The more you are able to focus on the other person's reactions, the more you will gain the insights necessary to make an effective presentation.

There is no limit to the number of imaginary dialogues you can conduct. If your audience is complex and you have reason to expect a variety of reactions, you should consider doing numerous dialogues.

One final point: After you become used to the imaginary dialogue technique and develop your confidence in using it, you will notice that a dialogue will often gather enough momentum to require little conscious direction from you. It will, in a sense, direct itself. When this happens, don't worry. It is a good sign, an indication that you have fully engaged your imagination and given yourself to the intellectual exchange with your imaginary opponent. Let the dialogue continue—what develops will usually be very useful. If it begins to turn away from the important concerns involved, just steer it back again.

WARM-UP EXERCISES

14.1. You have just heard a friend make the following statement. Decide whether his or her reasoning is sound or unsound. Then write a paragraph or two explaining your judgment.

I would vote this year if I could be reasonably sure any of the candidates would do a good job. But I have no way to be sure, so it's a waste of time to vote.

14.2. Follow the directions for Exercise 14.1.

Physical fitness is very fashionable today. Yet the great philosophers agree that the mind is more important than the body. So the physical fitness movement should be opposed.

14.3. Follow the directions for Exercise 14.1.

No honest lawyer would agree to represent a person accused of a crime because if the person is innocent, he doesn't need defending, and if he is guilty, he doesn't deserve defending.

APPLICATIONS

14.1. Each of the following cases was presented in an earlier chapter's applications. Turn back to the chapter in each case and reread the application. Then recall the position you took on it. (If you wish, you may rethink the problem now.) State your position on the matter and the reasons supporting your position. Then anticipate the negative reactions you would probably receive, proceeding as explained in this chapter.

  a. The marijuana warehouse case, Application 3.6, page 50.
  b. The adoption case involving the homosexual minister, Application 3.9, page 51.
  c. The case of the illiterate high school graduate, Application 3.10, page 51.
  d. The case involving the Jewish dietary laws, Application 3.7, page 50.
  e. The case of the owner's responsibility for the accident involving the loaned car, Application 6.5i, page 98.

    f.   The case of the woman ordered not to become pregnant, Application 6.5e, page 98.

14.2. The scandals involving televangelists Jimmy Swaggart and Jim and Tammy Bakker drew headlines for over two years. (Both Swaggart and Jim Bakker were allegedly involved in sexual dalliances, and Bakker was convicted of mismanaging his organization's funds.) These scandals have prompted some people to urge that all television ministries be stripped of their tax-exempt status. Identify and resolve this issue; then refine your view, giving special attention to your consideration of negative reactions.

14.3. The age of kiddie cosmetics has begun. A cosmetic company is now marketing a line of Tinkerbell products, including powders, perfumes, lip glosses, and nail polish, for girls aged 3 to 14. Other companies will undoubtedly follow suit. This marketing move has drawn the criticism of many individuals and groups who believe that kiddie cosmetics will make children mature too fast.[2] Identify and resolve this issue; if appropriate, refine your solution, giving special attention to your consideration of negative reactions.

14.4. Should the death penalty be permitted in this country? The controversy continues. Advocates of the death penalty argue that some crimes—for example, the brutal beating of infants, sex crimes against small children, the murder of on-duty police officers, and particularly vicious rapes and murders—are so heinous that nothing short of the death penalty would achieve justice. Opponents believe that for society to take a criminal's life is a criminal act. Proceed as you did in previous applications.

14.5. Eileen Stevens received the call at 1:20 in the morning. The dean of students at the college informed her that her son Chuck had died of an alcohol overdose. She was puzzled: He was not a drinker. She took the first plane available to the college, visited the hospital morgue, talked with the pathologist, visited the campus, and talked to students and college officials. Bit by bit she pieced the story together. Her son had been the victim of fraternity hazing. On a cold winter night the fraternity brothers had ordered Chuck and two other boys into the trunk of a car, handed them a bottle of wine, a six-pack of beer, and a pint of Jack Daniels, ordering them to drink it all. Hours later Chuck was dead of acute alcohol poisoning. The months and years that followed left Eileen Stevens not only grieving but also angry. The college, she felt, had handled the matter insensitively, perhaps trying to cover up what had happened. The district attorney concluded that no one was criminally responsible for Chuck's death and refused Mrs. Stevens access to his investigation. Moreover, Chuck's was not the only needless death from fraternity hazing. Mrs. Stevens knew that each year a number of pledges die in this country. She felt she should do something but didn't know what.[3] Identify Mrs. Stevens's problem and address it as you did the issues in the previous applications.

14.6. Jack Anderson reported some years ago that employees at a secret weapons-testing site in California were using sophisticated government video equipment, designed to test navy weapons, to show hard-core pornographic films for their own entertainment during working hours.[4] Many citizens consider such activities a moral outrage. Others believe there is no reason to be concerned. Address this issue as you did those in previous applications.

14.7. Occasionally the media carry a story about corporal punishment, like the story from Titusville, Florida, concerning the $45,000 lawsuit a couple brought against a Baptist grammar school. The principal of the school had paddled their 13-year-old son across the buttocks as punishment for not running in physical education class.[5] Informed people are divided on the issue of corporal punishment, some supporting its use in the schools (provided it is done in moderation and with restraint), others attacking it as barbaric. Proceed as you did in previous applications.

14.8. A great number of Americans find boxing not only distasteful but also a throwback to humankind's more violent past. A crowd of fans at a boxing arena seem to them the twentieth-century counterparts of the Roman Colosseum patrons who found the murder of one gladiator by another (or the feasting of lions on Christians) entertaining. Most boxing fans, of course, regard such a view as ignorant nonsense. Identify the issue here and proceed as you did in previous applications.

14.9. Every year, it seems, one or more school boards around the country decide to ban certain books from school library shelves, and the issue of censorship burns bright again. The banned books vary from case to case, but some recent examples are Bernard Malamud's *The Fixer,* Kurt Vonnegut's *Slaughterhouse Five,* and Eldridge Cleaver's *Soul on Ice.* (These books were characterized by one school board as "anti-American, anti-Christian, anti-Semitic, and just plain filthy.")[6] The school boards believe they act in the interests of the students and the community. But many individuals and community groups around the country disagree. They oppose censorship in any form. Proceed as you did in previous applications.

14.10. The issue of whether religion belongs in the schools continues to divide Americans. Many people believe that learning about a particular religion and saying prayers are activities that belong in the church and in the home but have no place in public schools. Others believe that these activities should be allowed in schools because the country was founded on religious principles and spiritual development makes better citizens and a more stable society. Proceed here as you did in previous applications.

14.11. Identify the issue in the following dialogue and address it as you did those in previous applications.

BETTY: I can't understand how anyone with any intelligence can argue in favor of freedom of thought.
GRACE: What do you mean?
BETTY: I mean it's ridiculous to allow people to think anything they wish.
GRACE: But thinking isn't the same as taking action.
BETTY: Wrong. Thinking is a form of action, a mental action that precedes physical action. Most rotten deeds are first conceived in the mind. Rape, burglary, shoplifting, treason, even the simple act of lying—all of them occur first as ideas. Then the person acts on the idea.
GRACE: Are you saying some thoughts are wrong and should be outlawed?
BETTY: Now you've got it. Even the Bible supports my view. It says, "Everyone who looks at a woman with lust for her has already committed the sin in his own heart."
GRACE: How would you outlaw them?
BETTY: I'd revise the laws to stipulate that thinking of a crime is the same as committing that crime. It won't always be possible to determine when a person is thinking of a crime, I admit, but where it can be determined, where there is evidence, he or she should be arrested and brought to trial. That would nip lawbreaking in the bud.

GRACE: I don't know. It seems to me such a law would do more harm than good.

BETTY: You've got to be kidding. Now the police and the courts can react only after a crime occurs. That puts us all at the mercy of criminals. With my law they'd be able to prevent crime from happening. This country would be a lot safer place to live.

GROUP DISCUSSION EXERCISE

Discuss the following issue with two or three of your classmates. Observe the guidelines to group discussion presented in Appendix B. Consider all sides of the matter and try to reach consensus. Be prepared to report your group's deliberations to the class, describing how your analysis proceeded, what questions were asked, and what agreements were reached. If differences of viewpoint remain unresolved, be prepared to report them objectively.

A group of black students at the University of Pennsylvania took offense at the writings of a conservative columnist on the student newspaper, the *Daily Pennsylvanian*. (He had, for example, accused the administration of a preferential admissions policy toward blacks.) In protest, the group of students, who called themselves "the black community," confiscated almost an entire issue of the newspaper, over 14,000 copies. Security officers caught some students in the act of stealing, but no charges were filed against the students. Rather, some security officers and a university administrator were reportedly reprimanded for trying to halt the theft. What should the university's response to the incident have been?

COMPOSITION OR SPEECH EXERCISE

Write a composition or, if your instructor specifies, a formal speech, presenting the view your group reached in the preceding group discussion exercise. (If you hold a dissenting view, present that instead.) Be sure to provide evidence that your view is the most reasonable one. Naturally your composition or speech will bear some resemblance to those of the other members of your group—you will have developed ideas as a team, so at least some of your ideas will be similar, even identical, to theirs. Don't be concerned about such similarities. Your composition or speech will be a unique effort if you (a) use supporting material from your own experience, observation, and research; (b) develop your own line of reasoning about that material; (c) employ your own ingenuity in designing an introduction and conclusion and in arranging the material in the body of your composition or speech; and (d) express your thoughts in your own words. For further guidance, consult the appropriate appendix—A for writing, B for speaking.

Build a Persuasive Case

Persuasive writing and speaking asks an audience to replace ideas they know and accept with ideas they have never heard before or, worse, have considered and rejected. In many cases, it also asks that they cooperate in the implementation of the ideas, investing time and money and taking risks. It is therefore not surprising that persuasiveness does not come easily. You are not likely to achieve it unless you approach the task seriously and prepare for it effectively.

HOW PERSUASION IS ACHIEVED

The first crucial requirement in persuading others is to put yourself in their place and determine where they are likely to stand on the problem or issue— that is, determine what they know, what they don't know, and what they believe. Their views will likely be shaped by a variety of factors, including age, gender, educational background, religion, income, race, nationality, and business or professional affiliation. You will seldom be able to learn all these details about an audience, but it is worth the effort to learn as many as you can. Even more important, you should consider the variety of views your audience might take of the issue and determine which of those views are most probable. The following questions provide a helpful checklist:

Is your audience likely to have been influenced by popular misconceptions? This question does not suggest that your audience is stupid or uneducated. As we saw in Chapter 1, there is a great deal of confusion today about such matters as free will, truth, knowledge, opinion, and morality. Many intelligent and educated people have fallen victim to ideas and attitudes that cripple their creative and critical faculties. By recognizing that your audience is inclined to think "one idea is as good as another" in, for example, sexual ethics, you are preparing to deal with that problem and to address the obstacle to understanding it poses.

Is your audience's perspective likely to be narrow? This question directs you to consider how your audience's tendencies to mine-is-better thinking, face saving, resistance to change, conformity, stereotyping, and self-deception may interfere with their comprehension of your views. A clue to the way those tendencies are likely to influence your audience on a particular problem or issue is the way they have influenced *you* in the past. (The more honest you are with yourself about your own occasional irrationality, the more sensitive you will be about your audience's irrationality.)

Is your audience likely to be unobservant about important considerations? We noted in Chapter 6 that most people give up their curiosity at a rather early age and never fully regain it. Chances are your own experience with the Chapter 6 applications and the later applications in this book have made you more aware of the difficulty of developing curiosity, even when you make a conscious and sustained effort to do so. If your audience has not made such an effort, their observation is likely to be careless, and they have probably missed many of the subtleties you have observed. By considering where the subtleties lie, you can determine what you need to explain more fully.

Is your audience's understanding of the problem or issue likely to be as clear as yours? We have seen how many people rush into a problem with only a vague notion of exactly what the problem is. You have learned the value of expressing the problem or issue in a number of ways and then selecting the best and most promising expression of it. Many members of your audience may not have done so. And if they haven't, they won't realize that your view of it is the best one. It may help open them to persuasion if you discuss the various views of the problem or at least explain your view and its advantage over other views.

Is your audience likely to be familiar with the facts you found in your investigation? It is easy to forget that once you have investigated a problem or issue, particularly a complex one, you have a tremendous advantage over those who have not investigated it. Their ignorance of the facts can be an obstacle to accepting your solution. By identifying what facts and interpretations they are likely to be unaware of, you are identifying matters that deserve emphasis in your writing.

Does your audience appreciate the various solutions possible? Have they considered them critically? Again, your effort to produce as many solutions as possible to the problem or issue sets you apart from most of your audience. The best way for them to appreciate your solution's soundness is to realize that other solutions are inferior. As long as they remain convinced that some inferior solution will work, they are not likely to be impressed by your solution. But if you show them how the others *don't* work, that their imperfections and complications are too great to overcome easily, you will have helped them to accept yours.

The more deeply you probe these matters, the more sensitive you will become to the demands of the particular situation. Beyond this sensitivity, you persuade in two ways: by using your evidence effectively and by presenting your ideas skillfully.

USING EVIDENCE EFFECTIVELY

To be persuasive you must not only know the best solution but also show that solution to your audience. In other words, you must help them to understand how it works in specific situations—particularly, if possible, in situations in which they tend to believe it won't work. This means you must help them to visualize the solution and appreciate why it is superior to other solutions. Doing this effectively means providing as many details as you can, consistent with the length of your presentation. In all but the most restricted presentations, in which you are required to be brief, you should consider including all the significant results of your investigation.

To ensure that you use your evidence effectively, ask and answer the following questions. They are based on the approach detailed in Chapter 8.

- What experiences and observations of your own did you find relevant to this issue? (Be sure to include in your answer any experiences or observations you originally classified under a different heading but then decided were connected with this problem or issue.)
- What experiences and observations of friends did you find relevant to this problem or issue?
- What information did you obtain from interviews with authorities?
- What information did you obtain from the library?

To be sure you squeeze your data for all their potential, don't settle for summary answers to these questions. Remember, you want your readers not only to understand your data but also to appreciate their significance. Therefore, try to recreate your experiences and observations. Make your audience see as you saw, feel what you felt. If they have never had similar experiences, this will be difficult, so aim for vividness wherever possible and try to convey a sense of the immediacy and drama of the original event. In addition, make your interpretation clear and reasonable.

Use the same kind of thoroughness with the data you obtain from interviews and library research. Your audience will probably be unaware of the authorities' views unless you make them aware. And if you cover these data in too brief and undeveloped a fashion and without the necessary emphasis, you will have failed to make your data serve your persuasive intent.

PRESENTING IDEAS SKILLFULLY

Presenting your ideas skillfully means, first, meeting the basic requirements of all good composition. These are discussed at some length in Appendix A. Second, it means applying these four guidelines:

- Respect your audience.
- Begin with the familiar.
- Select the most appropriate tone.
- Answer all significant objections.

Respect Your Audience

Whenever there is strong disagreement over ideas, as there is with controversial issues, there is also heightened potential for ill will. It is easy to believe, once we feel strongly about a point of view, that those who disagree with us are stupid or villainous or both. That kind of attitude not only poisons debate—it also makes persuasion difficult or impossible.

Since people are not likely to be persuaded by someone who shows disrespect for them, respecting your audience is not merely a matter of courtesy or good sportsmanship. It is a psychological imperative. You may be inclined to believe that you don't really have to respect your audience, that you can get by with pretending. But that is a mistake. Your own experience surely demonstrates that respect and disrespect are difficult to hide. Your manner or expression usually betrays strong feelings no matter how you try to hide them. Attitudes tend to show through what you say and the way you say it.

What can you do to make yourself feel respect for people whose views you disagree with? First, you can remember to distinguish between the idea and the person. It is possible for a decent, admirable person to have a foolish idea or a disreputable person to have a sound one. Second, in the case of a controversial issue, you can remind yourself that disagreement is more likely to reflect the complexity of the issue than any shortcoming in your opponent.

Begin with the Familiar

First impressions may not be very reliable, but they are usually quite strong and are therefore difficult to overcome. If you begin your presentation on a point your audience is unfamiliar with (or in disagreement with), they will be wary (or disagree) throughout your presentation. At best it will be difficult to change their reaction. That is why it makes sense to begin on a point they are familiar with, if possible a point on which they agree with you. This approach puts the psychology of first impressions to work for you instead of against you.

Beginning on a familiar point does not, however, mean that you should be dishonest and hide your disagreement. You are merely preparing your audience for the point of disagreement, helping them to see your solution more objectively than they otherwise would—not avoiding disagreement. There is nothing deceitful about this approach, nor does it require that you manufacture a point of agreement. If you look, you will usually be able to find at least several significant points of agreement, even where your basic views are sharply divergent. As a last resort, if you can't find anything else that you and your audience are likely to agree on, you can begin by stating the significance of the issue and pointing out that it, like all controversial issues, tends to fan emotions more than is helpful for debate.

Select the Most Appropriate Tone

The concept of tone is a subtle one. Tone may be defined as the mood or attitude suggested by a presentation. It is therefore closely related to the idea of respecting your audience. Certain tones are always inappropriate in persuasive writing and speaking. The now-hear-this tone, for example, goes beyond being authoritative to being *authoritarian* and suggests that the presenter is forcing his or her views on the audience. Another inappropriate tone is the only-an-idiot-would-think-as-you-do tone, characterized by mocking and sarcastic remarks. Still another inappropriate tone is the you've-got-to-agree-right-now-there's-no-time-left tone. Serious problems and issues demand careful consideration; it is irresponsible to make any important decision impulsively. Demanding an instant decision from your audience, therefore, only makes them suspicious of your motives. "If the writer [or speaker] really has a solid case," they reason, "why doesn't he or she want to give me time to examine it carefully and ponder it?"

The safest and most appropriate tone in persuasive writing and speaking is the calm, objective, courteous tone. This will reflect quiet competency and a sense of balance toward the issue, as well as a proper view of your audience.

Answer All Significant Objections

You may think that if you identify any valid objections to your solution and modify your solution to eliminate them, you have done enough. That view is incorrect. Even invalid objections may act as obstacles. Therefore, you must deal with all objections directly and thoroughly. This should be done subtly and smoothly, without reminding your audience that it is their objection and without interrupting the flow of your presentation.

THE IMPORTANCE OF TIMING

There is one additional element in building a persuasive case. It is not, properly speaking, a guideline for preparing your presentation. Nevertheless, it does have a major bearing on your presentation's effectiveness. It is your *timing* in presenting your case. Many a creative idea was defeated by simply being presented at the wrong time. People's attention, interest, and openness to ideas are not constant. At some times they are greater than others. It is not always possible to appraise an audience's state of mind, particularly when the audience is large and complex. Nevertheless, you should be aware of the most favorable conditions for persuasion and, whenever possible, time your presentation accordingly.

1. The audience should recognize that the problem or issue exists and be aware of its importance. A controversial issue should be currently in the news or at least have been there recently.
2. The audience should be relatively free to address your idea. That is, they should have no other pressing concerns commanding their attention.
3. The audience should have no commitment to a competing solution. It is not likely they will be interested in considering your solution to a

problem or issue if they have endorsed another, competing solution. In such cases, your wisest course of action is to withhold presentation until the competing idea proves unworkable.

A SAMPLE SITUATION

You are sitting in the cafeteria one day and happen to overhear the following conversation at the table next to yours:

FIRST PERSON: The matter is simple. Vince Lombardi summed up the intelligent perspective on winning when he said, "Winning isn't everything—it's the *only* thing."

SECOND PERSON: That's nonsense. Lombardi was a good football coach but a lousy philosopher. The traditional view is the right view: "It's not whether you win or lose, but how you play the game."

FIRST PERSON: With an attitude like that, how can you ever be a winner?

SECOND PERSON: Everyone who plays hard in sports can't help but be a winner.

FIRST PERSON: Wow! If only my Little League coach could hear that. He used to tell us, "If you lose, you're not the best, and if you're not the best, you're nothing." You know what he'd say to you? He'd say, "Man, you're a big nothing."

At that point the two get up and leave. But the conversation doesn't leave your mind, and you know why. It's because you were on a varsity team in a high school where winning was stressed above all else. Your coach taught the Lombardi philosophy; your teammates accepted it as gospel, and so did the fans. Even then you were not completely comfortable with it. You felt that it was wrong somehow, but you weren't quite sure how.

Now your curiosity is aroused. You begin to examine the issue the dialogue recalled, raising these question, among others: *What is the purpose of interscholastic and intercollegiate athletics, and how important is winning to its realization?* You begin talking to friends about it, then to several teachers, including your physical education instructor. Then you decide to do a little library research on the subject, purely for your own interest. Before long, you decide that there are a lot of people with the view of the first person in that cafeteria conversation, that our entire society seems to have an unhealthy view of winning. More importantly, you begin to want to persuade others that there is a better, more reasonable attitude. And so you decide to write an opinion piece for the campus newspaper.

After identifying the problem or issue, completing your investigation, producing a range of ideas, refining your best one, and anticipating negative reactions, you face the challenge of building a persuasive case. Let's see how you would use the approaches explained in the chapter to do this effectively.

Your readers will undoubtedly have mixed reactions to your presentation. Some will agree with you, but if your assessment of the extent of our society's emphasis on winning is correct, most will disagree—many strongly. Those are the ones you must consider carefully. Here are the questions suggested earlier in the chapter, with some of the most significant answers:

Is your audience likely to have been influenced by popular misconception? One problem that may exist for many readers concerns a moral question—is an action right and proper just because it proves successful? There is a tendency today to answer yes to this question. If you intend to argue that overemphasis on winning has the effect of promoting dishonesty on the court or playing field or a lack of respect for one's opponent, you should be prepared to have some readers think, "So what? If such actions help the person win, they're OK."

Is your audience's perspective likely to be narrow? A number of problems are likely to arise here. If many of your readers grew up thinking and being taught that the "winning philosophy" is the right philosophy, they will certainly tend to identify with that view. Undoubtedly, a good number of them apply it in their own athletic activities. Hence, your suggestion that it is wrong and harmful will trigger their mine-is-better, face-saving, and resistance-to-change responses. In addition, they are likely to view you stereotypically as a loser or someone who doesn't participate in or understand sports.

Is your audience likely to be unobservant about important considerations? Chances are that a number of your readers will never have wondered about the prevailing attitude toward competition. They will merely have accepted what they were told or shown by others' example. Moreover, because they lacked your curiosity, they may not have noticed the negative effects this philosophy produces at various levels of competition—from Little League to the professional levels of sport—and to fans as well as athletes. You'll need to show them.

Is your audience's understanding of the issue likely to be as clear as yours? Chances are most of your readers don't even see the matter as an issue. It hasn't nagged at them the way it has at you; they haven't felt the need to define it. They assume winning is the purpose of sports. The central question you have crystallized will seem new and strange, perhaps even pointless, to many of your readers. Therefore, you must present it with care and deepen their understanding of it gradually. Without helping them to understand that there is a real issue involved, you have no hope of gaining their acceptance.

Is your audience likely to be familiar with the facts you found in your investigation? There is little chance they will be familiar with views against winning, because this issue—unlike issues such as abortion and capital punishment—is not highly publicized. No widespread public debate has yet developed over it. For this reason, any important facts you find should be presented as if the readers are likely to be unaware and suspicious of them.

Does your audience appreciate the various solutions possible? Have they considered them critically? The answer to both questions is probably no. Most of them undoubtedly think that the only alternative to winning at all costs is *not caring about winning at all.* Thus, they tend to see any argument against the prevailing athletic philosophy as an argument against athletics. One of your greatest challenges will be to make them see that the enjoyment and satisfaction athletic competition offers exist independently of the "winning philosophy."

After answering these questions and deciding how to approach your readers most effectively, you would prepare the piece for the campus newspaper. Here is how that piece might read:

ONLY WINNERS

Only a fool would deny that winning is more pleasurable than losing. Anyone who has ever stood on the football field or the basketball court as those final seconds ticked away and victory was complete, or who watched the ball explode off the racquet and land out of his or her opponent's reach to end the tennis match, knows the emotions that accompany the experience. The joy, the excitement, the feeling of mastery are incomparable.

Those personal experiences are reason enough for preferring winning. But when you add to them the media effects created in the past 10 or 20 years—the on-field cameras capturing every emotion in the faces of the athletes, sweeping shots of cheering crowds, pregame buildup and postgame analysis—it's not surprising that winning has come to dominate the American view of sports. With phrases like "the thrill of victory and the agony of defeat" indelibly impressed on our minds, the traditional idea, "It's not whether you win or lose, but how you play the game," seems rather anemic.

But perhaps we've gone too far with the philosophy of winning. Vince Lombardi's famous expression, "Winning isn't everything—it's the only thing," was only the start. Lombardi said it in the context of coaching a professional team. But then many college coaches, high school coaches, and even Little League coaches adopted it as a philosophy. Some have gone far beyond it in their emphasis on winning.

A student at this college told me his high school soccer coach told his team before every game, "Defeat is worse than death, because you have to live with defeat." Another student said his Little League coach told his young players, "If you lose, you're not the best, and if you're not the best, you're nothing." I believe that is a terrible idea to plant in the minds of children. Terrible and false! After all, Fran Tarkenton, the great Minnesota Viking quarterback, was never on a championship team. And basketball star Wilt Chamberlain won a coveted championship ring very late in his phenomenal career. Those athletes were certainly not losers.

There are worse effects than slogans, too. In high school I played on a football team that won the state championship. We were winners, yes, and we were honored with a parade through town, a big dinner, and speeches by a lot of dignitaries. But one of the main reasons we won all those games was our coach's win-at-all-costs philosophy. He showed us films about how to hurt our opponents. He taught us to clip and to hold and how to pile on an opposing players in ways that would injure him. Whenever we played a team with an outstanding player, the coach would urge us to disable him. I can still remember him saying, "I want to see some stretchers out there today." More than once he got his wish. In one case, the opposing player, a boy with outstanding college prospects, suffered a permanent injury to his spine.

At the time we won the championship and were hailed as winners I was as happy as the next guy on the team. But today I see it differently. According to the win-at-all-costs philosophy, the fact that we won should be the only important thing; how we won shouldn't matter. Yet somehow it does matter to me. I've taken my trophy off the shelf and put it in the attic.

Bill Russell is certainly no loser. He played basketball on one of the winningest basketball teams in history, the Boston Celtics. And he is regarded by many authorities as one of the best players ever to set foot on a court. Yet he has some interesting things to say about winning in his book, *Second Wind.* To be sure, he doesn't advocate losing, and he expresses pride in the qualities that made the Celtics a winning team. But his view of winning is not the common view. He writes, for example, "If you fix your mind on the goal of winning and stay honest with yourself, you'll come to realize that winning isn't about right and wrong, or the good guys and the bad guys, or the pathway to good life and character, or statistics. Winning is about who has the best team, that's all."

Russell is remarkably balanced in his view of the importance of winning. He tells about something that was more important to him than winning: the feeling that the particular contest being played might be lifted to an unusual level of excellence on the part of both teams. At times like that he wasn't just rooting for his own team; he was rooting for his opponents, too. He wanted everyone to excel, to make the game something special. When that happened, he explains, he lost his feeling of competitiveness for a time, even while he was competing with every ounce of his strength. More important, when such a contest was over, he really didn't care who had won. The joy of participating in such a game was so fulfilling that winning was no longer important.

I believe amateur athletes would be much better if we returned to the traditional philosophy of "how you play the game." I'm not advocating trying to lose, nor even taking away the intense competitiveness that sports tend to generate. After all, competitiveness can be a positive force. The spirit that makes an athlete press forward in sports is the same spirit that makes men and women accept the challenges of invention and discovery and triumph over such formidable problems as poverty and disease and ignorance.

What I am advocating is a shifting of the emphasis from winning to excellence. With this emphasis, coaches can continue to teach team members to practice self-discipline, to extend their limits, and to perfect their talents. But they can also teach them to cope with failure, to accept losing gracefully and with honor, to deepen their understanding of life, and to gain self-knowledge and self-mastery. When the participants in athletics learn these things, whatever the final score of the game may be, everyone wins.

WARM-UP EXERCISES

15.1. Decide whether the reasoning in the following statement is sound or unsound. Then write a paragraph or two explaining your judgment.

If Sarah were a real friend, she'd agree with me, whether I was right or wrong in my idea. Even a stranger would agree when I was right. Friendship demands doing more than strangers do.

15.2. Three girls and three jealous boyfriends went to a distant movie theater on a motorcycle that would hold only two. How did they all get there without leaving any girl in the company of a boy other than her boyfriend unless her boyfriend was also present?[1]

15.3. Zane is sprawled on the dormitory lounge, holding forth on various matters of philosophic import. As you approach, he says the following:

One of the biggest problems in the criminal justice system today is the backlog of cases in the courts. And that backlog gets bigger every day. There's no hope of adding more judges with the economy in the shape that it's in. But there is an answer. It's to abolish trials for suspects who freely confess to crimes.

No one says anything. Zane turns to you and says, "Makes sense, doesn't it?" What do you answer? Be sure to explain your position thoroughly.

APPLICATIONS

15.1. Application 14.1 directed you to anticipate the negative reactions you would probably receive to your view on each of six specific cases. Take one of those cases, review your findings on it, and write a persuasive paper on it, following the approach explained in this chapter.

15.2. Choose one of the following issues. Then apply all the approaches you have learned in this book and write a persuasive paper in response to it.

   a. Should cigarette ads be outlawed?
   b. Is it wise for the average person to purchase a gun for protection?
   c. Should the speed limit be set at a uniform 65 on all interstate highways?
   d. Is the practice of acupuncture based on superstition? Does it have any therapeutic value?
   e. Do Head Start programs increase a child's chance of academic success?
   f. Does censorship always undermine democracy?
   g. Should colleges have open enrollment policies? (Such policies guarantee that everyone who wants to attend will be allowed to do so, at least in certain programs, regardless of high school performance.)

15.3. One of the most difficult considerations in divorce cases is who should be awarded custody of the children. Traditionally, the courts have favored the mother. Today, however, different judges decide differently. Given all the complex factors involved, there is no easy solution to the question of child custody. What guidelines would you follow if you were a family court judge? Apply all the approaches you have learned in this book and then write a persuasive paper in answer to this question.

15.4. Centuries ago, when there was little or no distinction between children and adults in daily life, children who committed crimes were treated exactly as adult offenders were treated. More recently, they have been treated quite differently: They are given special consideration for first offenses, receive lighter sentences for second and subsequent offenses, and are placed in special reform schools and rehabilitation centers rather than in prison. But in the past few years, many people have begun to question the wisdom of that special consideration. They reason that the crime in question, and not the criminal's age, should dictate the punishment. That thinking has begun to have an impact on legislative and judicial decisions. Vermont, for example, lowered the adult criminality age from 18 to 10. An Alabama court sentenced a 15-year-old boy to life imprisonment. In the same year, the Supreme Court refused to ban the death penalty for teenagers, and in Gainesville, Florida, a 6-year-old girl was scheduled to be tried as an adult for hitting another child in the nose with a stick. (The 6-year-old's case was later dismissed.) What is your position on the issue of whether children should be treated as adults for their crimes? Apply all the approaches you have learned in this book and then write a persuasive paper in answer to this question.

15.5. There has been a growing feeling in this country and abroad that the continued production of nuclear weapons must be halted soon or civilization itself will be imperiled. Some military experts disagree, arguing that the existence of sophisticated nuclear weapons is a deterrent to nuclear war, even urging that the United States be ready to use nuclear weapons first, if necessary. Decide your position on this issue and follow the directions in Application 15.4.

15.6. Most people in the United States today regard higher education as a necessity for a secure future. Yet some critics of education believe that the college degree should be abolished. They argue that it has little relation to the world of work, even in the professions. Many jobs that today carry a B.A. or M.A. education requirement, they claim, could be performed satisfactorily by a fairly bright high school graduate. And where further training is required, they believe, it could easily be given on the job. Decide your position on this issue and follow the directions given in previous applications.

15.7. Is it reasonable to believe that unidentified flying objects (UFOs) exist and that they are manned by intelligent beings from outer space? Decide your position on this issue and follow the directions given in previous applications.

15.8. Every morally sensitive person would agree that rape is a terrible crime and should carry a severe penalty. Everyone would agree, too, that for justice to be swift and meaningful, there should be no unnecessary obstacles to prosecuting rapists, and the victims should be spared further humiliation. But exactly how this is to be achieved is a matter of some controversy. Some propose accepting the victim's word that she (or less commonly, he) was raped and not requiring corroboration. Others disagree, arguing that this would provide no protection against false charges. False charges do sometimes occur. For example, a man who had served 2 years of a 12-year rape sentence was granted a new hearing when the victim admitted she had lied. In another case, a grade school teacher was acquitted of statutory rape charges when the two boys who had accused her were found to have lied. Where do you stand on the issue of whether to require corroboration in rape cases? Follow the directions given in previous applications.

15.9. The question of whether creationism should be taught in the schools remains controversial. Proponents believe it deserves equal time in the biology classroom because it is a science; that is, a theory about how the universe came to be. They point out that evolutionism is also a theory and argue that to give one theory preference over others is narrow-minded. Is this view reasonable?

15.10. Modern court trials can be long and costly. One way to save money would be to do away with the jury system and let all cases be decided by a judge. Would this be a good idea?

15.11. Some people believe that schools should have a dress code for students—for example, requiring skirts and blouses for girls and shirts and slacks for boys. Would such a code be likely to have any salutary effects?

15.12. Most of the assignments given in this book stop short of setting up the problem completely for you in order to give you practice in defining problems yourself. Nevertheless, in the great majority of cases some minor help was given; at very least the presentation suggested some possible directions for you to take. These last problems in the book will be different. They will give not even the slightest suggestion of the nature of the problem or issue or of the direction you should take. They merely present some interesting facts. What you do with them is entirely up to you. If you have learned your lessons well, each item will suggest a number of ideas.

a. The second amendment to the Bill of Rights states, "A well-regulated militia, being necessary to the security of a free State, the right of the people to keep and bear arms, shall not be infringed." The National Rifle Association (NRA) interprets this to mean that people have a constitutional right to own not only rifles and shotguns but pistols and assault weapons as well.

b. Some physicians believe that the disposal of the tissue from aborted fetuses is wasteful. They wish to use the tissue for skin grafts and other surgical procedures, as well as for medical research.

c. Polygamy is at present against the law in this country. This prohibition makes it impossible for many Mormons to act on their religious beliefs. It also, in the view of many people, seems insupportable at a time when numerous nontraditional forms of cohabitation are practiced, including gay "marriages" and serial monogamy.

d. Bill Tomaszewski, a Selkirk, New York, farmer, drenched a grainfield surrounding his cornfield with a pesticide the conservation department had restricted to be used as an insect repellent. Tomaszewski stated that his intention in using the pesticide was to protect his crop from birds. More than 2000 birds were killed by the pesticide.[2]

e. The National Coalition on Television Violence, a television monitoring coalition, reported that network television shows portray an average of six violent acts an hour.[3]

f. Each of the following products was banned from television advertising in 1952: feminine hygiene products, hemorrhoid remedies, tampons and sanitary napkins, body lice cures, enemas, pregnancy test kits, jock itch remedies, and incontinence products. The ban was lifted for every one of these products between then and now.[4]

g.   A nationwide Gallup poll, described as "the most comprehensive survey on beliefs about . . . the afterlife that has ever been undertaken," revealed that 67 percent of the American people believe in some kind of afterlife. In addition, according to the accompanying analysis of the survey, "college-educated Americans are more likely to hold such a belief than those with a high school education or less" and "eighteen-year-olds are just as likely to believe in life after death as people over fifty."[5]

h.   In many states the law requires that children be protected with seat belts or special seats. However, no such laws cover children riding on school buses.

i.   Political Action Committees (PACs) are organizations representing special business interests. By making (or withholding) donations to politicians' campaigns, they are often able to influence legislation. Many observers believe that PACs represent a serious threat to the democratic process.

j.   Public school teachers in New York State may not count attendance in grades, according to a decision by the state commissioner of education. The decision prohibits teachers from either giving bonus points for attendance or reducing students' grades for absence from class.[6]

k.   The national council of the Boy Scouts of America, in support of a local council decision, ruled that a youth who doesn't believe in God must be expelled from the organization.[7]

l.   An Iowa state legislator once proposed that students be allowed to get drunk under hospital supervision (and with parental permission) to teach them their drinking limitations.[8]

m. A mother who became pregnant after she was sterilized has filed a "wrongful birth" legal action against the doctors who performed the sterilization procedure and the hospital in which it was performed. She believes they are guilty of negligence and therefore should be made to pay for the upbringing of the child.[9]

n.   A federal government study revealed that more than 80 percent of convicted white-collar criminals spend little or no time behind bars.[10]

GROUP DISCUSSION EXERCISE

Discuss the following issue with two or three of your classmates. Observe the guidelines to group discussion presented in Appendix B. Consider all sides of the matter and try to reach consensus. Be prepared to report your group's deliberations to the class, describing how your analysis proceeded, what questions were asked, and what agreements were reached. If differences of viewpoint remain unresolved, be prepared to report them objectively.

When the school board in Hempstead, Texas, voted to ban pregnant girls from the cheerleading squad (and other extracurricular activities), a controversy arose. Three cheerleaders were reportedly affected by the ruling and were dropped from the squad. (A fourth, who had had an abortion, was allowed to remain.) Some charged racism because the three pregnant girls were all black and the one who had had the abortion was white. Others charged sexism because no boys were punished for their roles in the illegitimate pregnancies. Undoubtedly some regarded the pregnancies as a moral issue that was none of the school board's business. What would be the most reasonable regulation in such matters?

COMPOSITION OR SPEECH EXERCISE

Write a composition or, if your instructor specifies, a formal speech, presenting the view your group reached in the preceding group discussion exercise. (If you hold a dissenting view, present that instead.) Be sure to provide evidence that your view is the most reasonable one. Naturally your composition or speech will bear some resemblance to those of the other members of your group—you will have developed ideas as a team, so at least some of your ideas will be similar, even identical, to theirs. Don't be concerned about such similarities. Your composition or speech will be a unique effort if you (a) use supporting material from your own experience, observation, and research; (b) develop your own line of reasoning about that material; (c) employ your own ingenuity in designing an introduction and conclusion and in arranging the material in the body of your composition or speech; and (d) express your thoughts in your own words. For further guidance, consult the appropriate appendix—A for writing, B for speaking.

A Guide to Composition

Although it is possible to think without expressing our ideas, it is not possible to write well without thinking. Not only does thinking provide the substance of a composition; it also guides us as we proceed, enabling us to make important decisions about arrangement and style. This appendix will help you to understand what characteristics make a composition effective. It will also provide an efficient strategy for achieving those characteristics in your writing.

FOUR IMPORTANT CHARACTERISTICS

To be effective, a composition must display *unity, coherence, emphasis,* and *development.*

> To give your composition *unity,* develop a central idea and state it early in the composition.

Without a central idea, you have no basis for determining what arrangement of your thought is most effective. A central idea provides control over what to include in the composition and what to exclude, where to begin and where to end, and what arrangement of thoughts is best. To provide this guidance, the central idea should be clear to you *before you begin writing.* It saves no time to rush headlong into a composition expecting to find an idea somewhere along the way and then, half an hour later, after much head scratching and eyebrow furrowing, to decide that you are hopelessly lost or at a dead end. Never assume you know what you want to say. Put it down in a clear sentence or two; change it several times, if necessary, to be sure it is what you want to say; and refer back to it for direction while you are writing.

To give your composition *coherence,* choose a recognizable pattern of organization and follow it.

Immature writers have the idea that the world is waiting breathlessly to hear from them. Their attitude is "If the readers have trouble figuring out my meaning, let them struggle to do so; my thoughts are worth the effort." That attitude is naive. Readers of your writing will react to incoherence just as you do when you encounter it in others. In other words, they'll think to themselves, "This person is confused; if he or she couldn't make clear the meaning, I'm not going to waste my valuable time trying to figure it out." Then they'll throw it aside.

To avoid such a reaction and make your writing coherent, you must be sure that the order of your ideas is sensible. Whenever possible, you must also finish one idea before moving on to the next (so that your readers don't have to jump back and forth between ideas unnecessarily) and provide helpful connecting words or phrases to signal significant shifts from one idea to another.

To give your composition *emphasis,* give each of your ideas the degree of prominence it deserves.

There may be occasions when every idea in a composition has exactly the same degree of importance as every other. But those occasions are extremely rare. Much more often, the ideas differ significantly in their importance. To determine the relative importance of the ideas in a piece of writing, consider their exact relationship to your central idea. The larger the role they play in communicating that idea, the more important they are. Use these approaches to give greater emphasis to more important ideas.

1. Assign an important idea more space—that is, provide more information about it, and develop it further than other ideas.
2. Whenever possible, give important ideas the positions of greatest emphasis. The end is the most emphatic position and the beginning is the next most emphatic. Thus, if you had four points or arguments in the body of your composition, you'd put your most important point last, your next most important point first, and the others in the middle.
3. Repeat key words occasionally, or use echo words. The latter are words that do not repeat the key words but whose sense is similar enough to call them to mind. In a composition about love, words like *respect, devotion,* and *affection* would be echo words. One caution, though: Both repetition and echo words must be used judiciously or they will make your composition seem inflated.

To give your composition *development,* elaborate on important ideas.

It's not necessary to treat every idea in great detail. To do so would violate the principle of emphasis. It is necessary, however, to be sensitive to the development necessary to elicit the response you want from your readers, and then to provide that development—for example, by using cases in point, descriptions, definitions, explanations, and so on. When your purpose is to *persuade* your readers, many of your ideas may require considerable development.

A STRATEGY FOR COMPOSING

The basic strategy can be stated very simply—approach composing as a five-stage process* and give careful attention to each. Beginning writers often think they can cut corners and save time, but the result is usually unfortunate. Either they produce a shabby, ineffective piece of work that lacks one or more of the characteristics of good writing, or they make so many false starts that they spend more time writing rather than less. The five stages are prewriting, planning, drafting, revising, and editing.

Prewriting

This stage is the creative and critical thinking process that solves the problem or resolves the issue and thus provides the substance of an analytical (persuasive) piece of writing. This stage is comprised of virtually everything contained in the 15 chapters of this book. You may, of course, be using this appendix for guidance *before* you have read the entire book, so a brief discussion of the thinking process as prewriting activity is in order. That activity begins in your alertness to problems and issues, seeing them as exciting intellectual challenges as well as opportunities to enlarge your understanding and gain insights. Beyond being merely receptive to challenges that confront you, you should actively seek them out by practicing close observation, looking for imperfections in things, noting your own and other people's dissatisfactions, searching for causes, and being sensitive to implications.

When you find a problem or issue that you want to address, express it in as many ways as you can using the appropriate question—"How can . . . ?" for problems and "Is . . . ?" "Does . . . ?" or "Should . . . ?" for issues (see Chapter 7). Remember that the more expressions you produce, the more avenues of thought you open and the greater the chance that you will produce a genuine insight.

Next, investigate the problem or issue, starting with your own experience and that of people you know, then consulting appropriate authorities by means of interviews and reading (see Chapter 8). Your objective is to obtain the information necessary to deal effectively with the problem or issue. The modern library has a wide array of resources you can use to research almost any topic. Get to know your library and learn to use it imaginatively.

When you are in possession of all important facts and points of view about the problem or issue, produce answers to your initial questions ("How can?" or "Is?" "Does" or "Should?"). Resist the tendency to settle for a few answers. Strive for a large and varied number of conceivable answers, postponing judgment until the later evaluation stage. Remember that the habit of judging hastily can block the production of ideas and limit your perspective to the

---

*This process is not rigidly sequential but recursive. In other words, you will often find it helpful to move back and forth between stages.

common, the familiar, and the uncreative. Here are some proven ways to stimulate your imagination in producing ideas, most of them from Chapter 9:

1. *Freewriting.* Relax control of your mind and let one idea lead to another. Record all of them, then go back and pursue any that seem promising.
2. *Listmaking.* Since it involves only single words and short phrases, listmaking is faster and more efficient than freewriting. Keep a pen and paper handy at all times and briefly note ideas when they occur.
3. *Forcing uncommon responses.* After considering all the typical responses to the problem or issue, press yourself to think of some atypical ones, even those that you have never heard or thought of before.
4. *Making analogies.* Consider what the problem or issue or the items of evidence you have uncovered remind you of, what they are similar to in one or more respects. Such connections often prove insightful.
5. *Constructing unusual combinations.* Many useful inventions come from combining ideas or tools not previously considered related.
6. *Using visualizion.* Ask yourself "How would the situation change if the problem were solved?" Form a visual image and note the details.
7. *Constructing pro and con arguments.* You may be so inclined toward one side of an issue that you have difficulty thinking of anything worthwhile that could be said for the opposing view. Yet that's just what you must do to be fair-minded. Forcing yourself to list the arguments that could be advanced on either side of the issue is a way to achieve that more reasonable perspective. It sometimes reveals an insight you otherwise would have overlooked.
8. *Constructing relevant scenarios.* Scenarios are imaginatively conceived but realistic examples of situations and events that are relevant to the issue under consideration. For example, if you were evaluating a proposed change in registration procedure on your campus, you might consider what hardships, if any, it would create in the case of a part-time commuting student who has a full-time job.
9. *Playing devil's advocate.* Challenge popular beliefs, asking questions no one else seems to be raising. For example, if you encountered the notion that unconditional self-acceptance makes one emotionally healthy and more caring of others, you'd entertain the opposite idea— *that it makes one emotionally unhealthy and less caring of others.* (You will probably find that many common beliefs are perfectly reasonable, but don't be surprised to discover some that aren't.)
10. *Identifying implications.* Implications are ideas that are understood or suggested by what is said, though not directly expressed themselves. The highly publicized accounts of children "divorcing" their parents implies that members of families have the right to accept or reject the other members. Does this suggest, you'd wonder, that parents have the same right? If so, should they be permitted to "divorce" or disown their children?

11. *Noting ironic possibilities.* Ironic possibilities run counter to expectations or intentions. For example, if a health care plan is touted as costing less than existing plans and providing greater coverage, ask "What if it costs more and delivers less?" If someone proclaims that cultural diversity will reduce friction among ethnic groups, ask "Might it instead *increase* friction?"

Planning

In this stage you create a blueprint to follow in the writing stage. It is easier to experiment with different formats when ideas are in rough, abbreviated form than when they are fully developed in sentences and paragraphs. This is no small concern in situations (such as in the applications in this book) in which you are dealing with a large number of complex ideas and a number of different perspectives. These are the steps you should follow in planning your compositions:

1. *List your ideas.* There's no need for complete sentences here or for concern about neatness and correctness. This list is not a draft of your paper, just a gathering of its ingredients, and it is for your eyes only.

2. *Choose the arrangement.* Decide what arrangement of your ideas will be easiest for your readers to follow and most effective in persuading them. The following ways to organize ideas in a persuasive composition are among the most common. (Long or complex compositions often employ two or more of these organizational patterns.)

   Conclusion-to-evidence order, in which the conclusion is presented first, followed by the evidence that supports it. This is easy to follow, saying in effect, "This is what I believe and here is why I believe it."

   Evidence-to-conclusion order, in which you lead your readers to your conclusion in step-by-step fashion. This is the preferred pattern whenever you are disputing a popular and well-entrenched view.

   Cause-to-effect order, in which the causes of a phenomenon, such as the Great Depression, are discussed first and then the effects. (The reverse order, effect-to-cause, may also be used.)

   Order of importance, in which the supporting arguments are presented in ascending order from the less to the most important. A variation of this is modified order of importance, in which the second most important argument is presented first and the most important, last. This arrangement is designed to evoke both a good first impression and a good last impression from the readers.

   When you have decided how you will arrange your ideas, number them accordingly, so that you can follow along easily when drafting the composition.

3. ***Choose your introduction and conclusion.*** Prepare readers for your central idea and its development. How can you do that best? Here are some effective ways to *introduce* a composition:

Ask a salient question and discuss possible answers.

Tell a brief anecdote that will illustrate the problem or issue you are addressing.

Use a quotation from a respected person, one that leads into your central idea.

Concede a point to the opposing side of the issue—in other words, cite a point those who differ with you have made and that you agree with, and use that as a lead-in to your disagreement.

Here are some effective ways to *conclude* a composition:

Recommend an action consistent with the argument presented in the body.

Elaborate on something mentioned in your introduction—in other words, answer a question raised there, or comment on an anecdote or a quotation.

Use another quotation that reinforces your central idea or a main point.

Present a new adecdote, being sure that it reinforces your central idea *but avoids raising issues not covered earlier.*

State the benefits that will result if your ideas are implemented or the harmful consequences that are likely if your ideas are not implemented.

State, briefly and stirringly, why your audience should endorse the argument you have presented.

4. ***Note which ideas need support and how you will support them.*** Intelligent people are not persuaded by mere statements of opinion but by the quality of the evidence supporting them. If you have examined the issue carefully and fairly, you will know which of your statements are open to question and what evidence is most relevant and compelling. (That evidence will have guided your own judgment.) Check each of your assertions and decide what evidence you have for it, then present the assertion in one or more of the following ways:

Present factual details, such as statistics.

Describe someone or something.

Offer a summary of an article or book.

Quote or paraphrase an authority.

Trace a historical development.

Offer a brief or extended narrative of a real or hypothetical event.

Present a definition, literal or figurative.

Detail a process or procedure.

Compare or contrast, explaining similarities or differences.

Analyze causes or effects.

Evaluate someone's argument, demonstrating its strengths and/or weaknesses.

Drafting

In this stage, you carry out your composition plan and produce a rough draft. Complete the entire draft at a single sitting, with as few interruptions as possible. Choose your words as carefully as you can, write complete sentences, and break your writing into paragraphs. But do not let yourself get bogged down in doing these things. If the right word doesn't come to mind at once, write a similar word that does. If you aren't sure whether a paragraph break is appropriate, make a tentative decision. Never pause during the writing stage to look up the meaning or spelling of a word or to check some rule of usage or grammar. These are important tasks, but the time for them is later. The more carefully you follow this advice, the better the flow of your writing is likely to be.

Revising

Your purpose in this stage is to transform your rough draft into a polished composition. Begin by reading your rough draft critically, preferably aloud, since hearing plus seeing will reveal flaws more readily than will seeing by itself. Ask yourself the following questions, and make marginal notes wherever the need for revision is indicated:

How else might I express my central idea? What part of it needs fuller explanation to be meaningful to my readers?

How can I improve the coherence of my composition? What rearrangement of my sentences and paragraphs would make the progression of thoughts easier to follow? Where might I add transitions (connecting words) to signal the movement from one idea to another?

Which of my ideas deserve more emphasis? Which deserve less emphasis? What is the best way to change the emphasis?

For which ideas have I failed to provide adequate support? Which techniques will best provide that support?

Editing

Your purpose in this stage is to find and correct lapses in grammar, usage, diction, spelling, punctuation, and paragraphing. For best results, proofread your composition not once but a number of times: one reading for errors in general, followed by separate readings for each of the errors that tend to recur in your writing. Consult a dictionary and a composition handbook, as necessary. Write your final draft.

DEVELOPING A READABLE STYLE

As a literate person, a college student, you have done considerable reading. You have encountered a variety of prose styles, some of them so awkward and difficult to follow that you have almost wished you'd never learned to read, and others that have delighted you and made you sorry to come to the end of the work. Perhaps you've concluded that writing style must be a matter of genetic endowment. There's probably some truth to the idea—after all, some people do seem to have a special talent for verbal expression, just as some have a mechanical aptitude. But writing is essentially a learned activity, so habit is more significant than heredity. If the habits you acquired through trial and error or imitation are bad habits, you will be a poor writer. If they are good habits, you will be a good writer. Observing the following guidelines can help you build better habits.

1. **Make your writing sound good.** Many people who write poorly speak fairly well. In fact, some are very lively and interesting conversationalists. If you are such a person, you can improve your writing by making it reflect your speech. This doesn't mean, of course, all the little flaws of speaking—the *um*-ing, *ah*-ing, pausing and repeating yourself. It means the rhythm of your speaking voice. To accomplish this, read your rough draft aloud and note passages that don't sound natural. Revise them so that you feel comfortable saying them aloud.

2. **Strive for brevity.** The idea of brevity may seem inconsistent with writing longer papers and developing your ideas. But it is not inconsistent at all. A paper may be long because it has a lot of unnecessary words in it or because it is filled with ideas. You can develop your thoughts fully and still have your writing be a model of brevity. Simply express each idea in as few words as you can, consistent with conveying the meaning and creating the understanding you intend.

3. **Express your ideas in simple language.** This doesn't mean to avoid all big words, just the ones that are *unnecessarily* big. George Orwell said it best: "Never use a long word where a short word will do."

4. **Put some variety into your sentences.** What is the most boring quality in a speaker? Most people would say speaking in a monotone. A monotone is the use of a single, unvaried tone of voice. The word is derived from the same Greek word that gives us *monotonous*. Monotones are monotonous. The equivalent of monotone in writing is sentences that begin the same way, have the same structure, and are the same length. They are perfectly predictable; that's why they

put readers to sleep. To get the monotony out of your writing, begin some of your sentences differently, vary their structure, and include an occasional short sentence among a series of longer ones (or vice versa).

5. ***Paraphrase more often than you quote.*** Quotations are valuable. But used too often, they shift the focus from your style to someone else's. Whenever it is possible to paraphrase (to express the other writer's idea in *your* words) without making the idea suffer in the process, do so. You must, of course, give the same credit for paraphrased ideas as you do for quoted ideas; that is, by mentioning the person informally in your sentence or by including a formal footnote.

6. ***Be lively.*** Purge your writing of bland, mechanical expression. Try to express your ideas colorfully and imaginatively. Your writing will take on a new vitality when you do. Here are two brief examples of lively, imaginative expression:

As you turn the pages of that American history book, the story gets more and more polluted. The pilgrim lands in the New World and discovers a land that is already occupied. How do you find something that somebody else has and claim you discovered it? And we talk about crime in the streets!

That is like my wife and I walking down the street and seeing you and your wife sitting in your brand-new automobile. Suppose my wife says to me, "Gee, I'd like to have a car like that." And I answer, "Let's discover it." So I walk over to you and your wife and say, "Get out of that damned car. My wife and I just discovered it." The shock and surprise you would naturally feel gives you some idea of how the Indians must have felt.[1]

Only a very soft-headed, sentimental, and rather servile generation of men could possibly be affected by advertisements at all. People who are a little more hard-headed, humorous, and intellectually independent, see the rather simple joke and are not impressed by this or any other form of self-praise. If you had said to a man in the Stone Age, "Ugg says Ugg makes the best stone hatchets," he would have perceived a lack of detachment and disinterestedness in the testimonial. If you had said to a medieval peasant, "Robert the Bowyer proclaims, with three blasts of a horn, that he makes good bows," the peasant would have said, "Well, of course he does," and thought about something more important. It is only among people whose minds have been weakened by a sort of mesmerism that so transparent a trick as that of advertisement could ever have been tried at all.[2]

A SAMPLE ANALYTICAL PAPER

The following analytical paper illustrates how your responses to the end-of-chapter applications can be presented in traditional composition form, observing the principles of writing explained in this appendix. The composition is a response to the issue of violence in contemporary films. Specifically, it answers the question "What is the most reasonable reaction to the recent trend toward the graphic portrayal of violent scenes in films?"

FILM VIOLENCE SHOULD MAKE US SICK

I walked out of the movie after half an hour. It was either leave or throw up. The movie was *An American Werewolf in London*. In an early scene a wolf attacks two young men, killing one and badly slashing the other. Then, while recovering in the hospital, the survivor dreams he is running nude through the forest, spies a deer, pounces on it wolflike, and devours it.

Two more nightmares quickly follow. In one, the survivor's family is brutally assaulted and killed by monsters with hideous faces. In the other his nurse is similarly attacked. Soon the young man's dead friend visits him in the hospital to warn that he will become a werewolf. The camera lingers on the dead man's disgustingly mutilated face.

In each of these scenes, no gory detail is left to the imagination. Yet somehow many people around me in the theater found the visual assault enjoyable. They laughed and laughed. I left.

Like that audience, some critics have taken the film lightheartedly. The *Newsweek* critic, for example, titled his review "Cool Ghoul" and termed the film "a nearly perfect specimen of the wise-guy movie" in which the hero turns into a werewolf and "masticates half of Piccadilly before the bloody climax." That kind of critical reaction reflects a casual attitude toward film violence that has become very fashionable in recent years. That attitude rests on four widely accepted ideas, each of them flawed.

The first idea is that any time an audience is made to laugh, the effect is wholesome. This is nonsense. There's a big difference between laughing at someone making a fool of him- or herself or at an ironic development and laughing at someone being raped or torn to shreds. Some things—mental retardation, physical handicaps, and terminal illness, for example—just aren't funny.

The second idea is that films don't affect our attitudes and values. This view ignores the most obvious findings of psychology. Psychologists tell us that most people aren't born sensitive or insensitive, kind or cruel. Rather, they are shaped one way or the other by their experiences, including their vicarious experiences on the larger-than-life movie screen.

Chicago film critic Roger Ebert reports that in viewing another film on two separate occasions, he observed both audiences laughing in scenes showing a woman beaten, raped, and cut up. One respectable-looking man next to him kept murmuring, "That'll teach her. Give it to her." Ebert found that reaction frightening. So should we all. But we shouldn't be surprised by it. Like any powerful emotional experience, film viewing has the capacity to brutalize us, make us feel enjoyment where our humanity demands we feel revulsion.

The third popular notion is that films don't affect people's behavior. This idea is questionable at best. Consider the case of the 24-year-old Brockton, Massachusetts, man who, believing himself to be a vampire, killed his grandmother and drank her blood. Or the case of the Cincinnati publisher who marketed the 1982 Cat Hater's Calendar, featuring color photos of cats being hanged and wrapped in foil on a grill. No particular film may be responsible for inciting such actions, but surely the climate of violence generated by horror films contributed to them, at least by stimulating the person's imagination.

Finally, it is widely believed that the idea of democracy forbids any restriction on artistic expression, including that of filmmakers. To approve of even the most general guidelines is considered an attack on the U.S. Constitution. This belief is too extreme to be reasonable. Individual rights should not be allowed to take precedence over public rights. No one, for example, should be permitted to poison the air the rest of us breathe. And neither should a filmmaker have the right to poison the social climate.

This is not to say that the movie industry should be forbidden to explore the unpleasant side of reality. On the contrary, no subject should be forbidden to filmmakers because no subject is good or bad in itself. It is the *treatment* that makes the difference. In the hands of a genuine artist, even the most unspeakable violence can be handled inoffensively. Alfred Hitchcock's *Psycho* generated incomparable suspense without the knife once touching the victim on camera.

Not only is there no good reason to approve the kind and amount of film violence we have been subjected to in recent years—there is compelling reason to reject it. Across this country, from small communities to great cities, crime and violence are a daily threat to millions of people. If we are ever to conquer that threat, we must retain our capacity to be outraged by it. But it is precisely that capacity that is diminished every time we suppress revulsion and watch a succession of violent acts on the movie screen.

A Guide to Formal Speaking, Conversation, and Group Discussion

Thinking is as important in formal speaking, conversation, and group discussion as it is in writing. It provides the substance of what we say and helps us make appropriate decisions about organization and delivery. This appendix will help you understand and apply the principles of effective speaking.

FORMAL SPEAKING

In many ways the challenge of making a formal speech is identical to the challenge of writing a composition. So the basic goals and strategies discussed in Appendix A, "A Guide to Composition" (and Chapter 15, "Build a Persuasive Case") are applicable here. For any formal speeches you give in conjunction with this book, you will already have obtained your material in the course of analyzing a problem or issue. You also will have given careful consideration to the demands of the occasion and the characteristics of your audience. The discussion that follows will therefore be limited to those matters which are different in a speech than in a composition.

Types of Speeches

Formal speeches are classified as follows: *memorized* (delivered without notes), *manuscript* (read verbatim), *extemporaneous* (delivered from notes), and *impromptu* (unprepared, completely spontaneous). Impromptu speeches are the most difficult to give because the potential is greatest for rambling and incoherence. Memorized speeches can be effective, but if you forget or lose the sequence of the ideas, you'll be left standing in embarrassing silence.

Experienced speakers are often able to read manuscript speeches enthusiastically and animatedly without sacrificing eye contact; amateurs, on the other hand, almost always stare at the page, speak in a monotone, and bore the audience. The best choice for the majority of speakers, particularly the inexperienced, is the extemporaneous speech. It provides the security of notes without the temptation of fully written out sentences.

Organizing Your Material

A formal speech has three divisions: the introduction, the body, and the conclusion.

The Introduction   A successful introduction serves both to focus the audience's attention and to arouse their interest in what you are going to say. Effective techniques for doing so include making a startling statement, asking a question, recounting an anecdote, and reciting a quotation. (If the relevance of your introduction to your central idea is not self-evident, explain it.) Keep your introductions appropriately brief, generally no more than 10 or 15 percent of the overall presentation.

The Body   The body of a speech consists of the statement and support of your central idea. Unless you have a good reason for withholding your central idea until later in the speech, state it immediately after the introduction. Then present your evidence. Your goal is to have your audience remember your main points and understand how they support your central idea. Listening, of course, is more difficult than reading—even a brief lapse in attention will result in lost information because there is no looking back as in reading. (Remember: If the audience gets lost, they will usually blame you rather than themselves.) Accordingly, you will need to limit your main points. From three to five is standard; more than five is seldom effective.

In addition, use a clear and straightforward pattern of organization. For example, use time order when your evidence consists of a sequence of events, order of importance for a series of reasons, and cause-to-effect order when explaining how a phenomenon occurs. Don't make the mistake of reasoning, "My argument is complex, so the audience will just have to work to grasp it." The more complex the argument, the harder *the speaker* should work to present it clearly.

Following are three proven ways to make your speech even more accessible to your audience:

1. Use large, legible visual aids (charts, graphs, transparencies, and/or videos) whenever possible, being sure that they reinforce rather than substitute for your talk, that you continue to maintain eye contact with your audience while presenting them, and that you allow sufficient time for your audience to absorb each visual aid before putting it aside.
2. Use signal words and phrases to help your audience make connections among the parts of your speech, saying, for example, "One reason for . . . ," "A second reason for . . . ," and so on.
3. Summarize your main points just before the conclusion.

The Conclusion   In a persuasive speech, an effective conclusion underlines the central idea and reinforces the appeal to understanding and/or action. Among the most effective ways to conclude a composition are these:

1. Recommend an action consistent with the argument presented in the speech.
2. Elaborate on something mentioned in your introduction; in other words, answer a question raised there or comment on an anecdote or a quotation.
3. Present a new adecdote, being sure that it reinforces your central idea *but avoids raising issues not covered in your speech.*
4. Use another quotation.
5. State the benefits that will result if your ideas are implemented or the harmful consequences that are likely if your ideas are not implemented.
6. State, briefly and stirringly, why the audience should endorse the argument you have presented.

Sample Outline and Speech

You will speak more confidently and effectively if you plan your speech carefully, using an outline. Following are a sample outline and speech:

THE OUTLINE

Introduction	When your children watch a 15-second television commercial, they may be forced to shift their attention as many as 50 times. . . .
Body	
Central Idea	For the sake of our children and our country's future, the design and format of commercials must be regulated.
1st Main Point	Attention span is an essential factor in all learning. . . .
2nd Main Point	A mature attention span is an asset in everyday adult life. . . .
3rd Main Point	A highly developed attention span is indispensable in most careers. . . .
4th Main Point	The solution is to reduce the number of attention shifts in commercials and to cluster commercials at the end of each program. . . .
5th Main Point	Business leaders should take the initiative to implement this solution. . . .

Summary	To summarize, if America's children are to meet the challenges of learning, everyday living, and careers . . .
Conclusion	Parents and teachers could and should do a better job of educating young people. But they can hardly be expected to do so effectively as long as . . .

THE SPEECH

When your children watch a 15-second television commercial, they may be forced to shift their attention as many as 50 times. The camera will quickly cut from one scene or angle to another and then another, artificially creating excitement by multiplying images and accelerating the pace of change. Since there are 11 minutes of commercials in every viewing hour, if children watch 4 hours of television a day, they may shift their attention well over 8000 times. No one should be surprised that they find it difficult to concentrate on schoolwork.

For the sake of our children and our country's future, the design and format of commercials must be regulated. There is nothing radical or unprecedented about regulation. The Federal Communications Commission has always had the authority to set standards. In the early days of television the standard length of a commercial was a full minute. Over the next few decades the commission first approved 30-second commercials and then 15-second commercials. Meanwhile, advertisers were building in more and more attention shifts. Why is more stringent regulation desirable now? Because a short attention span is a serious handicap in every area of life.

To begin with, attention span is an essential factor in all learning. The more attentive the grade school child, the more that child will delight in hearing Dr. Seuss's books read and the more quickly he or she will master the fundamentals of reading, writing, and arithmetic. And the longer the child's attention span grows, the more adept he or she will become in reading complex material, struggling with difficult concepts, persevering in investigation and analysis, and engaging in thoughtful dialogue with others.

Second, a mature attention span is an asset in everyday adult life. Successful relationships with other people are not possible without communication skills. That means not only expressing ideas but also listening carefully to what others say and interpreting their nonverbal clues to meaning. It means being observant and reflective not just when the spirit moves us but also when the occasion demands. In short, it means exercising sufficient self-control to maintain concentration even in the midst of distractions. Individuals who have never learned how to focus their attention for more than a few minutes at a time can never engage in meaningful discussions with friends and family, and thus can never solve the problems that divide them or strengthen the bonds that unite them.

Third, a highly developed attention span is indispensable in most careers. Any rewarding job poses challenges to one's ingenuity, challenges that cannot be instantly overcome but require extended periods of concentration on small and unexciting details. In such instances, competency as well as excellence depends on painstaking effort. The lawyer labors over the brief, the accountant pores over the tax data, the doctor focuses, sometimes for hours, on the intricacies of the surgical procedure. People whose habits of mind have been shaped by kaleidoscopic commercials are doomed to mediocrity if not inadequacy in their careers. And their shortcomings deprive all who depend on them.

The solution to the problem is to reduce the number of attention shifts in commercials and to cluster commercials at the end of each program. The Federal Communications Commission already has outlawed subliminal messages—those that appear on the screen so briefly that viewers are not conscious of them. They should extend this regulation and limit the number of shifts of scene or camera angle per commercial, and perhaps return to the original 1-minute commercial. Moreover, the commission should do as many European countries do and eliminate interruptions within programs by moving all commercials to the end of the hour or half hour.

Business leaders should take the initiative to implement this solution because they alone have the necessary power and influence to do so. The advertising industry is often considered responsible for the commercials that are shown on television. Yet the final approval for commercials rests with the corporations that pay for them. If corporate executives said, "Here are our new guidelines—follow them," the advertising industry would comply. And corporations have every reason to issue such directives. The attention span of their employees affects their business; the attention span of their fellow citizens affects the strength of the nation.

To summarize, if America's children are to meet the challenges of learning, everyday living, and careers, television commercials must be prevented from retarding attention spans.

Many business leaders and representatives of the media criticize parents and teachers for failing to educate young people. The criticism may be justified in some cases. But the critics must not ignore their own responsibility to foster the development of a mature attention span in America's children.

If the above speech were delivered extemporaneously, the speaker would not take the entire text to the podium, only note cards containing key words or phrases, perhaps one or two for each paragraph.

Practicing the Delivery

When you hear an accomplished public speaker make a formal presentation, you may be impressed by his or her apparent spontaneity and envy the person's ability to choose the exact words to express thoughts and to connect ideas so clearly and logically. But in most cases that seeming effortlessness is actually the result of effort. Effective speaking, like effective writing, occurs less by chance than by diligence. That means rehearsing over and over, until your delivery is flawless. Keep the following points in mind when you rehearse and when you deliver the speech:

1. From the moment you rise and walk to the podium until you return to your seat, your audience will be forming impressions of you. Walk

(and stand) straight; gesture freely and naturally, but not frenetically or distractingly.

2. People tend to distrust anyone who doesn't look them in the eye. As you look out at your audience, aim for their eyes and not for the back wall or the ceiling. To be sure that everyone gets the impression you are speaking to him or her, shift your gaze from side to side and front to back of the room, pausing for a second or two after each movement. If you look down at your notes, do so briefly, and then quickly make eye contact again with your audience.

3. Be sure you speak loud enough that everyone in the room can hear you. Enunciate clearly. Keep your tone warm and friendly and don't be afraid to smile. If you have identified any bad vocal habits, such as the tendency to slur your words or to let the ends of your sentences trail off into a whisper, make a special effort to avoid them.

4. Remember that almost everyone is nervous when speaking in public, even the most accomplished professionals. The best way to overcome nervousness is to forget about yourself—think instead about the importance of what you are going to say and your audience's desire for you to succeed. (No audience wants to have a speaker punish them with a poor presentation. They want the speaker to do well.) Instead of trying to calm yourself, channel your energy into enthusiasm and dynamism.

CONVERSATION

Everyone knows how to carry on a productive conversation, right? Wrong. Believe it or not, many people converse without the slightest idea of what is occurring or whether their discussion is productive. The main reason for this is that many people's conversation is *egospeak*. The term was coined by Edmond Addeo and Robert Burger in their book of the same name. They define this common malady as "the art of boosting our own egos by speaking only about what *we* want to talk about, and not giving a hoot in hell about what the other person wants to talk about."[1]

Conversation is not serial monologue, in which one person speaks to him- or herself, followed by another person speaking to him- or herself, and so on. Instead, it is dialogue, a give-and-take communication in which each person bears responsibility not only for expressing his or her own thoughts and feelings but also for hearing and understanding the other's thoughts and feelings.

When conversation is serious rather than casual, as it is in business and professional contexts, the participants aim not merely to *share* meaning but also to *create* meaning. In other words, they exchange thoughts to generate or change ideas, build fresh interpretations and judgments, and produce solutions and decisions. To achieve these aims, of course, is not easy; a high level of conversational skill is needed.

Speaking Well

Conversation is less formal, more relaxed, and more personal than public speaking, thus allowing a fuller exchange of views. Nevertheless, many of the guidelines used for public speaking apply to conversation as well. The following ones are especially applicable:

> Maintain a professional bearing, sitting erect and controlling your gestures as you speak.

> Exercise care in your choice of wording, striving for exactness and clarity of expression, as well as for economy, vitality, and appropriate emphasis.

> Make frequent eye contact with the other person and monitor your voice quality, including enunciation, volume, pitch, and rate.

> If you have any annoying vocal habits or mannerisms, make a special effort to avoid them in conversation. (You may, of course, have never listened critically to your own voice. If that is the case, ask a friend for a candid assessment; better yet, tape-record your voice in normal conversation, and decide which of your vocal habits, if any, may be annoying to others.)

If you have never considered approaching conversation quite so meticulously, these recommendations may seem to preclude naturalness. Be assured that is not the case: With practice you will find them perfectly natural. More important, you will find that they help you make a more positive impression on others.

In addition to applying public speaking guidelines to conversation, you should also prepare for a conversation whenever it is scheduled in advance and you know its subject and purpose. More specifically, you should consider what questions are likely to arise and how you will respond to them, clarifying your views in your own mind so that you will be able to express them effectively in conversation. In addition, you should give some thought to *why* you think as you do; that is, consider the reasons and the evidence that underlie your positions. You may even wish to take along relevant factual material if it will be useful.

Whatever planning you do, be sure you do it in the right spirit. If the purpose of the conversation is to explore various positions and consider alternatives, it would be inappropriate to go with your mind made up in advance, expecting to persuade the other person. Remember that if you wish others to have open minds, you should make sure your mind is open, too. This doesn't mean that you should set aside genuine convictions. It only means that you should regard conversation as a cooperative, not a competitive, venture.

Listening Well

As important as speaking is in conversation, listening is even more important. Research reveals that people spend more time in listening than in any other single activity: more than reading and writing, more even than speaking (and undoubtedly more than thinking).[2] Nevertheless, most people achieve only 25 to 50 percent listening effectiveness.[3] In practical terms, that means that out of every four sentences that are spoken, only one or two are heard and understood by others. Small wonder there is so much misunderstanding among people. Small wonder, too, that so many business and professional conversations are unproductive.

In brief, to be a good conversationalist, not only must you be able to speak effectively—you must also have mastered the art of listening.

Improving Your Listening Skills

Here are six simple steps you can take to become a more effective listener:

Change your view of listening. Don't think of it as sitting passively, doing nothing, but as an active response, as *reading with your ears.* Practice using concentration in listening just as you use it in reading: to attend to the other person's words, steering your mind, as necessary, when distractions occur. It may help to remind yourself that listening intently to others will often reward you with valuable insights you would otherwise miss.

Each time the other person begins speaking, switch your attention from your thoughts to the speaker and keep them there until the speaker stops. If, like many people, you tend to plan what you will say next when you should be listening, you have simply not developed the habit of switching attention. All you need to develop it is practice. Start with casual conversation, where you will be less anxious about getting your words right and therefore less tempted to ignore the other person's words.

Maintain eye contact when the other person is speaking. You will be better able to enter into the person's frame of mind (and less likely to be distracted) if you are looking at his or her eyes rather than up, down, and around the room. Moreover, maintaining eye contact suggests that you respect the other person and are interested in his or her ideas.

Be prepared to have others disagree with you. Some people listen well when their ideas are accepted but stop listening as soon as the other person expresses even mild reservations. Not infrequently, such people grow visibly agitated and interrupt the other person. If you react this way, you probably misunderstand the nature of serious conversation. Disagreement is inevitable whenever informed people discuss complex issues. Differences of interpretation are worthwhile if handled constructively: They identify matters worthy of exploration. Reminding yourself of this from time to time will help you set ego aside and greet disagreement calmly and confidently.

In general, don't mix listening and analyzing. It is possible to listen to others and evaluate their words simultaneously, but it is inadvisable to do so until you have become an accomplished listener. The line between evaluation while listening and planning what to say next is too fine and too easily crossed.

Test your understanding of points the other person has indicated are important by restating what was said in your own words. This can be done smoothly by combining the restatement with a question or comment in this manner: "If I understand you correctly, you believe the frequent shifts to and from commercials on network television are preventing young people from developing a mature attention span. Am I correct?"

Don't expect to become an effective conversationalist overnight. Your present habits of speaking and listening were formed over the course of years. Replacing them with new ones will take time and effort. The best approach is to work on one or two at a time. For example, for the next few days you might concentrate on maintaining eye contact when the other person is speaking and steering your mind back to his or her words whenever it starts to wander. When you have made progress with those habits, you will be ready to work on others.

A final word of advice: Practice speaking and listening well in every conversation you have, not just serious or scheduled conversations. By doing so, you will master the art of conversation more quickly.

GROUP DISCUSSION

Although one-to-one conversation will always be a fundamental form of business and professional communication, group discussion continues to increase in importance. One reason for this is technological advance and the specialization that accompanies it: Today's decision making must reflect an ever-widening circle of expert opinion. Another reason is the realization that organizations reap substantial benefits from giving every employee a regular opportunity to contribute suggestions about policies and procedures. (The best-known approach to providing such opportunity is the "quality circle.")

Whether you are preparing for a career in business, public service, or a profession like law, medicine, teaching, or engineering, your preparation will not be complete unless you master the art of group discussion. Success in your career will depend, to a great extent, on your ability to discuss problems and issues with people who do not share your cultural background, level of education, or priorities and to maintain an attitude of respect and cooperation.

The best way to prepare yourself for this career challenge is to use this class—indeed, all your classes—as your training ground in group discussion. All you need to do is apply the following guidelines conscientiously.

Prepare for class discussions. If you are given a specific topic for subsequent class discussion, begin working on it early and complete your work before class. If you are not given a specific topic, try to anticipate what discussion might arise from lectures and reading assignments. Jot down questions and ideas you'd like to share with the class. If you can spare the time, do a little extra research on perplexing points, either in the library or in interviews with knowledgeable people on campus.

Monitor your contributions in class discussions. Be aware of how often you speak. If you find that you tend to speak more than anyone else, consider reducing the number of your contributions. If you are like most heavy contributors, you probably think faster than others and so are ready to speak before they are. Try waiting an extra half minute or so before contributing; you may find that others will express the same thought you were planning to express. Let them do so; wait to speak until you have a thought you have reason to believe is original.

If, on the other hand, you tend to speak less than anyone else, try to increase your contributions, particularly if no one else expresses ideas similar to yours. If it will make you feel more comfortable doing so, prepare some comments before the meeting or class and use them at appropriate times.

When you speak, try not to wander off the point; aim for clarity, directness, and economy of expression. When you offer interpretations and judgments, be prepared to support them with reasons and evidence should someone ask you to do so. And never take offense at such a request.

Be sensitive to the needs of the group. Be alert to the professor's or moderator's handling of the discussion. If you sense that he or she is trying to help the group through a "dry" period in which ideas are not flowing, make a special effort to contribute at that moment. This in no way means that you should be a slave to the group. It means only that you should accept your share of responsibility for the group's effort and not sit back waiting for others to take the initiative.

Listen to others' ideas. Make a special effort to leave your ego and preconceptions and private agendas outside the meeting room. Listen with special care to the views of those who do not share your perspective. After all, they will be the ones you will be tempted to deny a fair hearing. Before each class meeting, if necessary, remind yourself that differences of opinion provide valuable learning experience. Instead of fearing or resenting diversity, welcome it: If you disagree with something that is said, by all means express your disagreement and try to persuade others, but don't be disturbed if others continue to disagree. Be content with expressing yourself well.

Practice civility. A group can function effectively only in an atmosphere of mutual respect and good will. For that atmosphere to be maintained, everyone must practice good manners. To do your part, don't speak unless you are recognized by the professor or moderator, don't carry on side conversations while others have the floor, and never interrupt a speaker regardless of how strongly you feel prompted to speak.

The Fundamentals of Logic

Logic is the study of the principles of reasoning. Its main concerns are the structure of arguments and the process by which conclusions are derived from premises. Thus, its focus is not on statements as such, but on the *relationships* between them. In other words, in logic the question "Are the statements in this argument true or false?" is less important than the question "Is the conclusion in this argument validly drawn?"

THREE BASIC PRINCIPLES

Three principles underlie the subject of logic:

- The principle of identity: If a statement is true, then it is true.
- The principle of excluded middle: A statement is either true or false.
- The principle of contradiction: No statement can be both true and false.

Each of these principles has been challenged from time to time, but properly understood, each is true and does not admit exceptions. At first consideration we might, for example, think that some realities change and so the principle of identity isn't correct. The statement "Infant Charles Jackson weighs 8 pounds, 2 ounces" is true at birth but false for the rest of Charles Jackson's existence. Yet on closer inspection, we see that the statement is an assertion about his weight at a particular time. His later weight has no bearing on that truth.

Similarly, it might seem that the principle of excluded middle is challenged by a statement that is partly true and partly false, such as "Ronald Reagan, the thirty-fifth president of the United States, was at one time governor of California." But closer examination reveals that the statement is really two separate statements fused into one: the false statement that Reagan is thirty-fifth in the line of presidents and the true one about his prior office.

Finally, it may be possible to think of a statement that seems to be both true and false, but only if it is given two different interpretations. The sentence "Leonardo is Italian" cannot be both true and false at the same time in the same way. It may be, of course, that Leonardo is Italian by birth but American by naturalization. Yet to understand the sentence in that way is to read "is Italian" in two different senses. Such an example does not challenge the principle of contradiction.

FORMAL ARGUMENT

The traditional way of expressing a logical argument is in a syllogism. A syllogism is a kind of verbal mathematics: $a + b = c$ (or $1 + 2 = 3$). It is composed of three statements: the *major premise,* the *minor premise,* and the *conclusion.* Here is a famous example of a syllogism:

All men are mortal.

Socrates is a man.

Therefore, Socrates is mortal.

The major premise is the first statement. It is called major because it contains the *major term* of the syllogism (in this case *mortal*). The major term always appears as the predicate of the conclusion; the *minor term* (in this case *Socrates*) always appears as the subject of the conclusion. The *middle term* (*men/man*) does not appear in the conclusion but is the common element, the connector, between the premises.

For analytic ease, and to help themselves focus on structure instead of content, logicians often substitute symbols for the terms in a syllogism. The symbols most often used are *P, Q,* and *R.* The preceding syllogism would be expressed symbolically as follows:

All *P* are *Q.*

R is *P.*

Therefore, *R* is *Q.*

COMMON ERRORS IN SYLLOGISMS

Before we turn to specific errors, it is necessary to clarify the concept of *distribution.* Distribution means making an assertion about *every* member of a class. Thus, in the statement "All colleges offer degrees" the subject is distributed. However, in the sentence "Some colleges offer degrees" the subject is undistributed.

There are four errors that frequently occur in syllogisms and two related errors that, though technically not syllogistic, are similar in form:

- Undistributed middle
- Illicit process
- Affirming the consequent
- Denying the antecedent
- Converting a conditional
- Negating antecedent and consequent

Undistributed Middle

Each middle term in a syllogism must be distributed at least once. If it is not distributed in either of the premises that it is intended to connect, the error of undistributed middle exists and the reasoning is invalid.

SYMBOLIC EXPRESSION	EXAMPLE
All P are Q.	All hamsters are mammals.
All R are Q.	All elephants are mammals.
Therefore, all P are R.	Therefore, all hamsters are elephants.

Both the premises are true—both hamsters and elephants are mammals. But that shared quality is not sufficient reason to conclude that they are identical species. There are many kinds of mammals other than elephants.

Illicit Process

Any term in a syllogism that is distributed in the conclusion must also be distributed in the premise in which it occurs. If either the major or the minor term is distributed in the conclusion but not in the premise in which it occurs, the error of illicit process exists.

SYMBOLIC EXPRESSION	EXAMPLE
Illicit Major	
All P are Q.	All dalmatians are spotted.
No R are P.	No goldfish are dalmatians.
Therefore, no R are Q.	Therefore, no goldfish are spotted.

Having spots is indeed a characteristic of dalmatians, but they do not *own* that characteristic. Other animal species, such as butterflies and leopards, have it, too. So the fact that goldfish are not dalmatians does not mean that goldfish cannot have spots.

SYMBOLIC EXPRESSION	**EXAMPLE**
Illicit Minor	
All *P* are *Q*.	All Mensa members are intelligent.
Some *R* are *P*.	Some goatherds are Mensa members.
Therefore, all *R* are *Q*.	Therefore, all goatherds are intelligent.

It is true that all Mensa members are intelligent (at least in terms of the mental characteristics measured by intelligence tests). So it would be logical, even inescapable, to conclude that those goatherds that are Mensa members are intelligent. But the premise speaks only of *some* goatherds, not all of them. So it is improper to conclude that *all* of them are intelligent. Nonmembers may be positively brilliant but too modest to celebrate their intellectual gifts, or they may be dumber than the animals they tend. On the basis of what is given here, we simply can't say.

The four remaining errors occur in hypothetical (if-then) reasoning. They are all corruptions of the following *legitimate* form of hypothetical reasoning:

If *P*, then *Q*.

P.

Therefore *Q*.

Affirming the Consequent

SYMBOLIC EXPRESSION	**EXAMPLE**
If *P*, then *Q*.	If I try hard, I succeed.
Q.	I succeeded today.
Therefore, *P*.	Therefore, I tried hard [today].

The first premise doesn't say that trying hard is the only way to succeed. It just says it is *one way*. So there may be others: chance, for example, or good fortune. Thus it is incorrect to say that today's success proves that I tried hard. I may have just been lucky.

Denying the Antecedent

SYMBOLIC EXPRESSION	**EXAMPLE**
If *P*, then *Q*.	If Agnes knows, then Marie knows.
Not *P*.	Agnes doesn't know.
Therefore, not *Q*.	Therefore, Marie doesn't know.

The first premise asserts only that Marie knows when Agnes knows. It leaves open the possibility that Marie may also know when, as in this case, Agnes *doesn't* know.

Converting a Conditional

SYMBOLIC EXPRESSION	EXAMPLE
If *P*, then *Q*.	If the star retires, the show will be cancelled.
Therefore if *Q*, then *P*.	Therefore, if the show is cancelled, the star will retire.

The first premise asserts that there is a necessary connection between the star's presence on the show and the show's continuation. The meaning conveyed is that *the star is such an important factor in the show's success that it could not continue to succeed without him or her.* The conclusion asserts that because the star is so important, he or she cannot continue to be successful apart from the show. That assertion is absurd.

Negating Antecedent and Consequent

SYMBOLIC EXPRESSION	EXAMPLE
If *P*, then *Q*.	If I go to graduate school, then I'll get a high-paying job.
Therefore, if not *P*, then not *Q*.	Therefore, if I don't go to graduate school, I won't get a high-paying job.

Graduate school, the premise suggests, guarantees one a high-paying job. (Would that it were true!) But since the premise does not say that this route is the *only* one to such a job, the possibility remains open that one can get a high-paying job without going to graduate school.

Doing the Warm–up Exercises

The warm-up exercises at the end of each chapter are intended to limber up your mind for the thinking demanded by the applications. Try not to see them as a chore but as an enjoyable activity, an opportunity to develop the playful attitude toward problem solving that creative people have. Some of the problems will, of course, resist solution. Even more frustrating, some will be relatively simple to figure out but very difficult to explain clearly to your readers. However, none of these difficulties will be insurmountable if you apply the right strategy.

SEVEN HELPFUL STRATEGIES

1. If the exercise consists of a single statement to be analyzed, read it again carefully. Be sure you understand what it says. Ask yourself, "Does this make sense?" If you find yourself answering with a firm yes or no, decide precisely what makes you respond that way. Often that will be what you should explain to your audience.
2. If words fail you at the outset, try using a diagram to get you out of your rut. This will not work with all problems, but some lend themselves to the approach very nicely. If, for example, the passage were "All dogs are animals. Fido is a dog. Therefore, Fido is an animal," you might diagram it this way:

The diagram would suggest the way to explain your analysis:

> It is correct to classify dogs under the general heading *animals*. Moreover, this applies not just to some dogs but also to *all* dogs. There is no other category under which to classify dogs. Fido is correctly classified as a dog, so he must be an animal.

3. When the statement presents as fact something that is not fact, identify the error and explain how it invalidates the statement.
4. When the statement confuses two terms or ideas, identify the confusion and show its effect on the statement as a whole.
5. When the statement presents a conclusion as the only possible conclusion, and other conclusions are also possible, present the other conclusions and demonstrate that they, too, are reasonable (perhaps more reasonable).
6. When the statement, or some part of it, is open to interpretation, use the if-then approach to analysis. Consider, for example, the statement "Everyone must die." Here's how the if-then approach works:

> The statement as it stands is ambiguous. *If* it is taken to mean "At present there is no known way for human beings to avoid death," *then* it is a statement of fact. But *if* it is taken to mean "There will never be a way for human beings to avoid death," *then* it is presumptuous. For, however unlikely such a development may seem, we cannot say for certain it will never occur.

> The if-then approach is also useful when you are uncertain of the facts. In other words, you might say, "I am uncertain of the facts in this matter, but *if* they are as stated, *then* the conclusion is sound because. . . . *If*, however, they are not as stated, *then* the conclusion is not sound because. . . ."

7. If the exercise consists of a dialogue, read it several times, each time for a different purpose. First, read it to understand the discussion in its entirety. Then read each person's comments individually, noting the progression of his or her thoughts and the degree of logical consistency. Finally, read for implications and assumptions; these are ideas that are not stated directly but are nevertheless identifiable by what *is* stated directly. (The dialogue in Exercise 2, on page 241, contains an unstated idea.)

SAMPLE EXERCISES AND RESPONSES

Each exercise you do will have its own particular details and will therefore demand a special response. For that reason, no one formula can be given for responding to exercises. The following sample exercises and responses, though fairly typical, are illustrations of what can be done, but they are not models to be slavishly imitated.

Exercise 1

The Assignment   Analyze the following statement, deciding whether it is reasonable and, if so, to what degree. Explain your thinking thoroughly.

The results of a recent national examination reveal that 75 percent of America's high school students are below average in reading ability.

The Response

I don't know if the statement is a factual one. But I can say that it may have different meanings, depending on how the word *average* is interpreted. And the various meanings affect the reasonableness of the statement.

Below average may mean "below a score that half the high school seniors have achieved in previous years." Or it may mean "below a score now regarded as an acceptable minimum." In either of these cases, the statement is a reasonable one and could very well be factual.

But there is a more technical definition of below average. It may mean "below the arithmetic mean (the score derived from dividing the total scores of all high school students by the total number of high school students)." I am not sure whether it is even mathematically possible that 75 percent could fall below the mean. But I do know that it is highly unlikely. So if this is what the statement is saying, it is not very reasonable.

Exercise 2

The Assignment   Read the following dialogue carefully. Then decide whether what is stated (or implied) makes sense. Explain your reasoning thoroughly.

JOHN: Do you think the masses really have any power in the United States today?

BILL: That depends on what groups you include in "the masses." Would you include professional people—doctors, lawyers, teachers. . . ?

JOHN: *Teachers?* They don't make that much money.

The Response

John's last comment reveals the assumption that money is the basis for determining professional status. That assumption is unwarranted. If money were the measure, a lawyer with a small practice would not be considered a professional, but a plumber with a good business would be. If an apprentice clerk in a store inherited a large sum of money from his aunt, he would be a nonprofessional one day and a professional the next. No, a professional person is one engaged in one of the *professions:* those fields requiring a liberal arts or science education and some form of subsequent specialization. The amount of money a person earns is beside the point.

APPENDIX
E

Solutions to Sample Problems

THE THREE GLASSES PROBLEM

The key to solving this problem is to use one or more of the glasses as a measuring device. Here's how to proceed:

1. Fill the 3-ounce glass and empty it into the 5-ounce glass. Fill it a second time and empty as much as will fit into the 5-ounce glass. Now the 3-ounce glass will contain 1 ounce of liquid, the 5-ounce glass 5 ounces, and the 8-ounce glass 2 ounces.
2. Empty the 5-ounce glass into the 8-ounce glass. Then empty the 3-ounce glass into the 5-ounce glass. Now the 3-ounce glass will be empty, the 5-ounce glass will contain 1 ounce of liquid, and the 8-ounce glass 7 ounces.
3. Fill the 3-ounce glass from the 8-ounce glass. Then empty the 3-ounce glass into the 5-ounce glass. Now the 3-ounce glass will be empty and the 5- and 8-ounce glasses will each contain 4 ounces.

THE YOUNG GIRL/OLD WOMAN PROBLEM

The young girl is looking away from you. You can see only the side of her face. The old woman is looking down, her chin touching the top of her chest.

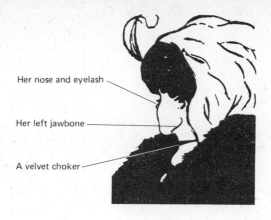

Her nose and eyelash

Her left jawbone

A velvet choker

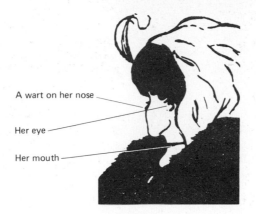

A wart on her nose

Her eye

Her mouth

THE VASE AND FACES PROBLEM

To see the vase, focus on the white object against a background of shadow. To see two faces, imagine a bright light shining through a window and two people standing nose to nose, in silhouette.

Notes

CHAPTER 1

1. Arthur Koestler, *The Act of Creation* (New York: Macmillan, 1964), p. 173.
2. James Mursell, *Using Your Mind Effectively* (New York: McGraw-Hill, 1951), pp. vi–vii.
3. For a more detailed discussion, see D. Galin, "Two Modes of Consciousness and the Two Halves of the Brain," in *Symposium on Consciousness,* eds. P. Lee et al. (New York: Viking, 1976).
4. "Research Synthesis on Right and Left Hemispheres." *Educational Leadership* 40, no. 4 (January 1983): 66–71.
5. See, for example, Sidney Parnes, *Creative Behavior Guidebook* (New York: Scribner's, 1967), p. 32.
6. E. Paul Torrance, *Guiding Creative Talent* (Englewood Cliffs, NJ: Prentice-Hall, 1962), p. 5.
7. Brewster Ghiselin, *The Creative Process: A Symposium* (Berkeley: University of California Press, 1954), p. 115.
8. See, for example, J. Dewey, *Art as Experience* (New York: Milton Balch, 1934), p. 73.
9. Quoted in W. I. B. Beveridge, *The Art of Scientific Investigation* (New York: Norton, 1951), p. 56.
10. Koestler, *Act of Creation,* p. 146.
11. This definition is Henry Hazlitt's, quoted ibid., pp. 72–73.
12. Benjamin Bloom and Lois J. Broder, *Problem-Solving Processes of College Students* (Chicago: University of Chicago Press, 1950), pp. 25–30.
13. Ernest Dimnet, *The Art of Thinking* (New York: Simon & Schuster, 1928), pp. 103–104.

CHAPTER 2

1. According to the CBS news program "60 Minutes," 17 September 1978, the most popular street names are, first, Park (avenue or street), and second, Washington. Main is thirty-second on the list, and Broadway is not in the top 50.

2. Israel Scheffler, *Reason and Teaching* (New York: Bobbs-Merrill, 1973).

3. Michael Brenson, "Scholars Re-Examining Rembrandt . . ." *New York Times,* 25 November 1985, p. 6.

4. John Phin, *The Seven Follies of Science,* 3rd ed. (New York: Van Nostrand, 1912), p. 202.

5. Ibid., p. 208.

6. Robert P. Crawford, *Think for Yourself* (New York: Fraser, 1937), p. 118.

7. Quoted in Harold A. Larrabee, *Reliable Knowledge,* rev. ed. (Boston: Houghton Mifflin, 1964), p. 22.

8. *New York Times,* 6 December 1981, p. 27.

9. "Computer Points to Single Author for Genesis," *New York Times,* 8 November 1981, p. 7.

10. The correct answers are as follows: (1) An English playwright. Although history books have traditionally credited Nathan Hale with the statement, Hale actually said, "It is the duty of every good officer to obey any orders given him by his commander-in-chief." His biographer borrowed the playwright's words. (2) The signal that was used is not known. The poet Henry Wadsworth Longfellow invented the well-known "one if by land and two if by sea" signal. (Both this and the answer to 1 are found in Michael T. Kaufman, "Myths of '76 Revolution Deflated at Yale Parley," *New York Times,* 4 May 1975, pp. 1f.) (3) Fur. The idea of a glass slipper occurred because the French word for *fur* was incorrectly translated. (4) Siberian squirrel fur. (Both this and the answer to 3 are found in Phin, *Seven Follies,* p. 208.)

11. *New York Times Magazine,* 1 December 1974, p. 31.

12. "The Great Change in Children," *Horizon,* Winter 1974, p. 4.

13. Walter Lippmann, *Public Opinion* (New York: Harcourt, Brace, 1922), p. 90.

14. George Seldes, *Freedom of the Press* (Indianapolis: Bobbs-Merrill, 1935).

15. *Oneonta* (New York) *Star,* 6 February 1982, p. 3.

16. Edwin L. Clarke, *The Art of Straight Thinking* (New York: Appleton, 1929), p. 269.

17. Frederick C. Bartlett, *Remembering: A Study in Experimental and Social Psychology* (New York: Cambridge University Press, 1932), pp. 205–207.

18. Columbia Associates in Philosophy, *An Introduction to Reflective Thinking* (Boston: Houghton Mifflin, 1923), p. 189. See also, Elizabeth Loftus, *Eyewitness Testimony* (Harvard University Press, 1979).

19. Larrabee, *Reliable Knowledge,* p. 203.

20. Martin Gardner, *Fads and Fallacies in the Name of Science* (New York: Dover, 1957), p. 123.

21. See, for example, John Altrocchi, *Abnormal Behavior* (New York: Harcourt Brace Jovanovich, 1980), pp. 17f.

22. Gardner, *Fads and Fallacies,* pp. 155–157.

23. The story of Raoul Wallenberg is detailed in John Bierman, *Righteous Gentile* (New York: Viking, 1982).

24. "Starving Children Saved by NYC Police," *Oneonta Star,* 13 October 1981, p. 13.

25. Joseph Jastrow, *Effective Thinking* (New York: Simon & Schuster, 1931), p. 121.

26. Warren Hoge, "Machismo 'Absolved' in Notorious Brazilian Trial," *New York Times,* 28 October 1979, p. 24.

27. Gordon W. Allport and Leo Postman, *The Psychology of Rumor* (New York: Henry Holt, 1947), pp. 214–215.

28. Quoted in E. L. McKitrick, ed., *Slavery Defended: The Views of the Old South* (Englewood Cliffs, NJ: Prentice-Hall, 1963), p. 53.

29. "CNN Headline News," 16 September 1989.

30. "Doctor Convicted of Rape Accused of Raping Others," *Oneonta Star,* 19 September 1981, p. 2.

31. "Respirator Plug Pulled, Girl Dies," *Oneonta Star,* 11 August 1977, p. 1.

32. "Family Steadfast Despite Girl's Death," *Oneonta Star,* 17 November 1981, p. 2.

33. Richard Haitch, "Defense Coup," *New York Times,* 20 September 1981, p. 49.

34. Diane Henry, "Parents of Three Retarded Girls . . . " *New York Times,* 2 October 1977, pp. 1f.

35. "A Current Affair," 28 April 1989.

36. Peter Monaghan, "Professor of Psychology Stokes a Controversy on the Reliability and Repression of Memory," *Chronicle of Higher Education,* 23 September 1992, pp. A9–10.

CHAPTER 3

1. John Godfrey Saxe, quoted in Don Fabun, *Communication: The Transfer of Meaning* (Encino, CA: Glencoe, 1968), p. 13.

2. D. Wallechinsky and I. Wallace, *The People's Almanac,* vol. 1 (New York: Doubleday, 1975), p. 1089.

3. Ibid.

4. D. S. Hiroto, "Locus of Control and Learned Helplessness," *Journal of Experimental Psychology* 102 (1974): 187–193. See also C. Diener and C. Dweck, "An Analysis of Learned Helplessness," *Journal of Personality and Social Psychology* 39 (1980): 5.

5. Maxwell Maltz, *Psycho-Cybernetics* (New York: Pocket Books, 1969), pp. 49f.

6. Gordon W. Allport, *Becoming* (New Haven, CT: Yale University Press, 1955), pp. 27–28.

7. Nancy Larrick, "Children of TV," *Teacher,* September 1975, pp. 75f.

8. Erich Fromm, "The Creative Attitude," in *Creativity and Its Cultivation,* ed. Harold H. Anderson (New York: Harper & Brothers, 1959), p. 48.

9. Rowland W. Jepson, *Clear Thinking* (New York: Longmans, Green, 1967), p. 79.

10. Koestler, *Act of Creation,* p. 75.

11. See, for example, May and Abraham Edel, *Anthropology and Ethics* (Springfield, IL: Charles C. Thomas, 1959), pp. 88f.

12. Jepson, *Clear Thinking,* p. 81.

13. Edwin A. Burtt, *Right Thinking*, 3rd ed. (New York: Harper & Brothers, 1946), p. 63.

14. Jepson, *Clear Thinking*, p. 81.

15. Sam Walter Foss, reprinted in Parnes, *Creative Behavior Guidebook,* p. 19.

16. Wallechinsky and Wallace, *People's Almanac,* vol. 1, p. 1091.

17. Abraham Maslow, *Toward a Psychology of Being,* 2nd ed. (Princeton, NJ: Van Nostrand, 1968), p. 34.

18. Lippman, *Public Opinion,* pp. 119–120.

19. William J. Reilly, *The Twelve Rules for Straight Thinking* (New York: Harper & Brothers, 1947), p. 15.

20. Quoted in Ghiselin, *The Creative Process,* p. 207.

21. Clarke, *Art of Straight Thinking,* p. 242.

22. Claudia Wallis, "Going Gentle Into That Good Night," *Time,* 8 February 1982, p. 79.

23. Quoted in Jastrow, *Effective Thinking,* pp. 130–131.

24. "Police Sell Marijuana, Then Make Arrests," *New York Times,* 10 December 1979, p. 28.

25. "Mother to Lose Child Over Kosher Food," *Oneonta Star,* 4 February 1982, p. 21.

26. "Nazis' 'Right to March' Upheld," *Oneonta Star,* 24 February 1978, p. 2.

27. "Gay's Adoption of Youth Approved," *Oneonta Star,* 21 June 1979, p. 2.

28. "Graduate Sues for One Million. . . " *New York Times,* 26 November 1972, p. 41.

29. "Accord Reached in Suit . . . " *New York Times,* 1 November 1981, p. 30.

30. "Minister Charged in Rooster Rite," *Oneonta Star,* 25 February 1982, p. 2.

CHAPTER 4

1. Mursell, *Using Your Mind Effectively,* p. 217.

2. James Harvey Robinson, *The Mind in the Making* (New York: Harper & Brothers, 1921), p. 46.

3. "Family Life No Longer That Vital to America," *Oneonta Star,* 1 September 1981, p. 3.

4. "Photo of Dinosaur Needs Some Help," *Oneonta Star,* 29 December 1981, p. 2.

5. *Time,* 25 January 1982, p. 31.

6. "Fear Lack Nullifies Rape Case," *Binghamton Press,* 8 August 1982, p. 12A.

7. *New York Times Magazine,* 7 November 1971, p. 30. © 1971 by the New York Times Company. Reprinted by permission.

CHAPTER 5

1. Paul Smith, ed., *Creativity: An Examination of the Creative Process* (New York: Hastings House, 1959), p. 17.

2. The best source of current works (as well as important older works) is the *Journal of Creative Behavior.*

3. George F. Kneller, *The Art and Science of Creativity* (New York: Holt, 1965), p. 2.

4. Quoted in Parnes, *Creative Behavior Guidebook,* p. 7.

5. J. W. Getzels and P. W. Jackson, *Creativity and Intelligence* (New York: Wiley, 1962), pp. 21f. Also Torrance, *Guiding,* pp. 5 and 63.

6. Ghiselin, *The Creative Process,* p. 9.

7. Eliot Dole Hutchinson, *How to Think Creatively* (Nashville: Abingdon-Cokesbury Press, 1949), p. 79.

8. Harold H. Anderson, "Creativity in Perspective," in Anderson, ed., *Creativity and Its Cultivation,* p. 258.

9. Good sources of studies include Getzels, *Creativity and Intelligence;* Torrance, *Guiding;* and Parnes, *Creative Behavior Guidebook.*

10. Quoted in C. P. Curtis and F. Greenslet, eds., *The Practical Cogitator* (Boston: Houghton Mifflin, 1945), p. 231.

11. Quoted in William J. J. Gordon, *Synectics: The Development of Creative Capacity* (New York: Harper & Brothers, 1961), p. 116.

12. Quoted in Getzels, *Creativity and Intelligence,* p. 53.

13. Joseph Rossman, *The Psychology of the Inventor* (Washington, DC: Inventors' Publishing Company, 1931), pp. 82f.

14. Alex Osborn, *Applied Imagination* (New York: Scribner's, 1957), p. 196.

15. Getzels, *Creativity and Intelligence,* p. 53.

16. "Couple Learns Golden Rule . . . " *Oneonta Star,* 29 August 1981, p. 1.

17. "In Divorce, Kids Get the House," *Oneonta Star,* 20 January 1982, p. 1.

18. *Chronicle of Higher Education,* 12 December 1987, p. A2.

19. *Time,* 14 November 1988, p. 75.

20. "Killer, Caught by New Technique, Gets Life Term," *Los Angeles Times,* 23 January 1988, part I, p. 3.

21. *Time,* 14 November 1988, p. 22.

22. "Grafitti Gobbler Gets Attention," *Oneonta Star,* 30 November 1981, p. 2.

23. "Crippled Inventor Is Standing Proud," *Oneonta Star,* 6 February 1982, p. 1.

24. "Trouble Sleeping? Call Up the Sandman," *Oneonta Star,* 7 July 1982, p. 1.

25. "Waterbabies," *Time,* 10 May 1982, p. 87.

26. "New Inventions from the Cornfield," *New York Times,* 10 January 1988, sect. 4, p. 36.

27. *U.S. News & World Report,* 7 March 1988, p. 53.

28. Hutchinson, *How to Think Creatively,* p. 38, for example, lists four stages, but one of them is "verification," which involves the process of solution refinement classified in this text as critical thinking.

29. "New Jersey Town Decides How to Bury Frozen Elephant," *Oneonta Star,* 22 January 1982, p. 10.

30. "Clone Hype," *Newsweek,* 8 November 1993, p. 61.

CHAPTER 6

1. F. Lorimer, *The Growth of Reason* (London: K. Paul, 1929). Quoted in Koestler, *Act of Creation*, pp. 616–618. Reprinted with permission.

2. Parnes, *Creative Behavior Guidebook*, p. 29.

3. Osborn, *Applied Imagination* p. 130.

4. Ibid., p. 172.

5. Interview in *Inc.*, December 1985, pp. 33f.

6. Beveridge, *The Art of Scientific Investigation*, p. 92.

7. Ibid., p. 28.

8. "Man Kills Wife in Spat Over Penny," *Oneonta Star*, 16 February 1982, p. 10.

9. Jane E. Brody, "Kinsey Study Shows Deep Predisposition," *New York Times*, 23 August 1981, pp. 1f.

10. "Shyness Traced to Genetic Base," *Oneonta Star*, 5 January 1982, p. 1.

11. "Tests Said to Predict Criminal Traits," *Oneonta Star*, 8 January 1982, p. 7.

12. "Court Rules Inmate May Starve Himself," *Oneonta Star*, 2 Febuary 1982, p. 2.

13. "Fickle Universe," *Time*, 25 January 1982, p. 61.

14. Associated Press wirephoto, *Oneonta Star*, 23 July 1981, p. 1.

15. "'Working Youth' Report Stresses Appearance," *New York Times*, 14 February 1982, p. 56.

16. *Oneonta Star*, 5 February 1982, p. 1.

17. *New York Times*, 27 March 1964.

18. "Paternity Battle," *New York Times*, 12 December 1982, p. 57.

19. "Minister Proposes Public Executions," *Oneonta Star*, 29 October 1975, p. 11.

20. "Split Decisions," *Time*, 8 February 1982, p. 67.

21. "Upstate Case Seen Expanding Definition . . . " *New York Times*, 6 December 1981, p. 82.

22. "No Children, Judge Orders," *Oneonta Star*, 25 April 1979, p. 1.

23. "Motorist Returns License," *Oneonta Star*, 22 January 1982, p. 3.

24. *New York Times*, 28 January 1982, p. 14.

25. Supreme Court of Washington, 119 Washington 547, 206, 6 (1922).

26. Debra Viadero, "Survey Finds Young People More Likely to Lie, Cheat, Steal," *Education Week*, 25 November 1992, p. 5.

CHAPTER 7

1. Dan Kaercher, "School Closings: What Can Parents Do?" *Better Homes and Gardens*, August 1982, p. 17.

2. "No Pass, No Drive," *U.S. News & World Report*, 5 June 1989, p. 49.

3. George Iles, *Inventors at Work* (New York: Doubleday, Page, 1906), p. 370.

4. "'Priestess' Is Convicted as Prostitute," *St. Petersburg Times,* 10 September 1989, p. 7A.

5. Interview on "Good Morning America," 29 August 1980.

6. "Recluse Leaves $57,000 to Jesus," *Oneonta Star,* 11 December 1981, p. 7.

7. From "If Japan Can . . . Why Can't We?" on NBC television, 24 June 1981.

8. "Tobacco Firm Cleared in Smoker's Death," *St. Petersburg Times,* 18 June 1993, p. 6A.

CHAPTER 8

1. A. E. Mander, *Logic for the Millions* (New York: Philosophical Library, 1947), p. 55.

2. "Child Abuse a Major Factor in Multiple Personalities," *Oneonta Star,* 31 October 1985, p. 5.

3. Parnes, *Creative Behavior Guidebook,* p. 40.

4. Koestler, *Act of Creation,* p. 123.

5. "Dolphins May Help Train Retarded Tots," *Binghamton Press,* 28 February 1982, p. 5a.

6. "America's Diet Wars," *U.S. News & World Report,* 20 January 1985, p. 62. See also "Obesity Depends on Genetics," *Oneonta Star,* 23 January 1986, pp. 1f.

7. "Nevada Man Says Rock Music Led to Suicide Attempt," *Binghamton Press,* 30 October 1988, p. 6F.

8. Marilyn Elias, "Inborn Traits Outweigh Environment," *USA Today,* 9 August 1989, pp. 1Df.

9. "Bank Robber, 10, Back in Trouble," *Oneonta Star,* 13 February 1982, p. 1.

10. "Tot's Testimony Crucial in Murder Trial," *Binghamton Press,* 26 October 1975, p. 2.

11. "A Man Called Jamison," *New York Times,* 26 January 1975, sect. 4, p. 9.

12. "Expert Warns on Testimony . . . " *New York Times,* 10 January 1982, p. 44.

13. *Wall Street Journal* quoted in "Kids' Dishonesty Sinks a Company," *Oneonta Star,* 26 January 1982, p. 4.

14. "Falsifying of College Records . . . " *New York Times,* 29 November 1981, pp. 1f.

15. "Birth Defects and Behavior . . . " *New York Times,* 21 January 1979, sect. 4, p. 9.

16. "Fetus Born Alive After . . . " *Binghamton Press,* 15 November 1981, p. 1a.

17. *New York Times,* 6 October 1985, sect. 4, p. 6.

18. *Time,* 24 June 1985, p. 69.

19. *New York Times,* 6 October 1985, sect. 4, p. 6.

20. "Should Animals Be Patented?" *Time,* 4 May 1987, p. 10.

21. "Plugging Away in Hollywood," *Time,* 2 January 1989, p. 103.

CHAPTER 9

1. This analogy was first made by Zbigniew Pietraskinski, *The Psychology of Efficient Thinking,* trans. B. Jankowski (New York: Pergamon Press, 1969), p. 134.

2. Parnes, *Creative Behavior Guidebook*, p. 57.

3. Osborn, *Implied Imagination*, p. 149.

4. Quoted in ibid., p. 151.

5. Parnes, *Creative Behavior Guidebook*, pp. 57–58.

6. Quoted in Beveridge, *The Art of Scientific Investigation*, p. 143.

7. Clarence D. Tuska, *Inventors and Inventions* (New York: McGraw-Hill, 1957), p. 88.

8. Parnes, *Creative Behavior Guidebook*, pp. 55–56.

9. Graham Wallas, *The Art of Thought* (New York: Harcourt, Brace, 1926), p. 139.

10. Parnes, *Creative Behavior Guidebook*, p. 57.

11. Max Wertheimer, *Productive Thinking* (New York: Harper & Brothers, 1945), pp. 169–173.

12. Quoted in Koestler, *Act of Creation*, p. 118.

13. See, for example, Hutchinson, *How to Think Creatively*, pp. 35–40.

14. "TV Fights Charges It Undercuts Reading," *Binghamton Press*, 29 November 1981, p. 1a.

CHAPTER 10

1. See, for example, Lenore Weitzman, *The Divorce Revolution* (New York: Free Press, 1986).

2. Jepson, *Clear Thinking*, p. 194.

3. "L.A.: Who's a Victim?" *U.S. News and World Report*, 1 November 1993, pp. 36f.

CHAPTER 11

1. Hutchinson, *How to Think Creatively*, pp. 182–183.

2. D. Wallechinsky and I. Wallace, *The People's Almanac*, vol. 2 (New York: Bantam, 1978), p. 817.

3. Wallechinsky and Wallace, *People's Almanac*, vol. 1, pp. 914–915.

4. Wallechinsky and Wallace, *People's Almanac*, vol. 2, p. 821.

5. Max Black, *Critical Thinking* (Englewood Cliffs, NJ: Prentice-Hall, 1952), pp. 156–157.

6. John Leo, "Single Parent, Double Trouble," *Time*, 4 January 1982, p. 81.

7. "Moneyball," *New York Times*, 28 March 1982, sect. 4, p. 22.

8. Laura Griffin, "Testing the Boundaries of Free Speech," *St. Petersburg Times*, 19 May 1993, p. 1A.

CHAPTER 12

1. "Frozen Embryo Plan Stirs Uproar," *Oneonta Star*, 29 January 1982, p. 8.

2. "Compulsory Alcoholism Treatment Gaining," *New York Times*, 9 May 1982, p. 10.
3. "Judge: No Child Abuse Against Fetus," *St. Petersburg Times*, 18 June 1993, p. 6A.

CHAPTER 13

1. "Texas Indictment . . . Mercy Killers," *New York Times*, 10 December 1981, p. 1.
2. "Slaying Confession Barred by Court," *New York Times*, 11 December 1981, p. 32.
3. "Poll Finds Insanity Plea Opposed," *Oneonta Star*, 21 October 1981, p. 2.
4. "No Tuition for Illegal Aliens," *Oneonta Star*, 28 June 1982, p. 3.

CHAPTER 14

1. Rudolph Verderber et al., "An Analysis of Student Communication Habits," unpublished study, University of Cincinnati, 1976.
2. "Selling Make-Believe Makeup," *Time*, 24 August 1981, p. 58.
3. James Stolz, "Death of a Fraternity Boy," *New York Daily News Magazine*, 24 January 1982, pp. 14f.
4. Jack Anderson, "Naval Base Runs Secret Porn Theater," *Oneonta Star*, 27 November 1981, p. 4.
5. "Student Awarded $10,000 for Spanking," *Oneonta Star*, 2 January 1982, p. 2.
6. Woodley B. Osborne, "High Court to Rule . . ." *On Campus*, December 1981/January 1982, p. 20.

CHAPTER 15

1. Roger W. Holmes, *The Rhyme of Reason* (New York: Appleton-Century, 1939), p. 458.
2. "Poisoned Cornfield Kills 2000 Birds," *Oneonta Star*, 2 January 1982, p. 1.
3. "Monitors Say TV Averaging . . ." *Oneonta Star*, 18 March 1982, p. 1.
4. "Contraceptive Ads Found Unacceptable," *Oneonta Star*, 18 January 1982, p. 15.
5. "Two-Thirds in Poll Believe . . ." *Oneonta Star*, 18 May 1982, p. 7.
6. "Teachers Can't Count Attendance in Grades," *Oneonta Star*, 14 May 1985, p. 10.
7. "Scouts Oust Atheist," *Binghamton Press*, 4 August 1985, p. 7a.
8. *USA Today*, International Edition, 18 September 1985, p. 5.
9. *Oneonta Star*, 25 March 1985, p. 9.
10. *Oneonta Star*, 17 November 1986, p. 1.

APPENDIXES

Appendix A

1. Dick Gregory, *Write Me In!* (New York: Bantam, 1968), p. 13.

2. Gilbert Keith Chesterton, "A Meditation in Broadway," in *The Man Who Was Chesterton,* ed. Raymond T. Bond (Garden City, NY: Doubleday, 1960), p. 150.

Appendix B

1. Edmond Addeo and Robert Burger, *Egospeak* (New York: Bantam 1974).
2. Albert J. Vasile and Harold K. Mintz, *Speak with Confidence* (Boston: Little, Brown, 1986), p. 38.
3. Stephen E. Lucas, *The Art of Public Speaking* (New York: Random House, 1983), p. 26.

Index

sample, 107–108, 136–138, 148–149, 174–175, 182–184
stages in creative handling of, 82–83

Jepson, Rowland, 41–43
Johnson, Samuel, 7
Judgment
  in analyzing an argument, 60–61, 173–174
  basis of moral, 29–31
  distinctions between taste and, 55
  opinions as, 27
  timing of, 131, 132
Judgment phase of thinking, 4, 74. *See also* Critical thinking

Kekulé, Friedrich August von, 133
Kepler, Johannes, 27
Key words, 214
Kneller, George, 75
Knowledge, 5
  information sources for, 113–116
  nature of, 21–23
  opinions and, 26–27
  remembering and, 25–26
  through direct experience, 23–24, 113–114
  through observation, 24
  through reports, 24–25
Koestler, Arthur, 8

Language
  distinctions between reality and, 57–58
  simple, 220
Laziness, 43, 190
Left hemisphere of brain, 3
Legitimate conclusion, 164–165
Levy, Jerre, 3
Library research, 118–120, 200, 215
Lippmann, Walter, 46
Listening, 117, 190, 230–232
Lister, Joseph, 189
Listmaking, 11, 216
Literal statements, 56–57
Location, of work, 7
Logic, 6, 234–238. *See also* Arguments
  basic principles of, 234–235
  errors in syllogisms, 235–238
  formal, 164

formal argument in, 235
Loud, John, 154
Luck, 87
Luther, Martin, 189

Mailer, Norman, 61
Major term, 235
Mander, A. E., 113
Manuscript speeches, 224, 225
Maslow, Abraham, 46, 76
May, Rollo, 76
Memorized speeches, 224
Memory
  note-taking and, 115, 118
  problem of, 25–26
Mental health, creativity and, 76
Metacognition, 49
Middle term, 235
Mine-is-better habit, 41–42, 48, 49, 104, 190, 198–199, 204
Minor term, 235
Moderation, appeal to, 173
Moral issues
  basis of judgment in, 29–31
  debating, 27–29
  dilemmas in, 32
  free will and, 19
Mozart, Wolfgang Amadeus, 6
Mursell, James, 3

Nader, Ralph, 93
Nathanson, David, 114
Negative reactions, 188–194
  anticipating specific, 191–194
  common, 191
  prevalence of, 189–190
  reasons for, 190–191
Newbold, Charles, 189
Newton, Isaac, 76–77, 126
Note–taking, 115, 118

Objections, significant, 200, 202
Obligations, 29, 31
Observation, 2, 24, 91–92, 113, 114, 199, 200, 215
Obstacles
  to critical thinking, 143–144
  to idea production, 131–133
Opinions, 5